ELMER RICE

Elmer Rice

THREE PLAYS

 HILL and WANG · New York

Hill and Wang
A division of Farrar, Straus and Giroux
19 Union Square West, New York 10003

Printed in the United States of America
Library of Congress catalog card number: 65-14528
First published in 1965 by Hill and Wang
First paperback edition, 1965
Twenty-second printing, 1997

OTHER PLAYS BY
ELMER RICE

*(Dates refer to first New York per-
formances unless otherwise noted.)*

1914 *On Trial*
1916 *The Passing of Chow Chow* (One Act)
1917 *The Home of the Free* (One Act)
1917 *The Iron Cross* (unpublished)
1918 *A Diadem of Snow* (One Act; not produced in New York)
1919 *For the Defense* (unpublished)
1921 *Wake Up, Jonathan* (in collaboration with Hatcher Hughes)
1922 *It Is the Law* (in collaboration with Hayden Talbot; unpublished)
1924 *Close Harmony* (also known as *The Lady Next Door*; in collaboration with Dorothy Parker)
1927 *The Blue Hawaii* (adaptation; not produced in New York; unpublished)
1928 *Cock Robin* (in collaboration with Philip Barry)
1929 *See Naples and Die*
1929 *The Subway*
1931 *The Left Bank*
1931 *Counsellor-at-Law*
1932 *Black Sheep*
1933 *We the People*
1934 *The Gay White Way* (One Act; not produced in New York)
1934 *Judgment Day*
1934 *Between Two Worlds*
1938 *American Landscape*

1938 *Life Is Real* (not produced in New York; unpublished)
1940 *Two on an Island*
1941 *Flight to the West*
1943 *A New Life*
1947 *Street Scene* (Musical version, in collaboration with Kurt Weill and Langston Hughes)
1951 *Not for Children*
1951 *The Grand Tour*
1954 *The Winner*
1958 *Cue for Passion*
1963 *Love Among the Ruins* (not produced in New York)

CONTENTS

THE ADDING MACHINE

A Play in Eight Scenes

(Originally presented at the Garrick Theatre, New York City, March 19, 1923)

CHARACTERS

(IN ORDER OF APPEARANCE)

MR. ZERO
MRS. ZERO
DAISY DIANA DOROTHEA DEVORE
THE BOSS
MR. ONE
MRS. ONE
MR. TWO
MRS. TWO
MR. THREE
MRS. THREE
MR. FOUR
MRS. FOUR
MR. FIVE
MRS. FIVE
MR. SIX
MRS. SIX
POLICEMAN
GUIDE
THE FIXER
A GUARD
JUDY O'GRADY
YOUNG MAN
SHRDLU
A HEAD
LIEUTENANT CHARLES
JOE

SIGHTSEERS

THE ADDING MACHINE

SCENE I

A *small bedroom containing an "installment plan" bed, dresser, and chairs. An ugly electric-light fixture over the bed with a single glaring, naked lamp. One small window with the shade drawn. The walls are papered with sheets of foolscap covered with columns of figures.*

MR. ZERO *is lying on the bed, facing the audience, his head and shoulders visible. He is thin, sallow, undersized, and partially bald.* MRS. ZERO *is standing before the dresser arranging her hair for the night. She is forty-five, sharp-featured, gray streaks in her hair. She is shapeless in her long-sleeved cotton nightgown. She is wearing her shoes, over which sag her ungartered stockings.*

MRS. ZERO [*as she takes down her hair*]. I'm gettin' sick o' them Westerns. All them cowboys ridin' around an' foolin' with them ropes. I don't care nothin' about that. I'm sick of 'em. I don't see why they don't have more of them stories like *For Love's Sweet Sake*. I like them sweet little love stories. They're nice an' wholesome. Mrs. Twelve was sayin' to me only yesterday, "Mrs. Zero," says she, "what I like is one of them wholesome stories, with just a sweet, simple little love story." "You're right, Mrs. Twelve," I says. "That's what I like too." They're showin' too many Westerns at the Rosebud. I'm gettin' sick of them. I think we'll start goin' to the Peter Stuyvesant. They got a good bill there Wednesday night. There's a Chubby Delano comedy called *Sea-Sick*. Mrs. Twelve was tellin' me about it. She says it's a scream. They're havin' a picnic in the country and they sit Chubby next to an old maid with a great big mouth. So he gets sore an' when she ain't lookin' he goes and catches a frog and drops it in her clam chowder. An' when she goes to eat the chowder the frog jumps out of it an' right into her mouth. Talk about laugh! Mrs. Twelve was tellin' me she laughed so she nearly passed out. He sure can pull some funny ones. An' they got that big Grace Darling feature, *A Mother's Tears*. She's sweet. But I don't like her clothes. There's no style to them. Mrs. Nine was tellin' me she read in *Pictureland* that she ain't

3

livin' with her husband. He's her second too. I don't know whether they're divorced or just separated. You wouldn't think it to see her on the screen. She looks so sweet and innocent. Maybe it ain't true. You can't believe all you read. They say some Pittsburgh millionaire is crazy about her and that's why she ain't livin' with her husband. Mrs. Seven was tellin' me her brother-in-law has a friend that used to go to school with Grace Darling. He says her name ain't Grace Darling at all. Her right name is Elizabeth Dugan, he says, an' all them stories about her gettin' five thousand a week is the bunk, he says. She's sweet though. Mrs. Eight was tellin' me that *A Mother's Tears* is the best picture she ever made. "Don't miss it, Mrs. Zero," she says. "It's sweet," she says. "Just sweet and wholesome. Cry!" she says, "I nearly cried my eyes out." There's one part in it where this big bum of an Englishman—he's a married man too—an' she's this little simple country girl. An' she nearly falls for him too. But she's sittin' out in the garden, one day, and she looks up and there's her mother lookin' at her, right out of the clouds. So that night she locks the door of her room. An' sure enough, when everybody's in bed, along comes this big bum of an Englishman an' when she won't let him in what does he do but go an' kick open the door. "Don't miss it, Mrs. Zero," Mrs. Eight was tellin' me. It's at the Peter Stuyvesant Wednesday night, so don't be tellin' me you want to go to the Rosebud. The Eights seen it downtown at the Strand. They go downtown all the time. Just like us—nit! I guess by the time it gets to the Peter Stuyvesant all that part about kickin' in the door will be cut out. Just like they cut out that big cabaret scene in *The Price of Virtue*. They sure are pullin' some rough stuff in the pictures nowadays. "It's no place for a young girl," I was tellin' Mrs. Eleven, only the other day. An' by the time they get uptown half of it is cut out. But you wouldn't go downtown—not if wild horses was to drag you. You can wait till they come uptown! Well, I don't want to wait, see? I want to see 'em when everybody else is seein' 'em an' not a month later. Now don't go tellin' me you ain't got the price. You could dig up the price all right, all right, if you wanted to. I notice you always got the price to go to the ball game. But when it comes to me havin' a good time, then it's always: "I ain't got the price, I gotta start savin'." A fat lot you'll ever save! I got all I can do now makin' both ends meet, an' you talkin' about savin'. [*She seats herself on a chair and begins removing her shoes and stockings.*] An' don't go pullin' that stuff about bein' tired. "I been workin' hard all day. Twice a day in the subway's enough for me." Tired! Where do you get that tired stuff, anyhow? What about me? Where do I come in? Scrubbin' floors an' cookin' your meals an' washin' your dirty clothes. An' you sittin' on a chair all day, just addin' figgers an' waitin' for five-thirty. There's no five-thirty for me. I don't wait for no whistle. I don't get no vacations neither. And what's more I don't get no pay envelope every Saturday night neither. I'd like to know where you'd be without me. An' what have I got to show for it?—slavin' my life away to give you a home. What's in it for me, I'd like to know? But it's my own fault, I guess. I was a fool for marryin' you. If I'd 'a' had any sense, I'd 'a' known what you were from the start. I wish I had it to do over again, I hope to tell you. You was goin' to do wonders, you was! You wasn't goin' to be a bookkeeper long—oh, no, not you. Wait till you got started—you was goin' to show 'em. There wasn't no job in the store that was too big for you. Well, I've been waitin' —waitin' for you to get started—see? It's been a good long wait too. Twenty-five years! An' I ain't seen nothin' happen. Twenty-five years in the same job. Twenty-five years tomorrow! You're proud of it, ain't you? Twenty-five years in the same job an' never missed a day! That's somethin' to be proud of, ain't it? Sittin' for twenty-five years on the same chair, addin' up figgers. What about bein' store manager? I guess you forgot about that, didn't you? An' me at home here lookin' at the same four walls an' workin' my fingers to the bone to make both ends meet. Seven years since you got a raise! An' if you don't get one tomorrow, I'll bet a nickel you won't have the guts to go an' ask for one. I didn't pick much when I picked you, I'll tell the world. You ain't much to be proud of. [*She rises, goes to the window, and raises the shade. A few lighted windows are visible on the other side of the closed court. Looking out for a moment.*] She ain't walkin' around tonight, you can bet your sweet life on that. An' she won't be walkin' around any more nights neither. Not in this house, anyhow. [*She turns away from the window.*] The dirty bum! The idea of her comin' to live in a house with respectable people. They should 'a' gave her six years, not six months. If I was the judge I'd of gave her life. A bum like that. [*She approaches the bed and stands there a moment.*] I guess you're sorry she's gone. I guess you'd like to sit home every night an' watch her goin's-on. You're somethin' to be proud of, you are! [*She stands on the bed and turns out the light. A thin stream of moonlight filters in from the court. The two figures are dimly visible. MRS. ZERO gets into bed.*] You'd better not start nothin' with women, if you know what's good for you. I've put up with a lot, but I won't put up with that. I've been slavin' away for twenty-five years, makin' a home for you an' nothin' to show for it. If you was any kind of a man you'd have a decent job by now an' I'd be gettin' some comfort out of life—instead of bein' just a slave, washin' pots an' standin' over the hot stove. I've stood it for twenty-five years an' I guess I'll have to stand it twenty-five more. But don't you go startin' nothin' with women——

She goes on talking as the curtain falls.

Curtain.

SCENE II

An office in a department store. Wood and glass partitions. In the middle of the room two tall desks back to back. At one desk on a high stool is ZERO. Opposite him at the other desk, also on a high stool, is DAISY DIANA DOROTHEA DEVORE, a plain, middle-aged woman. Both wear green eye-shades and paper sleeve-protectors. A pendent electric lamp throws light upon both desks. DAISY reads aloud figures from a pile of slips which lie before her. As she reads the figures ZERO enters them upon a large square sheet of ruled paper which lies before him.

DAISY [*reading aloud*]. Three ninety-eight. Forty-two cents. A dollar fifty. A dollar fifty. A dollar twenty-five. Two dollars. Thirty-nine cents. Twenty-seven fifty.

Zero [*petulantly*]. Speed it up a little, cancha?

Daisy. What's the rush? Tomorrer's another day.

Zero. Aw, you make me sick.

Daisy. An' you make me sicker.

Zero. Go on. Go on. We're losin' time.

Daisy. Then quit bein' so bossy. [*She reads.*] Three dollars. Two sixty-nine. Eighty-one fifty. Forty dollars. Eight seventy-five. Who do you think you are, anyhow?

Zero. Never mind who I think I am. You tend to your work.

Daisy. Aw, don't be givin' me so many orders. Sixty cents. Twenty-four cents. Seventy-five cents. A dollar fifty. Two fifty. One fifty. One fifty. Two fifty. I don't have to take it from you and what's more I won't.

Zero. Aw, quit talkin'.

Daisy. I'll talk all I want. Three dollars. Fifty cents. Fifty cents. Seven dollars. Fifty cents. Two fifty. Three fifty. Fifty cents. One fifty. Fifty cents.

She goes on, bending over the slips and transferring them from one pile to another. ZERO *bends over his desk, busily entering the figures.*

Zero [*without looking up*]. You make me sick. Always shootin' off your face about somethin'. Talk, talk, talk. Just like all the other women. Women make me sick.

Daisy [*busily fingering the slips*]. Who do you think you are, anyhow? Bossin' me around. I don't have to take it from you, and what's more I won't.

They both attend closely to their work, neither looking up. Throughout, each intones figures during the other's speeches.

Zero. Women make me sick. They're all alike. The judge gave her six months. I wonder what they do in the workhouse. Peel potatoes. I'll bet she's sore at me. Maybe she'll try to kill me when she gets out. I better be careful. Hello Girl Slays Betrayer. Jealous Wife Slays Rival. You can't tell what a woman's liable to do. I better be careful.

Daisy. I'm gettin' sick of it. Always pickin' on me about

somethin'. Never a decent word out of you. Not even the time o' day.

Zero. I guess she wouldn't have the nerve at that. Maybe she don't even know it's me. They didn't even put my name in the paper, the big bums. Maybe she's been in the workhouse before. A bum like that. She didn't have nothin' on that one time—nothin' but a shirt. [*He glances up quickly, then bends over again.*] You make me sick. I'm sick of lookin' at your face.

Daisy. Gee, ain't that whistle ever goin' to blow? You didn't used to be like that. Not even good mornin' or good evenin'. I ain't done nothin' to you. It's the young girls. Goin' around without corsets.

Zero. Your face is gettin' all yeller. Why don't you put some paint on it? She was puttin' on paint that time. On her cheeks and on her lips. And that blue stuff on her eyes. Just sittin' there in a shimmy puttin' on the paint. An' walkin' around the room with her legs all bare.

Daisy. I wish I was dead.

Zero. I was a goddam fool to let the wife get on to me. She oughta get six months at that. The dirty bum. Livin' in a house with respectable people. She'd be livin' there yet if the wife hadn't o' got on to me. Damn her!

Daisy. I wish I was dead.

Zero. Maybe another one'll move in. Gee, that would be great. But the wife's got her eye on me now.

Daisy. I'm scared to do it though.

Zero. You oughta move into that room. It's cheaper than where you're livin' now. I better tell you about it. I don't mean to be always pickin' on you.

Daisy. Gas. The smell of it makes me sick. [ZERO *looks up and clears his throat.* DAISY *looks up, startled.*] Whadja say?

Zero. I didn't say nothin'.

Daisy. I thought you did.

Zero. You thought wrong.

> *They bend over their work again.*

Daisy. A dollar sixty. A dollar fifty. Two ninety. One sixty-two.

Zero. Why the hell should I tell you? Fat chance of you forgettin' to pull down the shade!

Daisy. If I asked for carbolic they might get on to me.

Zero. Your hair's gettin' gray. You don't wear them shirtwaists any more with the low collars. When you'd bend down to pick somethin' up——

Daisy. I wish I knew what to ask for. Girl Takes Mercury After All-Night Party. Woman In Ten-Story Death Leap.

Zero. I wonder where'll she go when she gets out. Gee, I'd like to make a date with her. Why didn't I go over there the night my wife went to Brooklyn? She never woulda found out.

Daisy. I seen Pauline Frederick do it once. Where could I get a pistol though?

Zero. I guess I didn't have the nerve.

Daisy. I'll bet you'd be sorry then that you been so mean to me. How do I know though? Maybe you wouldn't.

Zero. Nerve! I got as much nerve as anybody. I'm on the level, that's all. I'm a married man and I'm on the level.

Daisy. Anyhow, why ain't I got a right to live? I'm as good as anybody else. I'm too refined, I guess. That's the whole trouble.

Zero. The time the wife had pneumonia I thought she was goin' to pass out. But she didn't. The doctor's bill was eighty-seven dollars. [*Looking up.*] Hey, wait a minute! Didn't you say eighty-seven dollars?

Daisy [*looking up*]. What?

Zero. Was the last you said eighty-seven dollars?

Daisy [*consulting the slip*]. Forty-two fifty.

Zero. Well, I made a mistake. Wait a minute. [*He busies himself with an eraser.*] All right. Shoot.

Daisy. Six dollars. Three fifteen. Two twenty-five. Sixty-five cents. A dollar twenty. You talk to me as if I was dirt.

Zero. I wonder if I could kill the wife without anybody findin' out. In bed some night. With a pillow.

Daisy. I used to think you was stuck on me.

Zero. I'd get found out though. They always have ways.

Daisy. We used to be so nice and friendly together when I first came here. You used to talk to me then.

Zero. Maybe she'll die soon. I noticed she was coughin' this mornin'.

Daisy. You used to tell me all kinds o' things. You were

goin' to show them all. Just the same, you're still sittin'
here.

Zero. Then I could do what I damn please. Oh, boy!

Daisy. Maybe it ain't all your fault neither. Maybe if
you'd had the right kind o' wife—somebody with a lot of
common sense, somebody refined—me!

Zero. At that, I guess I'd get tired of bummin' around.
A feller wants some place to hang his hat.

Daisy. I wish she would die.

Zero. And when you start goin' with women you're liable
to get into trouble. And lose your job maybe.

Daisy. Maybe you'd marry me.

Zero. Gee, I wish I'd gone over there that night.

Daisy. Then I could quit workin'.

Zero. Lots o' women would be glad to get me.

Daisy. You could look a long time before you'd find a
sensible, refined girl like me.

Zero. Yes, sir, they could look a long time before they'd
find a steady meal-ticket like me.

Daisy. I guess I'd be too old to have any kids. They say
it ain't safe after thirty-five.

Zero. Maybe I'd marry you. You might be all right, at
that.

Daisy. I wonder—if you don't want kids—whether—if
there's any way——

Zero [*looking up*]. Hey! Hey! Can't you slow up? What
do you think I am—a machine?

Daisy [*looking up*]. Say, what do you want, anyhow?
First it's too slow an' then it's too fast. I guess you don't
know what you want.

Zero. Well, never mind about that. Just you slow up.

Daisy. I'm gettin' sick o' this. I'm goin' to ask to be
transferred.

Zero. Go ahead. You can't make me mad.

Daisy. Aw, keep quiet. [*She reads.*] Two forty-five. A
dollar twenty. A dollar fifty. Ninety cents. Sixty-three cents.

Zero. Marry you! I guess not! You'd be as bad as the
one I got.

Daisy. You wouldn't care if I did ask. I got a good mind
to ask.

Zero. I was a fool to get married.

Daisy. Then I'd never see you at all.

Zero. What chance has a guy got with a woman tied around his neck?

Daisy. That time at the store picnic—the year your wife couldn't come—you were nice to me then.

Zero. Twenty-five years holdin' down the same job!

Daisy. We were together all day—just sittin' around under the trees.

Zero. I wonder if the boss remembers about it bein' twenty-five years.

Daisy. And comin' home that night—you sat next to me in the big delivery wagon.

Zero. I got a hunch there's a big raise comin' to me.

Daisy. I wonder what it feels like to be really kissed. Men —dirty pigs! They want the bold ones.

Zero. If he don't come across I'm goin' right up to the front office and tell him where he gets off.

Daisy. I wish I was dead.

Zero. "Boss," I'll say, "I want to have a talk with you." "Sure," he'll say, "sit down. Have a Corona Corona." "No," I'll say, "I don't smoke." "How's that?" he'll say. "Well, boss," I'll say, "it's this way. Every time I feel like smokin' I just take a nickel and put it in the old sock. A penny saved is a penny earned, that's the way I look at it." "Damn sensible," he'll say. "You got a wise head on you, Zero."

Daisy. I can't stand the smell of gas. It makes me sick. You coulda kissed me if you wanted to.

Zero. "Boss," I'll say, "I ain't quite satisfied. I been on the job twenty-five years now and if I'm gonna stay I gotta see a future ahead of me." "Zero," he'll say, "I'm glad you came in. I've had my eye on you, Zero. Nothin' gets by me." "Oh, I know that, boss," I'll say. That'll hand him a good laugh, that will. "You're a valuable man, Zero," he'll say, "and I want you right up here with me in the front office. You're done addin' figgers. Monday mornin' you move up here."

Daisy. Them kisses in the movies—them long ones— right on the mouth—

Zero. I'll keep a-goin' right on up after that. I'll show some of them birds where they get off.

Daisy. That one the other night—*The Devil's Alibi*—
he put his arms around her—and her head fell back and
her eyes closed—like she was in a daze.

Zero. Just give me about two years and I'll show them
birds where they get off.

Daisy. I guess that's what it's like—a kinda daze—when
I see them like that, I just seem to forget everything.

Zero. Then me for a place in Jersey. And maybe a little
Buick. No tin Lizzie for mine. Wait till I get started—I'll
show 'em.

Daisy. I can see it now when I kinda half close my eyes.
The way her head fell back. And his mouth pressed right up
against hers. Oh, Gawd! it must be grand!

There is a sudden shrill blast from a steam whistle.

Daisy and Zero [*together*]. The whistle!

*With great agility they get off their stools, remove their
eyeshades and sleeve-protectors and put them on the desks.
Then each produces from behind the desk a hat—*Zero*,
a dusty derby,* Daisy*, a frowsy straw.* Daisy *puts on her
hat and turns toward* Zero *as though she were about to
speak to him. But he is busy cleaning his pen and pays no
attention to her. She sighs and goes toward the door at
the left.*

Zero [*looking up*]. G'night, Miss Devore.

But she does not hear him and exits. Zero *takes up his hat
and goes left. The door at the right opens and the* Boss
enters—middle-aged, stoutish, bald, well dressed.

The Boss [*calling*]. Oh—er—Mister—er——

Zero *turns in surprise, sees who it is, and trembles nervously.*

Zero [*obsequiously*]. Yes, sir. Do you want me, sir?

Boss. Yes. Just come here a moment, will you?

Zero. Yes, sir. Right away, sir. [*He fumbles his hat,
picks it up, stumbles, recovers himself, and approaches the*
Boss, *every fiber quivering.*]

Boss. Mister—er—er——

Zero. Zero.

Boss. Yes, Mr. Zero. I wanted to have a little talk with
you.

Zero [*with a nervous grin*]. Yes, sir, I been kinda expectin' it.

Boss [*staring at him*]. Oh, have you?

Zero. Yes, sir.

Boss. How long have you been with us, Mister——er—— Mister——

Zero. Zero.

Boss. Yes, Mr. Zero.

Zero. Twenty-five years today.

Boss. Twenty-five years! That's a long time.

Zero. Never missed a day.

Boss. And you've been doing the same work all the time?

Zero. Yes, sir. Right here at this desk.

Boss. Then, in that case, a change probably won't be unwelcome to you.

Zero. No, sir, it won't. And that's the truth.

Boss. We've been planning a change in this department for some time.

Zero. I kinda thought you had your eye on me.

Boss. You were right. The fact is that my efficiency experts have recommended the installation of adding machines.

Zero [*staring at him*]. Addin' machines?

Boss. Yes, you've probably seen them. A mechanical device that adds automatically.

Zero. Sure. I've seen them. Keys—and a handle that you pull. [*He goes through the motions in the air.*]

Boss. That's it. They do the work in half the time and a high-school girl can operate them. Now, of course, I'm sorry to lose an old and faithful employee——

Zero. Excuse me, but would you mind sayin' that again?

Boss. I say I'm sorry to lose an employee who's been with me for so many years—— [*Soft music is heard—the sound of the mechanical player of a distant merry-go-round. The part of the floor upon which the desk and stools are standing begins to revolve very slowly.*] But, of course, in an organization like this, efficiency must be the first consideration—— [*The music becomes gradually louder and the revolutions more rapid.*] You will draw your salary for the full month. And I'll direct my secretary to give you a letter of recommendation——

Zero. Wait a minute, boss. Let me get this right. You mean I'm canned?

Boss [barely making himself heard above the increasing volume of sound]. I'm sorry—no other alternative—greatly regret—old   employee—efficiency—economy—business— business—BUSINESS——

His voice is drowned by the music. The platform is revolving rapidly now. ZERO and the Boss face each other. They are entirely motionless save for the Boss's jaws, which open and close incessantly. But the words are inaudible. The music swells and swells. To it is added every offstage effect of the theater: the wind, the waves, the galloping horses, the locomotive whistle, the sleigh bells, the automobile siren, the glass-crash. New Year's Eve, Election Night, Armistice Day, and Mardi Gras. The noise is deafening, maddening, unendurable. Suddenly it culminates in a terrific peal of thunder. For an instant there is a flash of red and then everything is plunged into blackness.

Curtain.

SCENE III

The ZERO dining room. Entrance door at right. Doors to kitchen and bedroom at left. The walls, as in the first scene, are papered with foolscap sheets covered with columns of figures. In the middle of the room, upstage, a table set for two. Along each side wall seven chairs are ranged in symmetrical rows.

At the rise of the curtain MRS. ZERO is seen seated at the table looking alternately at the entrance door and a clock on the wall. She wears a bungalow apron over her best dress.

After a few moments the entrance door opens and ZERO enters. He hangs his hat on a rack behind the door and, coming over to the table, seats himself at the vacant place. His movements throughout are quiet and abstracted.

MRS. ZERO [*breaking the silence*]. Well, it was nice of you to come home. You're only an hour late and that ain't very much. The supper don't get very cold in an hour. An' of course the part about our havin' a lot of company tonight don't matter. [*They begin to eat.*]

Ain't you even got sense enough to come home on time? Didn't I tell you we're goin' to have a lot o' company tonight? Didn't you know the Ones are comin'? An' the Twos? An' the Threes? An' the Fours? An' the Fives? And the Sixes? Didn't I tell you to be home on time? I might as well talk to a stone wall. [*They eat for a few moments in silence.*]

I guess you musta had some important business to attend to. Like watchin' the scoreboard. Or was two kids havin' a fight an' you was the referee? You sure do have a lot of business to attend to. It's a wonder you have time to come home at all. You gotta tough life, you have. Walk in, hang up your hat, an' put on the nosebag. An' me in the hot kitchen all day, cookin' your supper an' waitin' for you to get good an' ready to come home! [*Again they eat in silence.*]

Maybe the boss kept you late tonight. Tellin' you what a big noise you are and how the store couldn't 'a' got along if you hadn't been pushin' a pen for twenty-five years. Where's the gold medal he pinned on you? Did some blind old lady take it away from you or did you leave it on the seat of the boss's limousine when he brought you home? [*Again a few moments of silence.*]

I'll bet he gave you a big raise, didn't he? Promoted you from the third floor to the fourth, maybe. Raise? A fat chance you got o' gettin' a raise. All they gotta do is put an ad in the paper. There's ten thousand like you layin' around the streets. You'll be holdin' down the same job at the end of another twenty-five years—if you ain't forgot how to add by that time.

A noise is heard offstage, a sharp clicking such as is made by the operation of the keys and levers of an adding machine. ZERO *raises his head for a moment but lowers it almost instantly.*

Mrs. Zero. There's the doorbell. The company's here already. And we ain't hardly finished supper. [*She rises.*]

But I'm goin' to clear off the table whether you're finished or not. If you want your supper, you got a right to be home on time. Not standin' around lookin' at scoreboards. [*As she piles up the dishes* ZERO *rises and goes toward the entrance door.*] Wait a minute! Don't open the door yet. Do you want the company to see all the mess? An' go an' put on a clean collar. You got red ink all over it. [ZERO *goes toward bedroom door.*] I should think after pushin' a pen for twenty-five years, you'd learn how to do it without gettin' ink on your collar. [ZERO *exits to bedroom.* MRS. ZERO *takes dishes to kitchen, talking as she goes.*]

I guess I can stay up all night now washin' dishes. You should worry! That's what a man's got a wife for, ain't it? Don't he buy her her clothes an' let her eat with him at the same table? An' all she's gotta do is cook the meals an' do the washin' an' scrub the floor, an' wash the dishes when the company goes. But, believe me, you're goin' to sling a mean dish towel when the company goes tonight!

While she is talking ZERO *enters from bedroom. He wears a clean collar and is cramming the soiled one furtively into his pocket.* MRS. ZERO *enters from kitchen. She has removed her apron and carries a table cover which she spreads hastily over the table. The clicking noise is heard again.*

Mrs. Zero. There's the bell again. Open the door, cancha?

ZERO *goes to the entrance door and opens it. Six men and six women file into the room in a double column. The men are all shapes and sizes, but their dress is identical with that of* ZERO *in every detail. Each, however, wears a wig of a different color. The women are all dressed alike too, except that the dress of each is of a different color.*

Mrs. Zero [*taking the first woman's hand*]. How de do, Mrs. One.

Mrs. One. How de do, Mrs. Zero.

MRS. ZERO *repeats this formula with each woman in turn.* ZERO *does the same with the men except that he is silent throughout. The files now separate, each man taking a chair from the right wall and each woman one from the left wall. Each sex forms a circle with the chairs very close together. The men—all except* ZERO—*smoke cigars. The women munch chocolates.*

Six. Some rain we're havin'.

Five. Never saw the like of it.

Four. Worst in fourteen years, paper says.

Three. Y' can't always go by the papers.

Two. No, that's right too.

One. We're liable to forget from year to year.

Six. Yeh, come t' think, last year was pretty bad too.

Five. An' how about two years ago?

Four. Still, this year's pretty bad.

Three. Yeh, no gettin' away from that.

Two. Might be a whole lot worse.

One. Yeh, it's all the way you look at it. Some rain though.

Mrs. Six. I like them little organdie dresses.

Mrs. Five. Yeh, with a little lace trimmin' on the sleeves.

Mrs. Four. Well, I like 'em plain myself.

Mrs. Three. Yeh, what I always say is the plainer the more refined.

Mrs. Two. Well, I don't think a little lace does any harm.

Mrs. One. No, it kinda dresses it up.

Mrs. Zero. Well, I always say it's all a matter of taste.

Mrs. Six. I saw you at the Rosebud Movie Thursday night, Mr. One.

One. Pretty punk show, I'll say.

Two. They're gettin' worse all the time.

Mrs. Six. But who was the charming lady, Mr. One?

One. Now don't you go makin' trouble for me. That was my sister.

Mrs. Five. Oho! That's what they all say.

Mrs. Four. Never mind! I'll bet Mrs. One knows what's what, all right.

Mrs. One. Oh, well, he can do what he likes—'slong as he behaves himself.

Three. You're in luck at that, One. Fat chance I got of gettin' away from the frau even with my sister.

Mrs. Three. You oughta be glad you got a good wife to look after you.

The Other Women [*in unison*]. That's right, Mrs. Three.

Five. I guess I know who wears the pants in your house, Three.

Mrs. Zero. Never mind. I saw them holdin' hands at the movie the other night.

Three. She musta been tryin' to get some money away from me.

Mrs. Three. Swell chance anybody'd have of gettin' any money away from you.

General laughter.

Four. They sure are a loving couple.

Mrs. Two. Well, I think we oughta change the subject.

Mrs. One. Yes, let's change the subject.

Six [*sotto voce*]. Did you hear the one about the travelin' salesman?

Five. It seems this guy was in a sleeper.

Four. Goin' from Albany to San Diego.

Three. And in the next berth was an old maid.

Two. With a wooden leg.

One. Well, along about midnight——

They all put their heads together and whisper.

Mrs. Six [*sotto voce*]. Did you hear about the Sevens?

Mrs. Five. They're gettin' a divorce.

Mrs. Four. It's the second time for him.

Mrs. Three. They're two of a kind, if you ask me.

Mrs. Two. One's as bad as the other.

Mrs. One. Worse.

Mrs. Zero. They say that she——

They all put their heads together and whisper.

Six. I think this woman suffrage is the bunk.

Five. It sure is! Politics is a man's business.

Four. Woman's place is in the home.

Three. That's it! Lookin' after the kids, 'stead of hangin' around the streets.

Two. You hit the nail on the head that time.

One. The trouble is they don't know what they want.

Mrs. Six. Men sure get me tired.

Mrs. Five. They sure are a lazy lot.

Mrs. Four. And dirty.

Mrs. Three. Always grumblin' about somethin'.

Mrs. Two. When they're not lyin'!

Mrs. One. Or messin' up the house.

Mrs. Zero. Well, believe me, I tell mine where he gets off.

Six. Business conditions are sure bad.

Five. Never been worse.

Four. I don't know what we're comin' to.

Three. I look for a big smash-up in about three months.

Two. Wouldn't surprise me a bit.

One. We're sure headin' for trouble.

Mrs. Six. My aunt has gallstones.

Mrs. Five. My husband has bunions.

Mrs. Four. My sister expects next month.

Mrs. Three. My cousin's husband has erysipelas.

Mrs. Two. My niece has St. Vitus's dance.

Mrs. One. My boy has fits.

Mrs. Zero. I never felt better in my life. Knock wood!

Six. Too damn much agitation, that's at the bottom of it.

Five. That's it! Too damn many strikes.

Four. Foreign agitators, that's what it is.

Three. They oughta be run outa the country.

Two. What the hell do they want anyhow?

One. They don't know what they want, if you ask me.

Six. America for the Americans is what I say!

All [*in unison*]. That's it! Damn foreigners! Damn dagoes! Damn Catholics! Damn sheenies! Damn niggers! Jail 'em! Shoot 'em! Hang 'em! Lynch 'em! Burn 'em! [*They all rise. Sing in unison.*]

> My country 'tis of thee,
> Sweet land of liberty!

Mrs. Four. Why so pensive, Mr. Zero?

Zero [*speaking for the first time*]. I'm thinkin'.

Mrs. Four. Well, be careful not to sprain your mind. [*Laughter.*]

Mrs. Zero. Look at the poor men all by themselves. We ain't very sociable.

One. Looks like we're neglectin' the ladies.

The women cross the room and join the men, all chattering loudly. The doorbell rings.

Mrs. Zero. Sh! The doorbell!

The volume of sound slowly diminishes. Again the doorbell.

   Zero [*quietly*]. I'll go. It's for me.

They watch curiously as ZERO *goes to the door and opens it, admitting a* POLICEMAN. *There is a murmur of surprise and excitement.*

   Policeman. I'm lookin' for Mr. Zero. [*They all point to* ZERO.]

   Zero. I've been expectin' you.

   Policeman. Come along!

   Zero. Just a minute. [*He puts his hand in his pocket.*]

   Policeman. What's he tryin' to pull? [*He draws a revolver.*] I got you covered.

   Zero. Sure, that's all right. I just want to give you somethin'. [*He takes the collar from his pocket and gives it to the* POLICEMAN.]

   Policeman [*suspiciously*]. What's that?

   Zero. The collar I wore.

   Policeman. What do I want it for?

   Zero. It's got bloodstains on it.

   Policeman [*pocketing it*]. All right, come along!

   Zero [*turning to* MRS. ZERO]. I gotta go with him. You'll have to dry the dishes yourself.

   Mrs. Zero [*rushing forward*]. What are they takin' you for?

   Zero [*calmly*]. I killed the boss this afternoon. [*The* POLICEMAN *takes him off*.]

Quick Curtain.

SCENE IV

A court of justice. Three bare white walls without doors or windows except for a single door in the right wall. At the right is a jury box in which are seated MESSRS. ONE, TWO, THREE, FOUR, FIVE, *and* SIX *and their respective wives. On either side of the jury box stands a uniformed officer. Opposite the jury box is a long, bare oak table piled high with law books. Behind the books* ZERO *is seated, his face buried in his hands. There is no other furniture in the room. A moment after the rise of the curtain one of the officers rises and, going around the table, taps* ZERO *on the shoulder.* ZERO *rises and accompanies the officer. The officer escorts him to the great empty space in the middle of the courtroom, facing the jury. He motions to* ZERO *to stop, then points to the jury and resumes his place beside the jury box.* ZERO *stands there looking at the jury, bewildered and half afraid. The jurors give no sign of having seen him. Throughout they sit with folded arms, staring stolidly before them.*

ZERO [*beginning to speak, haltingly*]. Sure I killed him. I ain't sayin' I didn't, am I? Sure I killed him. Them lawyers! They give me a good stiff pain, that's what they give me. Half the time I don't know what the hell they're talkin' about. Objection sustained. Objection overruled. What's the big idea anyhow? You ain't heard me do any objectin', have you? Sure not! What's the idea of objectin'? You got a right to know. What I say is, if one bird kills another bird, why you got a right to call him for it. That's what I say. I know all about that. I been on the jury too. Them lawyers! Don't let 'em fill you full of bunk. All that bull about it bein' red ink on the bill file. Red ink nothin'! It was blood, see? I want you to get that right. I killed him, see? Right through the heart with the bill file, see? I want you to get that right—all of you. One, two, three, four, five, six, seven, eight, nine, ten, eleven, twelve. Twelve of you. Six and six. That makes twelve. I figgered it up often enough. Six and six makes twelve. And five is seventeen. And eight is twenty-five. And three is twenty-eight. Eight and carry two. Aw, cut it out! Them damn figgers! I can't forget 'em. Twenty-five years, see? Eight hours a day, exceptin' Sundays. And July and August half-day Saturday. One week's vacation with pay. And another week without pay if you want it. Who the hell wants it? Layin' around the house listenin' to the wife tellin' you where you get off. Nix! An' legal holidays. I nearly forgot them. New Year's, Washington's Birthday, Decoration Day, Fourth o' July, Labor Day, Election Day, Thanksgivin', Christmas. Good Friday if you want it. An' if you're a Jew, Young Kipper an' the other one—I forget what they call it. The dirty sheenies—always gettin' two to the other bird's one. An' when a holiday comes on Sunday, you get Monday off. So that's fair enough. But when the Fourth o' July comes on Saturday, why you're out o' luck on account of Saturday bein' a half-day anyhow. Get me? Twenty-five years—I'll tell you somethin' funny. Decoration Day an' the Fourth o' July are always on the same day o' the week. Twenty-five years. Never missed a day, and never more'n five minutes late. Look at my time card if you don't believe me. Eight twenty-seven, eight thirty, eight twenty-nine, eight twenty-seven, eight thirty-two. Eight an' thirty-two's forty an'— Goddam them figgers! I can't forget 'em. They're funny things, them figgers. They look like people sometimes. The eights, see? Two dots for the eyes and a dot for the nose. An' a line. That's the mouth, see? An' there's others remind you of other things—but I can't talk about them, on account of there bein' ladies here. Sure I killed him. Why didn't he shut up? If he'd only shut up! Instead o' talkin' an' talkin' about how sorry he was an' what a good guy I was an' this an' that. I felt like sayin' to him: "For Christ's sake, shut up!" But I didn't have the nerve, see? I didn't have the nerve to say that to the boss. An' he went on talkin', sayin' how sorry he was, see? He was standin' right close to me. An' his coat only had two buttons on it. Two an' two makes four an'—aw, can it! An' there was the bill file on the desk. Right where I could touch it. It ain't right to kill a guy. I know that. When I read all about him in the paper an' about his three kids I felt like a cheapskate, I tell you. They had the kids' pictures in the paper, right next to mine. An' his wife too. Gee, it must be swell to have a wife like that. Some guys sure is lucky. An' he left fifty thousand dollars just for a rest room for the girls in the store. He was a good guy at that. Fifty thousand. That's more'n twice as much as I'd have if I saved every nickel I ever made. Let's see. Twenty-five an' twenty-five an' twenty-five an'—aw, cut it out! An' the ads had a big, black border around 'em; an' all it said was that the store would be closed for three days on account of the boss bein' dead. That nearly handed me a laugh, that did. All them floor-walkers an' buyers an' high-muck-a-mucks havin' me to thank for gettin' three days off. I hadn't oughta killed him.

I ain't sayin' nothin' about that. But I thought he was goin' to give me a raise, see? On account of bein' there twenty-five years. He never talked to me before, see? Except one mornin' we happened to come in the store together and I held the door open for him and he said "Thanks." Just like that, see? "Thanks!" That was the only time he ever talked to me. An' when I seen him comin' up to my desk, I didn't know where I got off. A big guy like that comin' up to my desk. I felt like I was chokin' like and all of a sudden I got a kind o' bad taste in my mouth like when you get up in the mornin'. I didn't have no right to kill him. The district attorney is right about that. He read the law to you, right out o' the book. Killin' a bird—that's wrong. But there was that girl, see? Six months they gave her. It was a dirty trick tellin' the cops on her like that. I shouldn't 'a' done that. But what was I gonna do? The wife wouldn't let up on me. I hadda do it. She used to walk around the room, just in her under-shirt, see? Nothin' else on. Just her undershirt. An' they gave her six months. That's the last I'll ever see of her. Them birds—how do they get away with it? Just grabbin' women, the way you see 'em do in the pictures. I've seen lots I'd like to grab like that, but I ain't got the nerve— in the subway an' on the street an' in the store buyin' things. Pretty soft for them shoe salesmen, I'll say, lookin' at women's legs all day. Them lawyers! They give me a pain, I tell you—a pain! Sayin' the same thing over an' over again. I never said I didn't kill him. But that ain't the same as bein' a regular murderer. What good did it do me to kill him? I didn't make nothin' out of it. Answer yes or no! Yes or no, me elbow! There's some things you can't answer yes or no. Give me the once-over, you guys. Do I look like a murderer? Do I? I never did no harm to nobody. Ask the wife. She'll tell you. Ask anybody. I never got into trouble. You wouldn't count that one time at the Polo Grounds. That was just fun like. Everybody was yellin', "Kill the empire! Kill the empire!" An' before I knew what I was doin' I fired the pop bottle. It was on account of everybody yellin' like that. Just in fun like, see? The yeller dog! Callin' that one a strike—a mile away from the plate. Anyhow, the bottle didn't hit him. An'

when I seen the cop comin' up the aisle, I beat it. That
didn't hurt nobody. It was just in fun like, see? An' that
time in the subway. I was readin' about a lynchin', see?
Down in Georgia. They took the nigger an' they tied him
to a tree. An' they poured kerosene on him and lit a big
fire under him. The dirty nigger! Boy, I'd of liked to been
there, with a gat in each hand, pumpin' him full of lead.
I was readin' about it in the subway, see? Right at Times
Square where the big crowd gets on. An' all of a sudden this
big nigger steps right on my foot. It was lucky for him I
didn't have a gun on me. I'd of killed him sure, I guess. I
guess he couldn't help it all right on àccount of the crowd,
but a nigger's got no right to step on a white man's foot. I
told him where he got off all right. The dirty nigger. But
that didn't hurt nobody either. I'm a pretty steady guy,
you gotta admit that. Twenty-five years in one job an' I
never missed a day. Fifty-two weeks in a year. Fifty-two an'
fifty-two an' fifty-two an'— They didn't have t' look for me,
did they? I didn't try to run away, did I? Where was I goin'
to run to! I wasn't thinkin' about it at all, see? I'll tell you
what I was thinkin' about—how I was goin' to break it
to the wife about bein' canned. He canned me after twenty-
five years, see? Did the lawyers tell you about that? I forget.
All that talk gives me a headache. Objection sustained.
Objection overruled. Answer yes, or no. It gives me a headache. And I can't get the figgers outta my head neither.
But that's what I was thinkin' about—how I was goin' t'
break it to the wife about bein' canned. An' what Miss
Devore would think when she heard about me killin' him.
I bet she never thought I had the nerve to do it. I'd of
married her if the wife had passed out. I'd be holdin' down
my job yet if he hadn't o' canned me. But he kept talkin'
an' talkin'. An' there was the bill file right where I could
reach it. Do you get me? I'm just a regular guy like anybody else. Like you birds, now. [*For the first time the
jurors relax, looking indignantly at each other and whispering.*]
Suppose you was me, now. Maybe you'd 'a' done the
same thing. That's the way you oughta look at it, see?
Suppose you was me——
Jurors [*rising as one and shouting in unison*]. GUILTY!

ZERO *falls back, stunned for a moment by their vociferousness. The* JURORS *right-face in their places and file quickly out of the jury box and toward the door in a double column.*

Zero [*recovering speech as the* JURORS *pass out at the door*]. Wait a minute. Jest a minute. You don't get me right. Jest give me a chance an' I'll tell you how it was. I'm all mixed up, see? On account of them lawyers. And the figgers in my head. But I'm goin' to tell you how it was. I was there twenty-five years, see? An' they gave her six months, see?

He goes on haranguing the empty jury box as the curtain falls.

Curtain.

SCENE V

In the middle of the stage is a large cage with bars on all four sides. The bars are very far apart and the interior of the cage is clearly visible. The floor of the cage is about six feet above the level of the stage. A flight of wooden steps lead up to it on the side facing the audience. ZERO *is discovered in the middle of the cage seated at a table above which is suspended a single naked electric light. Before him is an enormous platter of ham and eggs which he eats voraciously with a large wooden spoon. He wears a uniform of very broad black and white horizontal stripes. A few moments after the rise of the curtain a man enters at left, wearing the blue uniform and peaked cap of a* GUIDE. *He is followed by a miscellaneous crowd of Men, Women, and Children—about a dozen in all.*

GUIDE [*stopping in front of the cage*]. Now ladies and gentlemen, if you'll kindly step right this way! [*The crowd straggles up and forms a loose semicircle around him.*]

Note: This scene was part of the original script. It was omitted, however, when the play was produced, and was performed for the first time (in its present revised form) when the play was revived at the Phoenix Theatre in New York in February, 1956.—ELMER RICE

Step right up, please. A little closer so's everybody can hear.
[*They move up closer.* ZERO *pays no attention whatever
to them.*] This, ladies and gentlemen, is a very in-ter-est-in'
specimen; the North American murderer, Genus homo
sapiens, Habitat North America. [*A titter of excitement.
They all crowd up around the cage.*] Don't push. There's
room enough for everybody.

Tall Lady. Oh, how interesting!

Stout Lady [*excitedly*]. Look, Charley, he's eating!

Charley [*bored*]. Yeh, I see him.

Guide [*repeating by rote*]. This specimen, ladies and
gentlemen, exhibits the characteristics which are typical of
his kind——

Small Boy [*in a Little Lord Fauntleroy suit, whiningly*].
Mama!

Mother. Be quiet, Eustace, or I'll take you right home.

Guide. He has the opposable thumbs, the large cranial
capacity, and the highly developed prefrontal areas which
distinguish him from all other species.

Youth [*who has been taking notes*]. What areas did you
say?

Guide [*grumpily*]. Pre-front-al areas. He learns by imi-
tation and has a language which is said by some eminent
philiologists to bear many striking resemblances to English.

Boy of Fourteen. Pop, what's a philiologist?

Father. Keep quiet, can't you, and listen to what he's
sayin'.

Guide. He thrives and breeds freely in captivity. This
specimen was taken alive in his native haunts shortly after
murdering his boss. [*Murmurs of great interest.*]

Tall Lady. Oh, how charming!

Youth [*again taking notes*]. What was that last? I didn't
get it.

Several [*helpfully*]. Murdering his boss.

Youth. Oh—thanks.

Guide. He was tried, convicted and sentenced in one
hour, thirteen minutes and twenty-four seconds, which sets
a new record for the territory east of the Rockies and north
of the Mason and Dixon line.

Little Lord Fauntleroy [*whiningly*]. Ma-ma!

Mother. Be quiet, Eustace, or Mama won't let you ride in the choo-choo.

Guide. Now take a good look at him, ladies and gents. It's his last day here. He's goin' to be executed at noon. [*Murmurs of interest.*]

Tall Lady. Oh, how lovely!

Man. What's he eating?

Guide. Ham and eggs.

Stout Lady. He's quite a big eater, ain't he?

Guide. Oh, he don't always eat that much. You see we always try to make 'em feel good on their last day. So about a week in advance we let them order what they want to eat on their last day. They can have eight courses and they can order anything they want—don't make no difference what it costs or how hard it is to get. Well, he couldn't make up his mind till last night and then he ordered eight courses of ham and eggs. [*They all push and stare.*]

Boy of Fourteen. Look, Pop! He's eatin' with a spoon. Don't he know how to use a knife and fork?

Guide [*overhearing him*]. We don't dare trust him with a knife and fork, sonny. He might try to kill himself.

Tall Lady. Oh, how fascinating!

Guide [*resuming his official tone*]. And now, friends, if you'll kindly give me your kind attention for just a moment. [*He takes a bundle of folders from his pocket.*] I have a little souvenir folder, which I'm sure you'll all want to have. It contains twelve beautiful colored views relating to the North American Murderer you have just been looking at. These include a picture of the murderer, a picture of the murderer's wife, the blood-stained weapon, the murderer at the age of six, the spot where the body was found, the little red schoolhouse where he went to school, and his vine-covered boyhood home in southern Illinois, with his sweet-faced, white-haired old mother plainly visible in the foreground. And many other interesting views. I'm now going to distribute these little folders for your examination. [*Sotto voce.*] Just pass them back, will you. [*In louder tones.*] Don't be afraid to look at them. You don't have to buy them if you don't want to. It don't cost anything to look at them. [*To the* YOUTH, *who is fumbling with a camera.*] Hey, there, young feller, no snapshots allowed. All right now, friends, if you'll just step this way. Keep close together and follow me. A lady lost her little boy here one time and by the time we found him, he was smoking cigarettes and hollering for a razor.

Much laughter as they all follow him off left. ZERO *finishes eating and pushes away his plate. As the crowd goes at left,* MRS. ZERO *enters at right. She is dressed in mourning garments. She carries a large parcel. She goes up the steps to the cage, opens the door, and enters.* ZERO *looks up and sees her.*

Mrs. Zero. Hello.

Zero. Hello, I didn't think you were comin' again.

Mrs. Zero. Well, I thought I'd come again. Are you glad to see me?

Zero. Sure. Sit down. [*She complies.*] You're all dolled up, ain't you?

Mrs. Zero. Yeh, don't you like it? [*She gets up and turns about like a mannequin.*]

Zero. Gee. Some class.

Mrs. Zero. I always look good in black. There's some weight to this veil though; I'll tell the world. I got a fierce headache.

Zero. How much did all that set you back?

Mrs. Zero. Sixty-four dollars and twenty cents. And I gotta get a pin yet and some writin' paper—you know, with black around the edges.

Zero. You'll be scrubbin' floors in about a year, if you go blowin' your coin like that.

Mrs. Zero. Well, I gotta do it right. It don't happen every day. [*She rises and takes up the parcel.*] I brought you somethin'.

Zero [*interested*]. Yeh, what?

Mrs. Zero [*opening the parcel*]. You gotta guess.

Zero. Er—er—gee, search me.

Mrs. Zero. Somethin' you like. [*She takes out a covered plate.*]

Zero [*with increasing interest*]. Looks like somethin' to eat.

Mrs. Zero [*nodding*]. Yeh. [*She takes off the top plate.*] Ham an' eggs!

Zero [*joyfully*]. Oh, boy! Just what I feel like eatin'. [*He takes up the wooden spoon and begins to eat avidly.*]

Mrs. Zero [*pleased*]. Are they good?

Zero [*his mouth full*]. Swell.

Mrs. Zero [*a little sadly*]. They're the last ones I'll ever make for you.

Zero [*busily eating*]. Uh-huh.

Mrs. Zero. I'll tell you somethin'—shall I?

Zero. Sure.

Mrs. Zero [*hesitantly*]. Well, all the while they were cookin' I was cryin'.

Zero. Yeh? [*He leans over and pats her hand.*]

Mrs. Zero. I jest couldn't help it. The thought of it jest made me cry.

Zero. Well—no use cryin' about it.

Mrs. Zero. I jest couldn't help it.

Zero. Maybe this time next year you'll be fryin' eggs for some other bird.

Mrs. Zero. Not on your life.

Zero. You never can tell.

Mrs. Zero. Not me. Once is enough for me.

Zero. I guess you're right at that. Still, I dunno. You might jest happen to meet some guy——

Mrs. Zero. Well, if I do, there'll be time enough to think about it. No use borrowin' trouble.

Zero. How do you like bein' alone in the house?

Mrs. Zero. Oh, it's all right.

Zero. You got plenty room in the bed now, ain't you?

Mrs. Zero. Oh yeh. [*A brief pause.*] It's kinda lonesome though—you know, wakin' up in the mornin' and nobody around to talk to.

Zero. Yeh, I know. It's the same with me.

Mrs. Zero. Not that we ever did much talkin'.

Zero. Well, that ain't it. It's just the idea of havin' somebody there in case you want to talk.

Mrs. Zero. Yeh, that's it. [*Another brief pause.*] I guess maybe I use t'bawl you out quite a lot, didn't I?

Zero. Oh well—no use talkin' about it now.

Mrs. Zero. We were always at it, weren't we?

Zero. No more than any other married folks, I guess.

Mrs. Zero [*dubiously*]. I dunno——

Zero. I guess I gave you cause, all right.

Mrs. Zero. Well, I got my faults too.

Zero. None of us are perfect.

Mrs. Zero. We got along all right, at that, didn't we?

Zero. Sure! Better'n most.

Mrs. Zero. Remember them Sundays at the beach, in the old days?

Zero. You bet. [*With a laugh.*] Remember that time I ducked you? Gee, you was mad!

Mrs. Zero [*with a laugh*]. I didn't talk to you for a whole week.

Zero [*chuckling*]. Yeh, I remember.

Mrs. Zero. And the time I had pneumonia and you brought me them roses. Remember?

Zero. Yeh, I remember. And when the doctor told me maybe you'd pass out, I nearly sat down and cried.

Mrs. Zero. Did you?

Zero. I sure did.

Mrs. Zero. We had some pretty good times at that, didn't we?

Zero. I'll say we did!

Mrs. Zero [*with a sudden soberness*]. It's all over now.

Zero. All over is right. I ain't got much longer.

Mrs. Zero [*rising and going over to him*]. Maybe—maybe—if we had to do it over again, it would be different.

Zero [*taking her hand*]. Yeh. We live and learn.

Mrs. Zero [*crying*]. If we only had another chance.

Zero. It's too late now.

Mrs. Zero. It don't seem right, does it?

Zero. It ain't right. But what can you do about it?

Mrs. Zero. Ain't there somethin'—somethin' I can do for you—before——

Zero. No. Nothin'. Not a thing.

Mrs. Zero. Nothin' at all?

Zero. No. I can't think of anything. [*Suddenly.*] You're takin' good care of that scrapbook, ain't you? With all the clippings in it?

Mrs. Zero. Oh, sure. I got it right on the parlor table. Right where everybody can see it.

Zero [*pleased*]. It must be pretty near full, ain't it?

Mrs. Zero. All but about three pages.

Zero. Well, there'll be more tomorrow. Enough to fill it, maybe. Be sure to get them all, will you?

Mrs. Zero. I will. I ordered the papers already.

Zero. Gee, I never thought I'd have a whole book full of clippings all about myself. [*Suddenly.*] Say, that's somethin' I'd like to ask you.

Mrs. Zero. What?

Zero. Suppose you should get sick or be run over or somethin', what would happen to the book?

Mrs. Zero. Well, I kinda thought I'd leave it to little Beatrice Elizabeth.

Zero. Who? Your sister's kid?

Mrs. Zero. Yeh.

Zero. What would she want with it?

Mrs. Zero. Well, it's nice to have, ain't it? And I wouldn't know who else to give it to.

Zero. Well, I don't want her to have it. That fresh little kid puttin' her dirty fingers all over it.

Mrs. Zero. She ain't fresh and she ain't dirty. She's a sweet little thing.

Zero. I don't want her to have it.

Mrs. Zero. Who do you want to have it then?

Zero. Well, I kinda thought I'd like Miss Devore to have it.

Mrs. Zero. Miss Devore?

Zero. Yeh. You know. Down at the store.

Mrs. Zero. Why should she have it?

Zero. She'd take good care of it. And anyhow, I'd like her to have it.

Mrs. Zero. Oh you would, would you?

Zero. Yes.

Mrs. Zero. Well, she ain't goin' to have it. Miss Devore! Where does she come in, I'd like to know, when I got two sisters and a niece.

Zero. I don't care nothin' about your sisters and your niece.

Mrs. Zero. Well, I do! And Miss Devore ain't goin' to get it. Now put that in your pipe and smoke it.

Zero. What have you got to say about it? It's my book, ain't it?

Mrs. Zero. No, it ain't. It's mine now—or it will be tomorrow. And I'm goin' to do what I like with it.

Zero. I should of given it to her in the first place, that's what I should of done.

Mrs. Zero. Oh, should you? And what about me? Am I your wife or ain't I?

Zero. Why remind me of my troubles?

Mrs. Zero. So it's Miss Devore all of a sudden, is it? What's been goin' on, I'd like to know, between you and Miss Devore?

Zero. Aw, tie a can to that!

Mrs. Zero. Why didn't you marry Miss Devore, if you think so much of her?

Zero. I would if I'd of met her first.

Mrs. Zero [*shrieking*]. Ooh! A fine way to talk to me. After all I've done for you. You bum! You dirty bum! I won't stand for it! I won't stand for it!

In a great rage Mrs. Zero *takes up the dishes and smashes them on the floor. Then crying hysterically she opens the cage door, bangs it behind her, comes down the steps, and goes off toward left.* Zero *stands gazing ruefully after her for a moment, and then with a shrug and a sigh begins picking up the pieces of broken crockery.*

As Mrs. Zero *exits at left a door in the back of the cage opens and a* Man *enters. He is dressed in a sky-blue padded silk dressing gown which is fitted with innumerable pockets. Under this he wears a pink silk union suit. His bare feet are in sandals. He wears a jaunty Panama hat with a red feather stuck in the brim. Wings are fastened to his sandals and to the shoulders of his dressing gown.* Zero, *who is busy picking up the broken crockery, does not notice him at first. The* Man *takes a gold toothpick and begins carefully picking his teeth, waiting for* Zero *to notice him.* Zero *happens to look up and suddenly sees the* Man. *He utters a cry of terror and shrinks into a corner of the cage, trembling with fear.*

Zero [*hoarsely*]. Who are you?

Man [*calmly, as he pockets his toothpick*] I'm the Fixer —from the Claim Department.

Zero. Whaddya want?

The Fixer. It's no use, Zero. There are no miracles.

Zero. I don't know what you're talkin' about.

The Fixer. Don't lie, Zero. [*Holding up his hand.*] And now that your course is run—now that the end is already in sight, you still believe that some thunderbolt, some fiery bush, some celestial apparition will intervene between you and extinction. But it's no use, Zero. You're done for.

Zero [*vehemently*]. It ain't right! It ain't fair! I ain't gettin' a square deal!

The Fixer [*wearily*]. They all say that, Zero. [*Mildly.*] Now just tell me why you're not getting a square deal.

Zero. Well, that addin' machine. Was that a square deal —after twenty-five years?

The Fixer. Certainly—from any point of view, except a sentimental one. [*Looking at his wrist watch.*] The machine is quicker, it never makes a mistake, it's always on time. It presents no problems of housing, traffic congestion, water supply, sanitation.

Zero. It costs somethin' to buy them machines, I'll tell you that!

The Fixer. Yes, you're right there. In one respect you have the advantage over the machine—the cost of manufacture. But we've learned from many years' experience, Zero, that the original cost is an inconsequential item compared to upkeep. Take the dinosaurs, for example. They literally ate themselves out of existence. I held out for them to the last. They were damned picturesque—but when it came to a question of the nitrate supply, I simply had to yield. [*He begins to empty and clean his pipe.*] And so with you, Zero. It costs a lot to keep up all that delicate mechanism of eye and ear and hand and brain which you've never put to any use. We can't afford to maintain it in idleness —and so you've got to go. [*He puts the pipe in one of his pockets.*]

Zero [*falling to his knees, supplicatingly*]. Gimme a chance, gimme another chance!

The Fixer. What would you do if I gave you another chance?

Zero. Well—first thing I'd go out and look for a job.

The Fixer. Adding figures?

Zero. Well, I ain't young enough to take up somethin' new.

THE FIXER *takes out a police whistle and blows shrilly. Instantly two guards enter.*

The Fixer. Put the skids under him, boys, and make it snappy. [*He strolls away to the other side of the cage, and taking a nail clipper from a pocket, begins to clip his nails as the* GUARDS *seize* ZERO.]

Zero [*struggling and shrieking*]. No! No! Don't take me away! Don't kill me! Gimme a chance! Gimme another chance!

Guard [*soothingly*]. Ah, come on! Be a good fellow! It'll all be over in a minute!

Zero. I don't want to die! I don't want to die! I want to live!

The GUARDS *look at each other dubiously. Then one of them walks rather timidly over to* THE FIXER, *who is busy with his nails.*

Guard [*clearing his throat*]. H'm!
The Fixer [*looking up*]. Well?
Guard [*timidly*]. He says he wants to live.
The Fixer. No. He's no good.
Guard [*touching his cap, deferentially*]. Yes sir! [*He goes back to his companion and the two of them drag* ZERO *out at the back of the cage, still struggling and screaming.*]

THE FIXER *puts away his nail clippers, yawns, then goes to the table and sits on the edge of it. From a pocket he takes an enoromous pair of horn-rimmed spectacles. Then from another pocket he takes a folded newspaper, which he unfolds carefully. It is a colored comic supplement. He holds it up in front of him and becomes absorbed in it.*

A moment later the door at the back of the cage opens and a tall, brawny, bearded MAN *enters. He wears a red flannel undershirt and carries a huge blood-stained axe.* THE FIXER, *absorbed in the comic supplement, does not look up.*

Man [*hoarsely*]. O.K.
The Fixer [*looking up*]. What?
Man. O.K.

The Fixer [nodding]. Oh, all right. [*The* MAN *bows deferentially and goes out at the back.* THE FIXER *puts away his spectacles and folds the comic supplement carefully. As he folds the paper.*] That makes a total of 2,137 black eyes for Jeff.

He puts away the paper, turns out the electric light over his head, and leaves the cage by the front door. Then he takes a padlock from a pocket, attaches it to the door, and saunters off.

Curtain.

SCENE VI

*A graveyard in full moonlight. It is a second-rate graveyard —no elaborate tombstones or monuments, just simple headstones and here and there a cross. At the back is an iron fence with a gate in the middle. At first no one is visible, but there are occasional sounds throughout: the hooting of an owl, the whistle of a distant whippoorwill, the croaking of a bullfrog, and the yowling of a serenading cat. After a few moments two figures appear outside the gate—a man and a woman. She pushes the gate and it opens with a rusty creak. The couple enter. They are now fully visible in the moonlight—*JUDY O'GRADY *and a* YOUNG MAN.

JUDY [*advancing*]. Come on, this is the place.

Young Man [hanging back]. This! Why this here is a cemetery.

Judy. Aw, quit yer kiddin'!

Young Man. You don't mean to say——

Judy. What's the matter with this place?

Young Man. A cemetery!

Judy. Sure. What of it?

Young Man. You must be crazy.

Judy. This place is all right, I tell you. I been here lots o' times.

Young Man. Nix on this place for me!

Judy. Ain't this place as good as another? Whaddya afraid of? They're all dead ones here! They don't bother you. [*With sudden interest.*] Oh, look, here's a new one.

Young Man. Come on out of here.

Judy. Wait a minute. Let's see what it says. [*She kneels on a grave in the foreground and putting her face close to the headstone spells out the inscription.*] Z-E-R-O. Z-e-r-o. Zero! Say, that's the guy——

Young Man. Zero? He's the guy killed his boss, ain't he?

Judy. Yeh, that's him, all right. But what I'm thinkin' of is that I went to the hoosegow on account of him.

Young Man. What for?

Judy. You know, same old stuff. Tenement House Law. [*Mincingly.*] Section blaa-blaa of the Penal Code. Third offense. Six months.

Young Man. And this bird——

Judy [*contemptuously*]. Him? He was mama's white-haired boy. We lived in the same house. Across the air-shaft, see? I used to see him lookin' in my window. I guess his wife musta seen him too. Anyhow, they went and turned the bulls on me. And now I'm out and he's in. [*Suddenly.*] Say—say—— [*She bursts into a peal of laughter.*]

Young Man [*nervously*]. What's so funny?

Judy [*rocking with laughter*]. Say, wouldn't it be funny —if—if—— [*She explodes again.*] That would be a good joke on him, all right. He can't do nothin' about it now, can he?

Young Man. Come on out of here. I don't like this place.

Judy. Aw, you're a bum sport. What do you want to spoil my joke for?

A cat yammers mellifluously.

Young Man [*half hysterically*]. What's that?

Judy. It's only the cats. They seem to like it here all right. But come on if you're afraid. [*They go toward the gate. As they go out.*] You nervous men sure are the limit.

They go out through the gate. As they disappear ZERO's *grave opens suddenly and his head appears.*

Zero [*looking about*]. That's funny! I thought I heard her talkin' and laughin'. But I don't see nobody. Anyhow,

what would she be doin' here? I guess I must 'a' been
dreamin'. But how could I be dreamin' when I ain't been
asleep? [*He looks about again.*] Well, no use goin' back.
I can't sleep anyhow. I might as well walk around a little.
[*He rises out of the ground, very rigidly. He wears a full-
dress suit of very antiquated cut and his hands are folded
stiffly across his breast. Walking woodenly.*] Gee! I'm stiff!
[*He slowly walks a few steps, then stops.*] Gee, it's lonesome here! [*He shivers and walks on aimlessly.*] I should
'a' stayed where I was. But I thought I heard her laughin'.
[*A loud sneeze is heard. ZERO stands motionless, quaking
with terror. The sneeze is repeated. ZERO says hoarsely.*]
What's that?

A *Mild Voice.* It's all right. Nothing to be afraid of.

From behind a headstone SHRDLU *appears. He is dressed in
a shabby and ill-fitting cutaway. He wears silver-rimmed
spectacles and is smoking a cigarette.*

Shrdlu. I hope I didn't frighten you.
Zero [*still badly shaken*]. No-o. It's all right. You see, I
wasn't expectin' to see anybody.
Shrdlu. You're a newcomer, aren't you?
Zero. Yeh, this is my first night. I couldn't seem to get
to sleep.
Shrdlu. I can't sleep either. Suppose we keep each other
company, shall we?
Zero [*eagerly*]. Yeh, that would be great. I been feelin'
awful lonesome.
Shrdlu [*nodding*]. I know. Let's make ourselves com-
fortable.

He seats himself easily on a grave. ZERO *tries to follow his
example but he is stiff in every joint and groans with pain.*

Zero. I'm kinda stiff.
Shrdlu. You mustn't mind the stiffness. It wears off in
a few days. [*He produces a package of cigarettes.*] Will you
have a Camel?
Zero. No, I don't smoke.
Shrdlu. I find it helps keep the mosquitoes away. [*He
lights a cigarette. Suddenly taking the cigarette out of his
mouth.*] Do you mind if I smoke, Mr.—Mr.—?

Zero. No, go right ahead.

Shrdlu [*replacing the cigarette*]. Thank you. I didn't catch your name. [ZERO *does not reply. Mildly.*] I say I didn't catch your name.

Zero. I heard you the first time. [*Hesistantly.*] I'm scared if I tell you who I am and what I done, you'll be off me.

Shrdlu [*sadly*]. No matter what your sins may be, they are as snow compared to mine.

Zero. You got another guess comin'. [*He pauses dramatically.*] My name's Zero. I'm a murderer.

Shrdlu [*nodding calmly*]. Oh, yes, I remember reading about you, Mr. Zero.

Zero [*a little piqued*]. And you still think you're worse than me?

Shrdlu [*throwing away his cigarette*]. Oh, a thousand times worse, Mr. Zero—a million times worse.

Zero. What did you do?

Shrdlu. I, too, am a murderer.

Zero [*looking at him in amazement*]. Go on! You're kiddin' me!

Shrdlu. Every word I speak is the truth, Mr. Zero. I am the foulest, the most sinful of murderers! You only murdered your employer, Mr. Zero. But I—I murdered my mother. [*He covers his face with his hands and sobs.*]

Zero [*horrified*]. The hell yer say!

Shrdlu [*sobbing*]. Yes, my mother! My beloved mother!

Zero [*suddenly*]. Say, you don't mean to say you're Mr.——

Shrdlu [*nodding*]. Yes. [*He wipes his eyes, still quivering with emotion.*]

Zero. I remember readin' about you in the papers.

Shrdlu. Yes, my guilt has been proclaimed to all the world. But that would be a trifle if only I could wash the stain of sin from my soul.

Zero. I never heard of a guy killin' his mother before. What did you do it for?

Shrdlu. Because I have a sinful heart—there is no other reason.

Zero. Did she always treat you square and all like that?

Shrdlu. She was a saint—a saint, I tell you. She cared for **me** and watched over me as only a mother can.

Zero. You mean to say you didn't have a scrap or nothin'?

Shrdlu. Never a harsh or an unkind word. Nothing except loving care and good advice. From my infancy she devoted herself to guiding me on the right path. She taught me to be thrifty, to be devout, to be unselfish, to shun evil companions, and to shut my ears to all the temptations of the flesh—in short, to become a virtuous, respectable, and God-fearing man. [*He groans.*] But it was a hopeless task. At fourteen I began to show evidence of my sinful nature.

Zero [*breathlessly*]. You didn't kill anybody else, did you?

Shrdlu. No, thank God, there is only one murder on my soul. But I ran away from home.

Zero. You did!

Shrdlu. Yes. A companion lent me a profane book—the only profane book I have ever read, I'm thankful to say. It was called *Treasure Island*. Have you ever read it?

Zero. No, I never was much on readin' books.

Shrdlu. It is a wicked book—a lurid tale of adventure. But it kindled in my sinful heart a desire to go to sea. And so I ran away from home.

Zero. What did you do—get a job as a sailor?

Shrdlu. I never saw the sea—not to the day of my death. Luckily my mother's loving intuition warned her of my intention and I was sent back home. She welcomed me with open arms. Not an angry word, not a look of reproach. But I could read the mute suffering in her eyes as we prayed together all through the night.

Zero [*sympathetically*]. Gee, that must 'a' been tough. Gee, the mosquitoes are bad, ain't they? [*He tries awkwardly to slap at them with his stiff hands.*]

Shrdlu [*absorbed in his narrative*]. I thought that experience had cured me of evil and I began to think about a career. I wanted to go in foreign missions at first, but we couldn't bear the thought of the separation. So we finally decided that I should become a proofreader.

Zero. Say, slip me one o' them Camels, will you? I'm gettin' all bit up.

Shrdlu. Certainly. [*He hands* ZERO *cigarettes and matches.*]

Zero [*lighting up*]. Go ahead. I'm listenin'.

Shrdlu. By the time I was twenty I had a good job reading proof for a firm that printed catalogues. After a year they promoted me and let me specialize in shoe catalogues.

Zero. Yeh? That must 'a' been a good job.

Shrdlu. It was a very good job. I was on the shoe catalogues for thirteen years. I'd been on them yet, if I hadn't —— [*He chokes back a sob.*]

Zero. They oughta put a shot o' citronella in that embalmin' fluid.

Shrdlu [*sighs*]. We were so happy together. I had my steady job. And Sundays we would go to morning, afternoon, and evening service. It was an honest and moral mode of life.

Zero. It sure was.

Shrdlu. Then came that fatal Sunday. Dr. Amaranth, our minister, was having dinner with us—one of the few pure spirits on earth. When he had finished saying grace, we had our soup. Everything was going along as usual—we were eating our soup and discussing the sermon, just like every other Sunday I could remember. Then came the leg of lamb—— [*He breaks off, then resumes in a choking voice.*] I see the whole scene before me so plainly—it never leaves me—Dr. Amaranth at my right, my mother at my left, the leg of lamb on the table in front of me, and the cuckoo clock on the little shelf between the windows. [*He stops and wipes his eyes.*]

Zero. Yeh, but what happened?

Shrdlu. Well, as I started to carve the lamb—— Did you ever carve a leg of lamb?

Zero. No, corned beef was our speed.

Shrdlu. It's very difficult on account of the bone. And when there's gravy in the dish there's danger of spilling it. So Mother always used to hold the dish for me. She leaned forward, just as she always did, and I could see the gold locket around her neck. It had my picture in it and one of my baby curls. Well, I raised my knife to carve the leg of lamb—and instead I cut my mother's throat! [*He sobs.*]

Zero. You must 'a' been crazy!

Shrdlu [*raising his head, vehemently*]. No! Don't try to justify me. I wasn't crazy. They tried to prove at the trial that I was crazy. But Dr. Amaranth saw the truth! He saw it from the first! He knew that it was my sinful nature—and he told me what was in store for me.

Zero [*trying to be comforting*]. Well, your troubles are over now.

Shrdlu [*his voice rising*]. Over! Do you think this is the end?

Zero. Sure. What more can they do to us?

Shrdlu [*his tones growing shriller and shriller*]. Do you think there can ever be any peace for such as we are—murderers, sinners? Don't you know what awaits us—flames, eternal flames!

Zero [*nervously*]. Keep your shirt on, buddy—they wouldn't do that to us.

Shrdlu. There's no escape—no escape for us, I tell you. We're doomed! We're doomed to suffer unspeakable torments through all eternity. [*His voice rises higher and higher.*]

A grave opens suddenly and a head appears.

The Head. Hey, you birds! Can't you shut up and let a guy sleep?

Zero *scrambles painfully to his feet.*

Zero [*to* Shrdlu]. Hey, put on the soft pedal.

Shrdlu [*too wrought up to attend*]. It won't be long now! We'll receive our summons soon.

The Head. Are you goin' to beat it or not? [*He calls into the grave.*] Hey, Bill, lend me your head a minute. [*A moment later his arm appears holding a skull.*]

Zero [*warningly*]. Look out! [*He seizes* Shrdlu *and drags him away just as* The Head *throws the skull.*]

The Head [*disgustedly*]. Missed 'em. Damn old tabby cats! I'll get 'em next time. [*A prodigious yawn.*] Ho-hum! Me for the worms!

The Head *disappears as the curtain falls.*

Curtain.

SCENE VII

*A pleasant place. A scene of pastoral loveliness. A meadow
dotted with fine old trees and carpeted with rich grass and
field flowers. In the background are seen a number of tents
fashioned of gay-striped silks, and beyond gleams a mean-
dering river. Clear air and a fleckless sky. Sweet distant
music throughout.*

At the rise of the curtain SHRDLU *is seen seated under a
tree in the foreground in an attitude of deep dejection. His
knees are drawn up and his head is buried in his arms. He
is dressed as in the preceding scene.*

A few minutes later ZERO *enters at right. He walks slowly
and looks about him with an air of half-suspicious curiosity.
He too is dressed as in the preceding scene. Suddenly he
sees* SHRDLU *seated under the tree. He stands still and looks
at him half fearfully. Then, seeing something familiar in
him, goes closer.* SHRDLU *is unaware of his presence. At last*
    ZERO *recognizes him and grins in pleased surprise.*

ZERO. Well, if it ain't——! [*He claps* SHRDLU *on the
shoulder.*] Hello, buddy!

SHRDLU *looks up slowly, then, recognizing* ZERO, *he rises
        gravely and extends his hand courteously.*

Shrdlu. How do you do, Mr. Zero? I'm very glad to see
you again.

Zero. Same here. I wasn't expectin' to see you either.
[*Looking about.*] This is a kinda nice place. I wouldn't
mind restin' here a while.

Shrdlu. You may if you wish.

Zero. I'm kinda tired. I ain't used to bein' outdoors. I
ain't walked so much in years.

Shrdlu. Sit down here, under the tree.

Zero. Do they let you sit on the grass?

Shrdlu. Oh, yes.

Zero [*seating himself*]. Boy, this feels good. I'll tell the
world my feet are sore. I ain't used to so much walkin'.
Say, I wonder would it be all right if I took my shoes off;
my feet are tired.

Shrdlu. Yes. Some of the people here go barefoot.

Zero. Yeh? They sure must be nuts. But I'm goin' t' leave 'em off for a while. So long as it's all right. The grass feels nice and cool. [*He stretches out comfortably.*] Say, this is the life of Riley all right, all right. This sure is a nice place. What do they call this place, anyhow?

Shrdlu. The Elysian Fields.

Zero. The which?

Shrdlu. The Elysian Fields.

Zero [*dubiously*]. Oh! Well, it's a nice place, all right.

Shrdlu. They say that this is the most desirable of all places. Only the most favored remain here.

Zero. Yeh? Well, that lets me out, I guess. [*Suddenly.*] But what are you doin' here? I thought you'd be burned by now.

Shrdlu [*sadly*]. Mr. Zero, I am the most unhappy of men.

Zero [*in mild astonishment*]. Why, because you ain't bein' roasted alive?

Shrdlu [*nodding*]. Nothing is turning out as I expected. I saw everything so clearly—the flames, the tortures, an eternity of suffering as the just punishment for my unspeakable crime. And it has all turned out so differently.

Zero. Well, that's pretty soft for you, ain't it?

Shrdlu [*wailingly*]. No, no, no! It's right and just that I should be punished. I could have endured it stoically. All through those endless ages of indescribable torment I should have exulted in the magnificence of divine justice. But this—this is maddening! What becomes of justice? What becomes of morality? What becomes of right and wrong? It's maddening—simply maddening! Oh, if Dr. Amaranth were only here to advise me! [*He buries his face and groans.*]

Zero [*trying to puzzle it out*]. You mean to say they ain't called you for cuttin' your mother's throat?

Shrdlu. No! It's terrible—terrible! I was prepared for anything—anything but this.

Zero. Well, what did they say to you?

Shrdlu [*looking up*]. Only that I was to come here and remain until I understood.

Zero. I don't get it. What do they want you to understand?

Shrdlu [*despairingly*]. I don't know—I don't know! If I only had an inkling of what they meant—— [*Interrupting himself.*] Just listen quietly for a moment: do you hear anything? [*They are both silent, straining their ears.*]

Zero [*at last*]. Nope.

Shrdlu. You don't hear any music? Do you?

Zero. Music? No, I don't hear nothin'.

Shrdlu. The people here say that the music never stops.

Zero. They're kiddin' you.

Shrdlu. Do you think so?

Zero. Sure thing. There ain't a sound.

Shrdlu. Perhaps. They're capable of anything. But I haven't told you of the bitterest of my disappointments.

Zero. Well, spill it. I'm gettin' used to hearin' bad news.

Shrdlu. When I came to this place my first thought was to find my dear mother. I wanted to ask her forgiveness. And I wanted her to help me to understand.

Zero. An' she couldn't do it?

Shrdlu [*with a deep groan*]. She's not here, Mr. Zero! Here where only the most favored dwell, that wisest and purest of spirits is nowhere to be found. I don't understand it.

A Woman's Voice [*in the distance*]. Mr. Zero! Oh, Mr. Zero! [ZERO *raises his head and listens attentively.*]

Shrdlu [*going on, unheedingly*]. If you were to see some of the people here—the things they do——

Zero [*interrupting*]. Wait a minute, will you? I think somebody's callin' me.

Voice [*somewhat nearer*]. Mr. Ze-ro! Oh! Mr. Ze-ro!

Zero. Who the hell's that now? I wonder if the wife's on my trail already. That would be swell, wouldn't it? An' I figgered on her bein' good for another twenty years anyhow.

Voice [*nearer*]. Mr. Ze-ro! Yoo-hoo!

Zero. No. That ain't her voice. [*Calling savagely.*] Yoo-hoo. [*To* SHRDLU.] Ain't that always the way? Just when a guy is takin' life easy an' havin' a good time! [*He rises and looks off left.*] Here she comes, whoever she is. [*In sudden amazement.*] Well, I'll be—! Well, what do you know about that!

He stands looking in wonderment as DAISY DIANA DORO-

THEA DEVORE *enters. She wears a much-beruffled white muslin dress which is a size too small and fifteen years too youthful for her. She is red-faced and breathless.*

Daisy [*panting*]. Oh! I thought I'd never catch up to you. I've been followin' you for days—callin' an' callin'. Didn't you hear me?

Zero. Not till just now. You look kinda winded.

Daisy. I sure am. I can't hardly catch my breath.

Zero. Well, sit down an' take a load off your feet. [*He leads her to the tree.*]

DAISY *sees* SHRDLU *for the first time and shrinks back a little.*

Zero. It's all right, he's a friend of mine. [*To* SHRDLU.] Buddy, I want you to meet my friend, Miss Devore.

Shrdlu [*rising and extending his hand courteously*]. How do you do, Miss Devore?

Daisy [*self-consciously*]. How do!

Zero [*to* DAISY]. He's a friend of mine. [*To* SHRDLU.] I guess you don't mind if she sits here a while an' cools off, do you?

Shrdlu. No, no, certainly not.

They all seat themselves under the tree. ZERO *and* DAISY *are a little self-conscious.* SHRDLU *gradually becomes absorbed in his own thoughts.*

Zero. I was just takin' a rest myself. I took my shoes off on account of my feet bein' so sore.

Daisy. Yeh, I'm kinda tired too. [*Looking about.*] Say, ain't it pretty here though?

Zero. Yeh, it is at that.

Daisy. What do they call this place?

Zero. Why—er—let's see. He was tellin' me just a minute ago. The—er—I don't know. Some kind o' fields. I forget now. [*To* SHRDLU.] Say, buddy, what do they call this place again? [SHRDLU, *absorbed in his thoughts, does not hear him. To* DAISY.] He don't hear me. He's thinkin' again.

Daisy [*sotto voce*]. What's the matter with him?

Zero. Why, he's the guy that murdered his mother—remember?

Daisy [*interested*]. Oh, yeh! Is that him?

Zero. Yeh. An' he had it all figgered out how they was goin' t' roast him or somethin'. And now they ain't goin' to do nothin' to him an' it's kinda got his goat.

Daisy [*sympathetically*]. Poor feller!

Zero. Yeh. He takes it kinda hard.

Daisy. He looks like a nice young feller.

Zero. Well, you sure are good for sore eyes. I never expected to see you here.

Daisy. I thought maybe you'd be kinda surprised.

Zero. Surprised is right. I thought you was alive an' kickin'. When did you pass out?

Daisy. Oh, right after you did—a coupla days.

Zero [*interested*]. Yeh? What happened? Get hit by a truck or somethin'?

Daisy. No. [*Hesitantly.*] You see—it's this way. I blew out the gas.

Zero [*astonished*]. Go on! What was the big idea?

Daisy [*falteringly*]. Oh, I don't know. You see, I lost my job.

Zero. I'll bet you're sorry you did it now, ain't you?

Daisy [*with conviction*]. No, I ain't sorry. Not a bit. [*Then hesitantly.*] Say, Mr. Zero, I been thinkin'—— [*She stops.*]

Zero. What?

Daisy [*plucking up courage*]. I been thinkin' it would be kinda nice—if you an' me—if we could kinda talk things over.

Zero. Yeh. Sure. What do you want to talk about?

Daisy. Well—I don't know—but you and me—we ain't really ever talked things over, have we?

Zero. No, that's right, we ain't. Well, let's go to it.

Daisy. I was thinkin' if we could be alone—just the two of us, see?

Zero. Oh, yeh! Yeh, I get you. [*He turns to* SHRDLU *and coughs loudly.* SHRDLU *does not stir.*]

Zero [*to* DAISY]. He's dead to the world. [*He turns to* SHRDLU.] Say, buddy! [*No answer.*] Say, buddy!

Shrdlu [*looking up with a start*]. Were you speaking to me?

Zero. Yeh. How'd you guess it? I was thinkin' that

maybe you'd like to walk around a little and look for your mother.

Shrdlu [*shaking his head*]. It's no use. I've looked everywhere. [*He relapses into thought again.*]

Zero. Maybe over there they might know.

Shrdlu. No, no! I've searched everywhere. She's not here.

ZERO *and* DAISY *look at each other in despair.*

Zero. Listen, old shirt, my friend here and me—see? —we used to work in the same store. An' we got some things to talk over—business, see?—kinda confidential. So if it ain't askin' too much——

Shrdlu [*springing to his feet*]. Why, certainly! Excuse me! [*He bows politely to* DAISY *and walks off.* DAISY *and* ZERO *watch him until he has disappeared.*]

Zero [*with a forced laugh*]. He's a good guy at that.

Now that they are alone, both are very self-conscious, and for a time they sit in silence.

Daisy [*breaking the silence*]. It sure is pretty here, ain't it?

Zero. Sure is.

Daisy. Look at the flowers! Ain't they just perfect! Why, you'd think they was artificial, wouldn't you?

Zero. Yeh, you would.

Daisy. And the smell of them. Like perfume.

Zero. Yeh.

Daisy. I'm crazy about the country, ain't you?

Zero. Yeh. It's nice for a change.

Daisy. Them store picnics—remember?

Zero. You bet. They sure was fun.

Daisy. One time—I guess you don't remember—the two of us—me and you—we sat down on the grass together under a tree—just like we're doin' now.

Zero. Sure I remember.

Daisy. Go on! I'll bet you don't.

Zero. I'll bet I do. It was the year the wife didn't go.

Daisy [*her face brightening*]. That's right! I didn't think you'd remember.

Zero. An' comin' home we sat together in the truck.

Daisy [*eagerly, rather shamefacedly*]. Yeh! There's somethin' I've always wanted to ask you.

Zero. Well, why didn't you?

Daisy. I don't know. It didn't seem refined. But I'm goin' to ask you now anyhow.

Zero. Go ahead. Shoot.

Daisy [*falteringly*]. Well—while we was comin' home —you put your arm up on the bench behind me—and I could feel your knee kinda pressin' against mine. [*She stops.*]

Zero [*becoming more and more interested*]. Yeh—well, what about it?

Daisy. What I wanted to ask you was—was it just kinda accidental?

Zero [*with a laugh*]. Sure it was accidental. Accidental on purpose.

Daisy [*eagerly*]. Do you mean it?

Zero. Sure I mean it. You mean to say you didn't know it?

Daisy. No. I've been wantin' to ask you——

Zero. Then why did you get sore at me?

Daisy. Sore? I wasn't sore! When was I sore?

Zero. That night. Sure you was sore. If you wasn't sore why did you move away?

Daisy. Just to see if you meant it. I thought if you meant it you'd move up closer. An' then when you took your arm away I was sure you didn't mean it.

Zero. An' I thought all the time you was sore. That's why I took my arm away. I thought if I moved up you'd holler and then I'd be in a jam, like you read in the paper all the time about guys gettin' pulled in for annoyin' women.

Daisy. An' I was wishin' you'd put your arm around me —just sittin' there wishin' all the way home.

Zero. What do you know about that? That sure is hard luck, that is. If I'd 'a' only knew! You know what I felt like doin'—only I didn't have the nerve?

Daisy. What?

Zero. I felt like kissin' you.

Daisy [*fervently*]. I wanted you to.

Zero [*astonished*]. You would 'a' let me?

Daisy. I wanted you to! I wanted you to! Oh, why didn't you—why didn't you?

Zero. I didn't have the nerve. I sure was a dumbbell.

Daisy. I would 'a' let you all you wanted to. I wouldn't 'a' cared. I know it would 'a' been wrong but I wouldn't 'a' cared. I wasn't thinkin' about right an' wrong at all. I didn't care—see? I just wanted you to kiss me.

Zero [*feelingly*]. If I'd only knew. I wanted to do it, I swear I did. But I didn't think you cared nothin' about me.

Daisy [*passionately*]. I never cared nothin' about nobody else.

Zero. Do you mean it—on the level? You ain't kiddin' me, are you?

Daisy. No, I ain't kiddin'. I mean it. I'm tellin' you the truth. I ain't never had the nerve to tell you before—but now I don't care. It don't make no difference now. I mean it—every word of it.

Zero [*dejectedly*]. If I'd only knew it.

Daisy. Listen to me. There's somethin' else I want to tell you. I may as well tell you everything now. It don't make no difference now. About my blowin' out the gas—see? Do you know why I done it?

Zero. Yeh, you told me—on account o' bein' canned.

Daisy. I just told you that. That ain't the real reason. The real reason is on account o' you.

Zero. You mean to say on account o' me passin' out?

Daisy. Yeh. That's it. I didn't want to go on livin'. What for? What did I want to go on livin' for? I didn't have nothin' to live for with you gone. I often thought of doin' it before. But I never had the nerve. An' anyhow I didn't want to leave you.

Zero. An' me bawlin' you out, about readin' too fast an' readin' too slow.

Daisy [*reproachfully*]. Why did you do it?

Zero. I don't know, I swear I don't. I was always stuck on you. An' while I'd be addin' them figgers, I'd be thinkin' how if the wife died, you an' me could get married.

Daisy. I used to think o' that too.

Zero. An' then before I knew it I was bawlin' you out.

Daisy. Them was the times I'd think o' blowin' out the gas. But I never did till you was gone. There wasn't nothin' to live for then. But it wasn't so easy to do anyhow. I never could stand the smell o' gas. An' all the while I was gettin' ready, you know, stuffin' up all the cracks, the way you read about in the paper—I was thinkin' of you and hopin' that maybe I'd meet you again. An' I made up my mind if I ever did see you, I'd tell you.

Zero [*taking her hand*]. I'm sure glad you did. I'm sure glad. [*Ruefully.*] But it don't do much good now, does it?

Daisy. No, I guess it don't. [*Summoning courage.*] But there's one thing I'm goin' to ask you.

Zero. What's that?

Daisy [*in a low voice*]. I want you to kiss me.

Zero. You bet I will! [*He leans over and kisses her cheek.*]

Daisy. Not like that. I don't mean like that. I mean really kiss me. On the mouth. I ain't never been kissed like that.

ZERO *puts his arms about her and presses his lips to hers. A long embrace. At last they separate and sit side by side in silence.*

Daisy [*putting her hands to her cheeks*]. So that's what it's like. I didn't know it could be like that. I didn't know anythin' could be like that.

Zero [*fondling her hand*]. Your cheeks are red. They're all red. And your eyes are shinin'. I never seen your eyes shinin' like that before.

Daisy [*holding up her hand*]. Listen—do you hear it? Do you hear the music?

Zero. No, I don't hear nothin'!

Daisy. Yeh—music. Listen an' you'll hear it. [*They are both silent for a moment.*]

Zero [*excitedly*]. Yeh! I hear it! He said there was music, but I didn't hear it till just now.

Daisy. Ain't it grand?

Zero. Swell! Say, do you know what?

Daisy. What?

Zero. It makes me feel like dancin'.

Daisy. Yeh? Me too.

Zero [*springing to his feet*]. Come on! Let's dance! [*He seizes her hands and tries to pull her up.*]

Daisy [*resisting laughingly*]. I can't dance. I ain't danced in twenty years.

Zero. That's nothin'. I ain't neither. Come on! I feel just like a kid! [*He pulls her to her feet and seizes her about the waist.*]

Daisy. Wait a minute! Wait till I fix my skirt. [*She turns back her skirts and pins them above the ankles.*]

ZERO *seizes her about the waist. They dance clumsily but with gay abandon.* DAISY'S *hair becomes loosened and tumbles over her shoulders. She lends herself more and more to the spirit of the dance. But* ZERO *soon begins to tire and dances with less and less zest.*

Zero [*stopping at last, panting for breath*]. Wait a minute! I'm all winded. [*He releases* DAISY, *but before he can turn away, she throws her arms about him and presses her lips to his. Freeing himself.*] Wait a minute! Let me get my wind! [*He limps to the tree and seats himself under it, gasping for breath.* DAISY *looks after him, her spirits rather dampened.*] Whew! I sure am winded! I ain't used to dancin'. [*He takes off his collar and tie and opens the neckband of his shirt.* DAISY *sits under the tree near him, looking at him longingly. But he is busy catching his breath.*] Gee, my heart's goin' a mile a minute.

Daisy. Why don't you lay down an' rest? You could put your head on my lap.

Zero. That ain't a bad idea. [*He stretches out, his head in* DAISY's *lap.*]

Daisy [*fondling his hair*]. It was swell, wasn't it?

Zero. Yeh. But you gotta be used to it.

Daisy. Just imagine if we could stay here all the time—you an' me together—wouldn't it be swell?

Zero. Yeh. But there ain't a chance.

Daisy. Won't they let us stay?

Zero. No. This place is only for the good ones.

Daisy. Well, we ain't so bad, are we?

Zero. Go on! Me a murderer an' you committin' suicide. Anyway, they wouldn't stand for this—the way we been goin' on.

Daisy. I don't see why.

Zero. You don't! You know it ain't right. Ain't I got a wife?

Daisy. Not any more you ain't. When you're dead that

ends it. Don't they always say "until death do us part"?

Zero. Well, maybe you're right about that but they wouldn't stand for us here.

Daisy. It would be swell—the two of us together—we could make up for all them years.

Zero. Yeh, I wish we could.

Daisy. We sure were fools. But I don't care. I've got you now. [*She kisses his forehead and cheeks and mouth.*]

Zero. I'm sure crazy about you. I never saw you lookin' so pretty before, with your cheeks all red. An' your hair hangin' down. You got swell hair. [*He fondles and kisses her hair.*]

Daisy [*ecstatically*]. We got each other now, ain't we?

Zero. Yeh. I'm crazy about you. Daisy! That's a pretty name. It's a flower, ain't it? Well—that's what you are—just a flower.

Daisy [*happily*]. We can always be together now, can't we?

Zero. As long as they'll let us. I sure am crazy about you. [*Suddenly he sits upright.*] Watch your step!

Daisy [*alarmed*]. What's the matter?

Zero [*nervously*]. He's comin' back.

Daisy. Oh, is that all? Well, what about it?

Zero. You don't want him to see us layin' around like this, do you?

Daisy. I don't care if he does.

Zero. Well, you oughta care. You don't want him to think you ain't a refined girl, do you? He's an awful moral bird, he is.

Daisy. I don't care nothin' about him. I don't care nothin' about anybody but you.

Zero. Sure, I know. But we don't want people talkin' about us. You better fix your hair an' pull down your skirts. [DAISY *complies rather sadly. They are both silent as* SHRDLU *enters. With feigned nonchalance.*] Well, you got back all right, didn't you?

Shrdlu. I hope I haven't returned too soon.

Zero. No, that's all right. We were just havin' a little talk. You know—about business an' things.

Daisy [*boldly*]. We were wishin' we could stay here all the time.

Shrdlu. You may if you like.

Zero and Daisy [*in astonishment*]. What!

Shrdlu. Yes. Anyone who likes may remain——

Zero. But I thought you were tellin' me——

Shrdlu. Just as I told you, only the most favored do remain. But anyone may.

Zero. I don't get it. There's a catch in it somewheres.

Daisy. It don't matter as long as we can stay.

Zero [*to* SHRDLU]. We were thinkin' about gettin' married, see?

Shrdlu. You may or may not, just as you like.

Zero. You don't mean to say we could stay if we didn't, do you?

Shrdlu. Yes. They don't care.

Zero. An' there's some here that ain't married?

Shrdlu. Yes.

Zero [*to* DAISY]. I don't know about this place, at that. They must be kind of a mixed crowd.

Daisy. It don't matter, so long as we got each other.

Zero. Yeh, I know, but you don't want to mix with people that ain't respectable.

Daisy [*to* SHRDLU]. Can we get married right away? I guess there must be a lot of ministers here, ain't there?

Shrdlu. Not as many as I had hoped to find. The two who seem most beloved are Dean Swift and the Abbé Rabelais. They are both much admired for some indecent tales which they have written.

Zero [*shocked*]. What! Ministers writin' smutty stories! Say, what kind of a dump is this anyway?

Shrdlu [*despairingly*]. I don't know, Mr. Zero. All these people here are so strange, so unlike the good people I've known. They seem to think of nothing but enjoyment or of wasting their time in profitless occupations. Some paint pictures from morning until night, or carve blocks of stone. Others write songs or put words together, day in and day out. Still others do nothing but lie under the trees and look at the sky. There are men who spend all their time reading books and women who think only of adorning themselves. And forever they are telling stories and laughing and singing and drinking and dancing. There **are**

drunkards, thieves, vagabonds, blasphemers, adulterers.
There is one——

Zero. That's enough. I heard enough. [*He seats himself
and begins putting on his shoes.*]

Daisy [*anxiously*]. What are you goin' to do?

Zero. I'm goin' to beat it, that's what I'm goin' to do.

Daisy. You said you liked it here.

Zero [*looking at her in amazement*]. Liked it! Say, you
don't mean to say you want to stay here, do you, with a
lot of rummies an' loafers an' bums?

Daisy. We don't have to bother with them. We can
just sit here together an' look at the flowers an' listen to
the music.

Shrdlu [*eagerly*]. Music! Did you hear music?

Daisy. Sure. Don't you hear it?

Shrdlu. No, they say it never stops. But I've never heard
it.

Zero [*listening*]. I thought I heard it before but I don't
hear nothin' now. I guess I must 'a' been dreamin'. [*Looking about.*] What's the quickest way out of this place?

Daisy [*pleadingly*]. Won't you stay just a little longer?

Zero. Didn't yer hear me say I'm goin'? Good-by, Miss
Devore. I'm goin' to beat it. [*He limps off at the right.*
Daisy *follows him slowly.*]

Daisy [*to* Shrdlu]. I won't ever see him again.

Shrdlu. Are you goin' to stay here?

Daisy. It don't make no difference now. Without him I
might as well be alive.

She goes off right. Shrdlu *watches her a moment, then
sighs and seating himself under the tree, buries his head
on his arm.*

Curtain.

SCENE VIII

*Before the curtain rises the clicking of an adding machine
is heard. The curtain rises upon an office similar in appearance to that in Scene II except that there is a door in*

*the back wall through which can be seen a glimpse of the
corridor outside. In the middle of the room* ZERO *is seated
completely absorbed in the operation of an adding machine.
He presses the keys and pulls the lever with mechanical
precision. He still wears his full-dress suit but he has added
to it sleeve-protectors and a green eyeshade. A strip of
white paper-tape flows steadily from the machine as* ZERO
*operates. The room is filled with this tape—streamers,
festoons, billows of it everywhere. It covers the floor and
the furniture, it climbs the walls and chokes the doorways.
A few moments later* LIEUTENANT CHARLES *and* JOE *enter
at the left.* LIEUTENANT CHARLES *is middle-aged and in-
clined to corpulence. He has an air of world-weariness. He
is barefooted, wears a Panama hat, and is dressed in bright
red tights which are a very bad fit—too tight in some
places, badly wrinkled in others.* JOE *is a youth with a
smutty face dressed in dirty blue overalls.*

CHARLES [*after contemplating* ZERO *for a few moments*].
All right, Zero, cease firing.

Zero [*looking up, surprised*]. Whaddja say?

Charles. I said stop punching· that machine.

Zero [*bewildered*]. Stop? [*He goes on working mechanically.*]

Charles [*impatiently*]. Yes. Can't you stop? Here, Joe,
give me a hand. He can't stop.

JOE *and* CHARLES *each take one of* ZERO's *arms and with
enormous effort detach him from the machine. He resists
passively—mere inertia. Finally they succeed and swing
him around on his stool.* CHARLES *and* JOE *mop their
foreheads.*

Zero [*querulously*]. What's the idea? Can't you lemme
alone?

Charles [*ignoring the question*]. How long have you been
here?

Zero. Jes' twenty-five years. Three hundred months,
ninety-one hundred and thirty-one days, one hundred
thirty-six thousand——

Charles [*impatiently*]. That'll do! That'll do!

Zero [*proudly*]. I ain't missed a day, not an hour, not
a minute. Look at all I got done. [*He points to the maze of
paper.*]

Charles. It's time to quit.

Zero. Quit? Whaddya mean quit? I ain't goin' to quit!

Charles. You've got to.

Zero. What for? What do I have to quit for?

Charles. It's time for you to go back.

Zero. Go back where? Whaddya talkin' about?

Charles. Back to earth, you dub. Where do you think?

Zero. Aw, go on, Cap, who are you kiddin'?

Charles. I'm not kidding anybody. And don't call me Cap. I'm a lieutenant.

Zero. All right, Lieutenant, all right. But what's this you're tryin' to tell me about goin' back?

Charles. Your time's up, I'm telling you. You must be pretty thick. How many times do you want to be told a thing?

Zero. This is the first time I heard about goin' back. Nobody ever said nothin' to me about it before.

Charles. You didn't think you were going to stay here forever, did you?

Zero. Sure. Why not? I did my bit, didn't I? Forty-five years of it. Twenty-five years in the store. Then the boss canned me and I knocked him cold. I guess you ain't heard about that——

Charles [*interrupting*]. I know all about that. But what's that got to do with it?

Zero. Well, I done my bit, didn't I? That oughta let me out.

Charles [*jeeringly*]. So you think you're all through, do you?

Zero. Sure, I do. I did the best I could while I was there and then I passed out. And now I'm sittin' pretty here.

Charles. You've got a fine idea of the way they run things, you have. Do you think they're going to all of the trouble of making a soul just to use it once?

Zero. Once is often enough, it seems to me.

Charles. It seems to you, does it? Well, who are you? And what do you know about it? Why, man, they use a soul over and over again—over and over until it's worn out.

Zero. Nobody ever told me.

Charles. So you thought you were all through, did you? Well, that's a hot one, that is.

Zero [*sullenly*]. How was I to know?

Charles. Use your brains! Where would we put them all! We're crowded enough as it is. Why, this place is nothing but a kind of repair and service station—a sort of cosmic laundry, you might say. We get the souls in here by the bushelful. Then we get busy and clean them up. And you ought to see some of them. The muck and the slime. Phoo! And as full of holes as a flour sifter. But we fix them up. We disinfect them and give them a kerosene rub and mend the holes and back they go—practically as good as new.

Zero. You mean to say I've been here before—before the last time, I mean?

Charles. Been here before! Why, you poor boob—you've been here thousands of times—fifty thousand at least.

Zero [*suspiciously*]. How is it I don't remember nothin' about it?

Charles. Well—that's partly because you're stupid. But it's mostly because that's the way they fix it. [*Musingly.*] They're funny that way—every now and then they'll do something white like that—when you'd least expect it. I guess economy's at the bottom of it though. They figure that the souls would get worn out quicker if they remembered.

Zero. And don't any of 'em remember?

Charles. Oh, some do. You see there's different types: there's the type that gets a little better each time it goes back—we just give them a wash and send them right through. Then there's another type—the type that gets a little worse each time. That's where you belong!

Zero [*offended*]. Me? You mean to say I'm gettin' worse all the time?

Charles [*nodding*]. Yes. A little worse each time.

Zero. Well—what was I when I started? Somethin' big? A king or somethin'?

Charles [*laughing derisively*]. A king! That's a good one! I'll tell you what you were the first time—if you want to know so much—a monkey.

Zero [*shocked and offended*]. A monkey!

Charles [*nodding*]. Yes, sir—just a hairy, chattering, long-tailed monkey.

Zero. That musta been a long time ago.

Charles. Oh, not so long. A million years or so. Seems like yesterday to me.

Zero. Then look here, whaddya mean by sayin' I'm gettin' worse all the time?

Charles. Just what I said. You weren't so bad as a monkey. Of course, you did just what all the other monkeys did, but still it kept you out in the open air. And you weren't woman-shy—there was one little red-headed monkey— Well, never mind. Yes, sir, you weren't so bad then. But even in those days there must have been some bigger and brainier monkey that you kowtowed to. The mark of the slave was on you from the start.

Zero [*sullenly*]. You ain't very particular about what you call people, are you?

Charles. You wanted the truth, didn't you? If there ever was a soul in the world that was labeled slave it's yours. Why, all the bosses and kings that there ever were have left their trademarks on your backside.

Zero. It ain't fair, if you ask me.

Charles [*shrugging his shoulders*]. Don't tell me about it. I don't make the rules. All I know is, you've been getting worse—worse each time. Why, even six thousand years ago you weren't so bad. That was the time you were hauling stones for one of those big pyramids in a place they call Africa. Ever hear of the pyramids?

Zero. Them big pointy things?

Charles [*nodding*]. That's it.

Zero. I seen a picture of them in the movies.

Charles. Well, you helped build them. It was a long step down from the happy days in the jungle, but it was a good job—even though you didn't know what you were doing and your back was striped by the foreman's whip. But you've been going down, down. Two thousand years ago you were a Roman galley slave. You were on one of the triremes that knocked the Carthaginian fleet for a goal. Again the whip. But you had muscles then—chest muscles, back muscles, biceps. [*He feels* ZERO's *arm gingerly and turns away in disgust.*] Phoo! A bunch of mush! [*He notices that* JOE *has fallen asleep. Walking over, he kicks him in the shin.*] Wake up, you mutt! Where do you think you are! [*He turns to* ZERO *again.*] And then another thousand years and you were a serf—a lump of clay digging up other lumps of clay. You wore an iron collar then—white ones hadn't been invented yet. Another long step down. But where you dug, potatoes grew, and that helped fatten the pigs. Which was something. And now—well, I don't want to rub it in——

Zero. Rub it in is right! Seems to me I got a pretty healthy kick comin'. I ain't had a square deal! Hard work! That's all I've ever had!

Charles [*callously*]. What else were you ever good for?

Zero. Well, that ain't the point. The point is I'm through! I had enough! Let 'em find somebody else to do the dirty work. I'm sick of bein' the goat! I quit right here and now! [*He glares about defiantly. There is a thunderclap and a bright flash of lightning. Screaming.*] Ooh! What's that? [*He clings to* CHARLES.]

Charles. It's all right. Nobody's going to hurt you. It's just their way of telling you that they don't like you to talk that way. Pull yourself together and calm down. You can't change the rules—nobody can—they've got it all fixed. It's a rotten system—but what are you going to do about it?

Zero. Why can't they stop pickin' on me? I'm satisfied here—doin' my day's work. I don't want to go back.

Charles. You've got to, I tell you. There's no way out of it.

Zero. What chance have I got—at my age? Who'll give me a job?

Charles. You big boob, you don't think you're going back the way you are, do you?

Zero. Sure, how then?

Charles. Why, you've got to start all over.

Zero. All over?

Charles [*nodding*]. You'll be a baby again—a bald, red-faced little animal, and then you'll go through it all again. There'll be millions of others like you—all with their mouths open, squalling for food. And then when you get a little older you'll begin to learn things—and you'll learn all the wrong things and learn them all in the wrong way. You'll eat the wrong food and wear the wrong clothes, and you'll live in swarming dens where there's no light and no air! You'll learn to be a liar and a bully and a braggart and a coward and a sneak. You'll learn to fear the sunlight and to hate beauty. By that time you'll be ready for school. There they'll tell you the truth about a great many things that you don't give a damn about, and they'll tell you lies about all the things you ought to know—and about all the things you want to know they'll tell you nothing at all. When you get through you'll be equipped for your life work. You'll be ready to take a job.

Zero [*eagerly*]. What'll my job be? Another adding machine?

Charles. Yes. But not one of these antiquated adding machines. It will be a superb, super-hyper-adding machine, as far from this old piece of junk as you are from God. It will be something to make you sit up and take notice, that adding machine. It will be an adding machine which will be installed in a coal mine and which will record the individual output of each miner. As each miner down in the lower galleries takes up a shovelful of coal, the impact of his shovel will automatically set in motion a graphite pencil in your gallery. The pencil will make a mark in white upon a blackened, sensitized drum. Then your work comes in. With the great toe of your right foot you release a lever which focuses a violet ray on the drum. The ray, playing upon and through the white mark, falls upon a selenium cell which in turn sets the keys of the adding apparatus in motion. In this way the individual output of each miner is recorded without any human effort except the slight pressure of the great toe of your right foot.

Zero [*in breathless, round-eyed wonder*]. Say, that'll be some machine, won't it?

Charles. Some machine is right. It will be the culmination of human effort—the final triumph of the evolutionary process. For millions of years the nebulous gases swirled in space. For more millions of years the gases cooled and then through inconceivable ages they hardened into rocks. And then came life. Floating green things on the waters that covered the earth. More millions of years and a step upward—an animate organism in the ancient slime. And so on—step by step, down through the ages—a gain here, a gain there—the mollusk, the fish, the reptile, then mammal, man! And all so that you might sit in the gallery of a coal mine and operate the super-hyper-adding machine with the great toe of your right foot!

Zero. Well, then—I ain't so bad after all.

Charles. You're a failure, Zero, a failure. A waste product. A slave to a contraption of steel and iron. The animal's instincts, but not his strength and skill. The animal's appetites, but not his unashamed indulgence of them. True, you move and eat and digest and excrete and reproduce. But any microscopic organism can do as much. Well—time's up! Back you go—back to your sunless groove—the raw material of slums and wars—the ready prey of the first jingo or demagogue or political adventurer who takes the trouble to play upon your ignorance and credulity and provincialism. You poor, spineless, brainless boob—I'm sorry for you!

Zero [*falling to his knees*]. Then keep me here! Don't send me back! Let me stay!

Charles. Get up. Didn't I tell you I can't do anything for you? Come on, time's up!

Zero. I can't! I can't! I'm afraid to go through it all again.

Charles. You've got to, I tell you. Come on, now!

Zero. What did you tell me so much for? Couldn't you just let me go, thinkin' everythin' was goin' to be all right?

Charles. You wanted to know, didn't you?

Zero. How did I know what you were goin' to tell me? Now I can't stop thinkin' about it! I can't stop thinkin'! I'll be thinkin' about it all the time.

Charles. All right! I'll do the best I can for you. I'll send a girl with you to keep you company.

Zero. A girl? What for? What good will a girl do me?

Charles. She'll help make you forget.

Zero [*eagerly*]. She will? Where is she?

Charles. Wait a minute, I'll call her. [*He calls in a loud voice.*] Oh! Hope! Yoo-hoo! [*He turns his head aside and speaks in the manner of a ventriloquist imitating a distant feminine voice.*] Ye-es. [*Then in his own voice:*] Come here, will you? There's a fellow who wants you to take him back. [*Ventriloquously again.*] All right. I'll be right over,

Charlie dear. [*He turns to* Zero.] Kind of familiar, isn't she? Charlie dear!

Zero. What did you say her name is?

Charles. Hope. H-o-p-e.

Zero. Is she good-lookin'?

Charles. Is she good-looking! Oh, boy, wait until you see her! She's a blonde with big blue eyes and red lips and little white teeth and——

Zero. Say, that listens good to me. Will she be long?

Charles. She'll be here right away. There she is now! Do you see her?

Zero. No. Where?

Charles. Out in the corridor. No, not there. Over farther. To the right. Don't you see her blue dress? And the sunlight on her hair?

Zero. Oh, sure! Now I see her! What's the matter with me anyhow? Say, she's some jane! Oh, you baby vamp!

Charles. She'll make you forget your troubles.

Zero. What troubles are you talkin' about?

Charles. Nothing. Go on. Don't keep her waiting.

Zero. You bet I won't! Oh, Hope! Wait for me! I'll be right with you! I'm on my way! [*He stumbles out eagerly.* Joe *bursts into uproarious laughter.*]

Charles [*eying him in surprise and anger*]. What in hell's the matter with you?

Joe [*shaking with laughter*]. Did you get that? He thinks he saw somebody and he's following her! [*He rocks with laughter.*]

Charles [*punching him in the jaw*]. Shut your face!

Joe [*nursing his jaw*]. What's the idea? Can't I even laugh when I see something funny?

Charles. Funny! You keep your mouth shut or I'll show you something funny. Go on, hustle out of here and get something to clean up this mess with. There's another fellow moving in. Hurry now. [*He makes a threatening gesture.* Joe *exits hastily.* Charles *goes to chair and seats himself. He looks weary and dispirited. Shaking his head.*] Hell, I'll tell the world this is a lousy job! [*He takes a flask from his pocket, uncorks it, and slowly drains it.*]

Curtain.

STREET SCENE

A Play in Three Acts

(Originally presented at The Playhouse, New York City, January 10, 1929)

CHARACTERS

ABRAHAM KAPLAN
GRETA FIORENTINO
EMMA JONES
OLGA OLSEN
WILLIE MAURRANT
ANNA MAURRANT
FRANK MAURRANT
GEORGE JONES
STEVE SANKEY
AGNES CUSHING
CARL OLSEN
SHIRLEY KAPLAN
FILIPPO FIORENTINO
ALICE SIMPSON
LAURA HILDEBRAND
MARY HILDEBRAND
CHARLIE HILDEBRAND
SAMUEL KAPLAN
ROSE MAURRANT
HARRY EASTER
DANIEL BUCHANAN

MAE JONES
DICK MCGANN
VINCENT JONES
DR. JOHN WILSON

A MILKMAN
A LETTER CARRIER
AN ICEMAN
TWO COLLEGE GIRLS
A MUSIC STUDENT
MARSHALL JAMES HENRY
FRED CULLEN
AN OLD-CLOTHES MAN
INTERN
AN AMBULANCE DRIVER
FURNITURE MOVERS
TWO NURSEMAIDS
OFFICER HARRY MURPHY
TWO APARTMENT HUNTERS
PASSERS-BY

SCENE

There is only one setting, which is described in detail in the text.

The action takes place on an evening in June and on the morning and afternoon of the following day.

STREET SCENE

ACT ONE

The exterior of a "walk-up" apartment house in a mean quarter of New York. It is of ugly brownstone and was built in the nineties. Between the pavement of large gray flagstones and the front of the house is a deep and narrow areaway, guarded by a rusted, ornamental iron railing. At the right, a steep flight of rotting wooden steps leads down to the cellar and to the janitor's apartment, the windows of which are just visible above the street level. Spanning the areaway is a "stoop" of four shallow stone steps flanked on either side by a curved stone balustrade. Beyond the broad fourth step another step leads to the double wooden outer doors of the house; and as these are open, the vestibule and the wide, heavy glass-paneled entrance door beyond are visible. Above the outer doors is a glass fanlight upon which appears the half-obliterated house number. At the left side of the doorway is a sign which reads: "Flat To Let. 6 Rooms. Steam Heat."

On either side of the stoop are the two narrow windows of the ground-floor apartments. In one of the windows, at the left, is a sign bearing the legend: "Prof. Filippo Fiorentino. Music for all occasions. Also instruction." Above are the six narrow windows of the first-floor apartments, and above that the stone sills of the second-floor windows can just be seen.

To the left of the house, part of the adjoining building is visible: the motor entrance to a storage warehouse. Crude boarding across the large driveway and rough planks across the sidewalk and curb indicate that an excavation is in progress. On the boarding is painted in rude lettering: "Keep Out"; and at the curb is a small barrel bearing a sign with the words: "Street Closed." To the wall of the warehouse is affixed a brass plate bearing the name: "Patrick Mulcahy Storage Warehouse Co. Inc."

To the right of the house, scaffolding and a wooden sidewalk indicate that the house next door is being demolished.

65

On the scaffolding is a large wooden sign reading: "Man-
hattan House-Wrecking Corp."

In the close foreground, below the level of the curb, is a
mere suggestion of the street.

At rise of curtain the house is seen in the white glare of an
arc-light, which is just offstage to the right. The windows
in the janitor's apartment are lighted, as are also those of
the ground-floor apartment at the right and the two
windows at the extreme left of the first floor. A dim red
light is affixed to the boarding of the excavation at the left.

In the lighted ground-floor window, at the right of the
doorway, ABRAHAM KAPLAN *is seated in a rocking chair,*
reading a Yiddish newspaper. He is a Russian Jew, well
past sixty: clean-shaven, thick gray hair, hooked nose, horn-
rimmed spectacles. To the left of the doorway, GRETA
FIORENTINO *is leaning out of the window. She is forty, a*
blonde, ruddy-faced, stout German. She wears a wrapper
of light, flowered material, and a large pillow supports her
left arm and her ample, uncorseted bosom. In her right
hand is a folding paper fan, which she waves languidly.

Throughout the act, and, indeed, throughout the play, there
is constant noise. The noises of the city rise, fall, intermingle:
the distant roar of El trains, automobile sirens, and the
whistles of boats on the river; the rattle of trucks and the
indeterminate clanking of metals; fire engines, ambulances,
musical instruments, a radio, dogs barking, and human
voices calling, quarreling, and screaming with laughter. The
noises are subdued and in the background, but they never
wholly cease.

A moment after the rise of the curtain an elderly man
enters at the right and walks into the house, exchanging a
nod with MRS. FIORENTINO. *A man, munching peanuts,*
crosses the stage from left to right.

A VOICE [*offstage*]. Char-lie!

EMMA JONES *appears at the left. She is middle-aged, tall,*
and rather bony. She carries a small parcel.

  Mrs. Fiorentino [*she speaks with a faint German accent*].
Good evening, Mrs. Jones.

  Mrs. Jones [*stopping beneath* MRS. FIORENTINO'S *win-*

dow]. Good evenin', Mrs. F. Well, I hope it's hot enough for you.

Mrs. Fioretino. Ain't it joost awful? When I was through with the dishes, you could take my clothes and joost wring them out.

Mrs. Jones. Me too. I ain't got a dry stitch on me.

Mrs. Fiorentino. I took off my shoes and my corset and made myself nice and comfortable, and tonight before I go to bed, I take a nice bath.

Mrs. Jones. The trouble with a bath is, by the time you're all through, you're as hot as when you started. [*As* OLGA OLSEN, *a thin, anemic Scandinavian with untidy fair hair, comes up the cellar steps and onto the sidewalk.*] Good evenin', Mrs. Olsen. Awful hot, ain't it?

Mrs. Olsen [*coming over to the front of the stoop*]. Yust awful. Mrs. Forentiner, my hoosban' say vill you put de garbage on de doomvaider?

Mrs. Fiorentino. Oh, sure, sure! I didn't hear him vistle. [*As* MRS. JONES *starts to cross to the stoop.*] Don't go 'vay, Mrs. Jones. [*She disappears from the window.*]

Mrs. Olsen [*pushing back some wisps of hair*]. I tank is more cooler in de cellar.

Mrs. Jones [*sitting on the stoop and fanning herself with her parcel*]. Phew! I'm just about ready to pass out.

Mrs. Olsen. My baby is crying, crying, all day.

Mrs. Jones. Yeah, I often say they mind the heat more'n we do. It's the same with dogs. My Queenie has jes' been layin' aroun' all day.

Mrs. Olsen. The baby get new teet'. It hurt her.

Mrs. Jones. Don't tell me! If you was to know what I went t'roo with my Vincent. Half the time he used to have convulsions.

WILLIE MAURRANT, *a disorderly boy of twelve, appears at the left on roller skates. He stops at the left of the stoop and takes hold of the railing with both hands.*

Willie [*raising his head and bawling*]. Hey, Ma!

Mrs. Jones [*disapprovingly*]. If you want your mother, why don't you go upstairs, instead o' yellin' like that?

Willie [*without paying the slightest attention to her, bawls louder*]. Hey, Ma!

Mrs. Maurrant [*appearing at one of the lighted first-floor windows*]. What do you want, Willie? [*She is a fair woman of forty, who looks her age, but is by no means unattractive.*]

Willie. Gimme a dime, will ya? I wanna git a cone.

Mrs. Maurrant [*to* Mrs. Olsen *and* Mrs. Jones]. Good evening.

Mrs. Olsen and Mrs. Jones. Good evenin', Mrs. Maurrant.

Mrs. Maurrant [*to* Willie]. How many cones did you have today already?

Willie [*belligerently*]. I'm hot! All de other guys is havin' cones. Come on, gimme a dime.

Mrs. Maurrant. Well, it's the last one. [*She disappears.*]

Mrs. Jones. You certainly don't talk very nice to your mother. [*To* Mrs. Olsen.] I'd like to hear one o' mine talkin' that way to me!

Mrs. Maurrant [*appearing at the window*]. Remember, this is the last one.

Willie. Aw right. T'row it down.

Mrs. Fiorentino *reappears and leans out of the window again.*

Mrs. Maurrant. Catch it!

She throws out a twist of newspaper. Willie *scrambles for it, hastily extracts the dime, drops the newspaper on the pavement, and skates off at the left.*

Mrs. Fiorentino [*twisting her neck upward*]. Good evening, Mrs. Maurrant.

Mrs. Maurrant. Good evening, Mrs. Fiorentino. [*Calling after* Willie.] And don't come home too late, Willie! [*But* Willie *is already out of earshot.*]

Mrs. Fiorentino. Why don't you come down and be sociable?

Mrs. Maurrant. I'm keeping some supper warm for my husband. [*A slight pause.*] Well, maybe I will for just a minute. [*She leaves the window. The lights in her apartment go out.*]

Mrs. Fiorentino. She has her troubles with dot Willie.

Mrs. Jones. I guess it don't bother her much. [*Significantly.*] She's got her mind on other things.

Mrs. Olsen [*looking about cautiously and coming over to the left of the stoop between the two women*]. He vas comin' again today to see her.

Mrs. Jones [*rising excitedly, and leaning over the balustrade*]. Who—Sankey?

Mrs. Olsen [*nodding*]. Yes.

Mrs. Fiorentino. Are you sure, Mrs. Olsen?

Mrs. Olsen. I seen him. I vas doostin' de halls.

Mrs. Fiorentino. Dot's terrible!

Mrs. Jones. Wouldn't you think a woman her age, with a grown-up daughter——!

Mrs. Olsen. Two times already dis veek I see him here.

Mrs. Jones. I seen him meself one day last week. He was comin' out o' the house, jest as I was comin' in wit' de dog. "Good mornin', Mrs. Jones," he says to me, as if butter wouldn't melt in his mouth. "Good mornin'," says I, lookin' him straight in the eye—— [*Breaking off suddenly as the vestibule door opens.*] Be careful, she's comin'.

MRS. MAURRANT *comes out of the house and stops for a moment on the top step.*

Mrs. Maurrant. Goodness, ain't it hot! I think it's really cooler upstairs. [*She comes down the steps to the sidewalk.*]

Mrs. Jones. Yeah, jes' what I was sayin' meself. I feel like a wet dishrag.

Mrs. Maurrant. I would have liked to go to the Park concert tonight if Rose had got home in time. I don't get much chance to go to concerts. My husband don't care for music. But Rose is more like me—just crazy about it.

Mrs. Jones. Ain't she home yet?

Mrs. Maurrant. No. I think maybe she had to work overtime.

Mrs. Jones. Well, all mine ever comes home for is to sleep.

Mrs. Fiorentino. The young girls nowadays——!

Mrs. Olsen. My sister was writin' me in Schweden is same t'ing——

Mrs. Jones. It ain't only the young ones either.

A baby is heard crying in the cellar.

Olsen's Voice [*from the cellar*]. Ol-ga!

A man, in a dinner jacket and straw hat, appears at the

*left, whistling a jazz tune. He crosses the stage and goes
off at the right.*

Mrs. Olsen [hurrying to the right]. I betcha the baby,
she's cryin' again.

Olsen's Voice. Ol-ga!

Mrs. Olsen. Yes, I come right away. [*She goes down the
cellar steps.*]

Mrs. Jones. What them foreigners don't know about
bringin' up babies would fill a book.

Mrs. Fiorentino [a little huffily]. Foreigners know joost
as much as other people, Mrs. Jones. My mother had eight
children and she brought up seven.

Mrs. Jones [tactfully]. Well, I'm not sayin' anythin'
about the Joimans. The Joimans is different—more like
the Irish. What I'm talkin' about is all them squareheads
an' Polacks—[*with a glance in* KAPLAN's *direction*]—an'
Jews.

Buchanan's Voice [from a third-story window]. Good
evening, ladies.

The Women [in unison, looking upward]. Oh, good evening, Mr. Buchanan.

Buchanan's Voice. Well, is it hot enough for you?

Mrs. Jones. I'll say!

Buchanan's Voice. I was just saying to my wife, it's not
the heat I mind as much as it is the humidity.

Mrs. Jones. Yeah, that's it! Makes everything stick to
you.

Mrs. Maurrant. How's your wife feeling in this weather?

Buchanan's Voice. She don't compain about the weather.
But she's afraid to go out of the house. Thinks maybe she
couldn't get back in time, in case—you know.

Mrs. Jones [to the other women]. I was the same way
with my Vincent—afraid to take a step. But with Mae, I
was up an' out till the very last minute.

Mrs. Fiorentino [craning her neck upward]. Mr. Buchanan, do you think she would eat some nice minestrone
—good Italian vegetable soup?

Buchanan's Voice. Why, much obliged, Mrs. F., but I
really can't get her to eat a thing.

Mrs. Jones [rising and looking upward]. Tell her she

ought to keep up her strength. She's got two to feed, you know.

Buchanan's Voice. Excuse me, she's calling.

Mrs. Jones [*crossing to the railing at the left of* Mrs. Fiorentino]. You'd think it was him that was havin' the baby.

Mrs. Maurrant. She's such a puny little thing.

Mrs. Fiorentino [*with a sigh*]. Well, that's the way it goes. The little skinny ones have them and the big strong ones don't.

Mrs. Maurrant. Don't take it that way, Mrs. Fiorentino. You're a young woman yet.

Mrs. Fiorentino [*shaking her head*]. Oh, well!

Mrs. Jones. My aunt, Mrs. Barclay, was forty-two—— [*Breaking off.*] Oh, good evenin', Mr. Maurrant!

Frank Maurrant *appears at the left with his coat on his arm. He is a tall, powerfully built man of forty-five, with a rugged, grim face.*

Mrs. Fiorentino. Good evening, Mr. Maurrant.

Maurrant. 'Evenin'. [*He goes to the stoop and seats himself, mopping his face.*] Some baby of a day!

Mrs. Maurrant. Have you been working all this while, Frank?

Maurrant. I'll say I've been workin'. Dress rehearsin' since twelve o'clock, with lights—in this weather. An' tomorra I gotta go to Stamford for the tryout.

Mrs. Maurrant. Oh, you're going to Stamford tomorrow?

Maurrant. Yeah, the whole crew's goin'. [*Looking at her.*] What about it?

Mrs. Maurrant. Why, nothing. Oh, I've got some cabbage and potatoes on the stove for you.

Maurrant. I just had a plate o' beans at the Coffee Pot. All I want is a good wash. I been sweatin' like a horse all day. [*He rises and goes up the steps.*]

Mrs. Fiorentino. My husband too; he's sweating terrible.

Mrs. Jones. Mine don't. There's some people that just naturally do, and then there's others that don't.

Maurrant [*to Mrs. Maurrant*]. Is anybody upstairs?

Mrs. Maurrant. No. Willie's off playing with the boys. I can't keep him home.

Maurrant. What about Rose?

Mrs. Maurrant. I think maybe she's working overtime.

Maurrant. I never heard o' nobody workin' nights in a real-estate office.

Mrs. Maurrant. I thought maybe on account of the office being closed tomorrow—— [*To the others.*] Mr. Jacobson, the head of the firm, died Tuesday, and tomorrow's the funeral, so I thought maybe——

Mrs. Jones. Yeah. Leave it to the Jews not to lose a workin' day without makin' up for it.

Maurrant [*to* Mrs. Maurrant]. She shouldn't be stayin' out nights without us knowin' where she is.

Mrs. Maurrant. She didn't say a word about not coming home.

Maurrant. That's what I'm sayin', ain't it? It's a mother's place to know what her daughter's doin'.

Mrs. Fiorentino [*soothingly*]. Things are different nowadays, Mr. Maurrant, from what they used to be.

Maurrant. Not in my family, they're not goin' to be no different. Not so long as I got somethin' to say.

A *Girl's Voice* [*offstage*]. Red Rover! Red Rover! Let Freddie come over!

George Jones, *a short, rather plump, red-faced man, cigar in mouth, comes out of the house as* Maurrant *enters the vestibule.*

Jones. Hello, Mr. Maurrant.

Maurrant [*curtly*]. 'Evenin'.

He enters the house. Jones *looks after him in surprise for a moment.* Mrs. Maurrant *seats herself on the stoop.*

Jones. Good evenin', ladies.

Mrs. Fiorentino and Mrs. Maurrant. Good evening, Mr. Jones.

Jones [*seating himself on the left balustrade*]. What's the matter with your hubby, Mrs. Maurrant? Guess he's feelin' the heat, huh?

Mrs. Maurrant. He's been working till just now and I guess he's a little tired.

Mrs. Jones. Men are all alike. They're all easy to get along with, so long as everythin's goin' the way they want it to. But once it don't—good night!

Mrs. Fiorentino. Yes, dot's true, Mrs. Jones.

Jones. Yeah, an' what about the women?

Mrs. Maurrant. I guess it's just the same with the women. I often think it's a shame that people don't get along better together. People ought to be able to live together in peace and quiet, without making each other miserable.

Mrs. Jones. The way I look at it, you get married for better or worse, an' if it turns out to be worse, why, all you can do is make the best of it.

Mrs. Maurrant. I think the trouble is people don't make allowances. They don't realize that everybody wants a kind word, now and then. After all, we're all human, and we can't just go along by ourselves, all the time, without ever getting a kind word.

While she is speaking STEVE SANKEY *appears at the right. He is in his early thirties and is prematurely bald. He is rather flashily dressed in a patently cheap, light gray suit and a straw hat with a plaid band. As he appears* MRS. JONES *and* MRS. FIORENTINO *exchange a swift, significant look.*

Sankey [*stopping at the right of the stoop and removing his hat*]. Good evening, folks! Is it hot enough for you?

The Others. Good evening.

Mrs. Maurrant [*self-consciously*]. Good evening, Mr. Sankey.

Throughout the scene MRS. MAURRANT *and* SANKEY *try vainly to avoid looking at each other.*

Sankey. I don't know when we've had a day like this. Hottest June fifteenth in forty-one years. It was up to ninety-four at three P.M.

Jones. Six dead in Chicago. An' no relief in sight, the evenin' paper says.

MAURRANT *appears at the window of his apartment and stands there, looking out.*

Mrs. Fiorentino. It's joost awful!

Sankey. Well, it's good for the milk business. You know the old saying, it's an ill wind that blows nobody any good.

Mrs. Maurrant. Yes. You hardly get the milk in the morning before it turns sour.

Mrs. Jones. I'm just after pourin' half a bottle down the sink.

MAURRANT *leaves the window.*

Mrs. Fiorentino. You shouldn't throw it avay. You should make—what do you call it?—*schmier-käs'*.

Sankey. Oh, I know what you mean—pot cheese. My wife makes it too once in a while.

Mrs. Maurrant. Is your wife all right again, Mr. Sankey? You were telling me last time, she had a cold.

MRS. JONES *and* MRS. FIORENTINO *exchange another look.*

Sankey. Was I? Oh, sure, sure. That was a couple weeks ago. Yes, sure, she's all right again. That didn't amount to anything much.

Mrs. Jones. You got a family too, ain't you?

Sankey. Yes. Yes, I have. Two little girls. Well, I got to be going along. [*He goes to the left of the stoop and stops again.*] I told my wife I'd go down to the drugstore and get her some nice cold ginger ale. You want something to cool you off in this kind of weather.

Mrs. Jones [*as* SANKEY *passes her*]. If you ask me, all that gassy stuff don't do you a bit of good.

Sankey. I guess you're right, at that. Still it cools you off. Well, good night, folks. See you all again.

He strolls off at the left with affected nonchalance; but when he is almost out of sight he casts a swift look back at MRS. MAURRANT. *A dowdy* WOMAN, *wheeling a dilapidated baby carriage, appears at the left and crosses the stage.*

Jones. What's his name—Sankey?

Mrs. Jones. Yeah—Mr. Sankey.

Mrs. Maurrant. He's the collector for the milk company.

AGNES CUSHING *comes out of the house. She is a thin, dried-up woman, past fifty.*

Miss Cushing [*coming down the steps*]. Good evening.

The Others. Good evening, Miss Cushing.

Mrs. Maurrant. How is your mother today, Miss Cushing?

Miss Cushing [*passing at the left of the stoop*]. Why, she complains of the heat. But I'm afraid it's really her

heart. She's seventy-two, you know. I'm just going down
to the corner to get her a little ice cream.

As she goes off at the left OLSEN, *the janitor, a lanky
Swede, struggles up the cellar steps with a large, covered,
tin garbage barrel. The others look around in annoyance
as he bangs the garbage barrel upon the pavement.*

Olsen. Phew! Hot! [*He mops his face and neck with a
dingy handkerchief, then lights his pipe and leans against
the railing.*]

Mrs. Jones [*significantly, as she crosses to the center of
the stoop and sits*]. Between you and I, I don't think her
mother's got long for this world. Once the heart starts goin'
back on you——!

Mrs. Fiorentino. It's too bad.

Mrs. Maurrant. Poor soul! She'll have nothing at all
when her mother dies. She's just spent her whole life looking after her mother.

Mrs. Jones. It's no more than her duty, is it?

Mrs. Fiorentino. You could not expect that she should
neglect her mother.

A Voice [*offstage*]. Char-lie!

Mrs. Maurrant. It's not a matter of neglecting. Only—
it seems as if a person should get more out of life than
just looking after somebody else.

Mrs. Jones. Well, I hope to tell you, after all I've done
for mine, I expect 'em to look after me, in my old age.

Mrs. Maurrant. I don't know. It seems to me you might
just as well not live at all, as the way she does. [*Rising,
with affected casualness.*] I don't know what's become of
Willie. I think I'd better walk down to the corner and look
for him. My husband don't like it if he stays out late.

*She goes off at the left. They all watch her, in dead silence,
until she is out of earshot. Then the storm breaks.*

Mrs. Jones [*rising excitedly*]. Didja get that? Goin' to
look for Willie! Can ya beat it?

Mrs. Fiorentino. It's joost terrible!

Jones. You think she's just goin' out lookin' for this guy
Sankey?

Mrs. Jones [*scornfully*]. Ain't men the limit? What do
you think he come walkin' by here for? [*Mincingly.*] Just

strolled by to get the wife a little ginger ale. A fat lot he cares whether his wife has ginger ale!

Mrs. Fiorentino. Two little girls he's got too!

Jones. Yeah, that ain't right—a bird like that, wit' a wife an' two kids of his own.

Mrs. Fiorentino. The way he stands there and looks and looks at her!

Mrs. Jones. An' what about the looks she was givin' him! [*Seating herself again.*] You'd think he was the Prince of Wales instead of a milk collector. And didja get the crack about not seein' him for two weeks?

Mrs. Fiorentino. And joost today he was upstairs, Mrs. Olsen says.

OLSEN *approaches the stoop and removes his pipe from his mouth.*

Olsen [*pointing upward*]. Someday her hoosban' is killing him. [*He replaces his pipe and goes back to his former position.*]

Mrs. Fiorentino. Dot would be terrible!

Jones. He's li'ble to, at that. You know, he's got a wicked look in his eye, dat baby has.

Mrs. Jones. Well, it's no more than he deserves, the little rabbit—goin' around breakin' up people's homes. [*Mockingly.*] Good evenin', folks! Jes' like Whozis on the radio.

Jones. D'ya think Maurrant is wise to what's goin' on?

Mrs. Jones. Well, if he ain't, there must be somethin' the matter with him. But you never can tell about men. They're as blind as bats. An' what I always say is, in a case like that, the husband or the wife is always the last one to find out.

MISS CUSHING, *carrying a small paper bag, hurries on at the left in a state of great excitement.*

Miss Cushing [*breathlessly, as she comes up the left of the stoop*]. Say, what do you think! I just saw them together—the two of them!

Mrs. Jones [*rising excitedly*]. What did I tell you?

Mrs. Fiorentino. Where did you see them, Miss Cushing?

Miss Cushing. Why, right next door, in the entrance to

the warehouse. They were standing right close together. And he had his hands up on her shoulders. It's awful, isn't it?

Jones. Looks to me like this thing is gettin' pretty serious.

Mrs. Jones. You didn't notice if they was kissin' or anythin', did you?

Miss Cushing. Well, to tell you the truth, Mrs. Jones, I was so ashamed for her that I hardly looked at all.

Jones [*sotto voce, as the house door opens*]. Look out! Maurrant's comin'.

A conspirators' silence falls upon them as MAURRANT, *pipe in mouth, comes out of the house.*

Miss Cushing [*tremulously*]. Good evening, Mr. Maurrant.

Maurrant [*on the top step*]. 'Evenin'. [*To the others.*] What's become of me wife?

Mrs. Jones. Why, she said she was goin' around the corner to look for Willie.

Maurrant [*grunts*]. Oh.

Mrs. Jones. They need a lot of lookin' after when they're that age.

A momentary silence.

Miss Cushing. Well, I think I'd better get back to my mother. [*She goes up the steps.*]

Mrs. Jones, Mrs. Fiorentino, and Jones. Good night, Miss Cushing.

Miss Cushing. Good night. [*As she passes* MAURRANT.] Good night, Mr. Maurrant.

Maurrant. 'Night.

She looks at him swiftly and goes into the vestibule.

A Boy's Voice [*offstage*]. Red Rover! Red Rover! Let Mary come over!

As MISS CUSHING *enters the house* SHIRLEY KAPLAN *appears at the ground-floor window, at the extreme right, with a glass of steaming tea in her hand. She is a dark, unattractive Jewess, past thirty. She wears a light housedress.* KAPLAN *goes on reading.*

Shirley [*to the neighbors outside; she speaks with the faintest trace of accent*]. Good evening.

The Others [*not very cordially*]. Good evenin'.

Shirley. It's been a terrible day, hasn't it?

Jones and Mrs. Jones. Yeah.

Shirley [*going to the other window*]. Papa, here's your tea. Haven't you finished your paper yet? It makes it so hot, with the lights on.

Kaplan [*lowering his newspaper*]. Oll right! Oll right! Put it out! Put it out! There is anahoo notting to read in de papers. Notting but deevorce, skendal, and moiders. [*He speaks with a strong accent, overemphatically, and with much gesticulation. He puts his paper away, removes his glasses, and starts to drink his tea.*]

Shirley. There doesn't seem to be a breath of air anywhere.

No one answers. SHIRLEY *goes away from the window and puts out the lights.*

Mrs. Jones [*sotto voce*]. You wouldn't think anybody would want to read that Hebrew writin', would ya? I don't see how they make head or tail out of it, meself.

Jones. I guess if you learn it when you're a kid——

Mrs. Jones [*suddenly*]. Well, will you look at your hubby, Mrs. F.! He's sure got his hands full!

She looks toward the left, greatly amused. SHIRLEY *reappears at the window at the extreme right and seats herself on the sill.*

Mrs. Fiorentino [*leaning far out*]. Joost look at him! [*Calling.*] Lippo, be careful you don't drop any!

Lippo [*offstage*]. 'Allo, Margherita!

They all watch in amusement as FILIPPO FIORENTINO, *a fat Italian, with thick black hair and mustache, comes on at the left. He is clutching a violin in his left arm and balancing five ice-cream cones in his right hand.*

Lippo [*shouting*]. Who wantsa da ice-cream cone? Nica, fresha ice-cream cone!

Mrs. Fiorentino. Lippo, you will drop them!

Mrs. Jones [*going up to him*]. Here, gimme your violin. [*She relieves him of the violin, and he shifts two of the cones to his left hand.*]

Lippo [*as* MRS. JONES *hands the violin to* MRS. FIOREN-

TINO]. T'ank you, Messes Jones. 'Ere's for you a nica, fresha ice-cream cone.

MRS. FIORENTINO *puts the violin on a chair behind her.*

Mrs. Jones [taking a cone]. Why, thank you very much, Mr. F.

Lippo [going up to the window]. Meeses Fiorentino, 'ere's for you a nica, fresha ice-cream cone.

Mrs. Fiorentino [taking the cone]. It makes me too fat.

Lippo. Ah, no! Five, ten poun' more, nobody can tell da deef! [*He laughs loudly at his own joke and crosses to the stoop.*]

Mrs. Jones [enjoying her cone]. Ain't he a sketch though?

Lippo. Meester Jones, you eata da cone, ha?

Jones. Why, yeah, I will at that. Thanks. Thanks.

Lippo. Meester Maurrant?

Maurrant. Naw; I got me pipe.

Lippo. You lika better da pipe den da ice cream? [*Crossing the stoop.*] Meesa Kaplan, nica, fresha cone, yes?

Shirley. No, thanks. I really don't want any.

Lippo. Meester Kaplan, yes?

Kaplan [waving his hand]. No, no! Tenks! tenks!

Mrs. Jones [to JONES]. You oughta pay Mr. F. for the cones.

Jones [reluctantly reaching into his pocket]. Why, sure.

Lippo [excitedly]. Ah, no, no! I don' taka da mon'. I'm treata da whole crowd. I deedn' know was gona be such a biga crowd or I bringa doz'. [*Crossing to* OLSEN.] Meester Olsen, you like da cone, ha?

Olsen. Sure. Much oblige'. [*He takes the pipe from his mouth and stolidly licks the cone.*]

Lippo [seating himself on the stoop with a long sigh of relaxation]. Aaah! [*He tastes the cone and, smacking his lips, looks about for approval.*] Ees tasta good, ha?

Jones [his mouth full]. You betcha!

Mrs. Jones. It cools you off a little.

Lippo. Sure. Dassa right. Cool you off. [*He pulls at his clothing and sits on the stoop.*] I'ma wat, wat—like I jus' come outa da bad-tub. Ees 'ota like hal in da Park. Two, t'ree t'ousan' people, everybody sweatin'—ees smal lika menageria.

While he is speaking ALICE SIMPSON, *a tall, spare spinster, appears at the right. She goes up the steps, enters the vestibule, and is about to push one of the buttons on the side wall.*

Mrs. Jones [*sotto voce*]. She's from the Charities. [*Coming over to the stoop and calling into the vestibule.*] If you're lookin' for Mrs. Hildebrand, she ain't home yet.

Miss Simpson [*coming to the doorway*]. Do you know when she'll be back?

Mrs. Jones. Well, she oughta be here by now. She jus' went aroun' to the Livingston. That's the pitcher theayter.

Miss Simpson [*outraged*]. You mean she's gone to a moving-picture show?

Olsen [*calmly*]. She's comin' now.

Lippo [*rising to his feet and calling vehemently*]. Mees Hil'brand! Hurry up! Hurry up! Ees a lady here.

He motions violently to her to hurry. LAURA HILDEBRAND *appears at the right with her two children,* CHARLIE *and* MARY. *She is a small, rather young woman, with a manner of perpetual bewilderment. Both children are chewing gum, and* MARY *comes on skipping a rope and chanting:* "Apple, peach, pear, plum, banana." CHARLIE *carefully avoids all the cracks in the sidewalk.*

Miss Simpson [*coming out on the steps*]. Well, good evening, Mrs. Hildebrand!

Mrs. Hildebrand [*flustered*]. Good evening, Miss Simpson.

Miss Simpson. Where have you been—to a moving-picture show?

Mrs. Hildebrand. Yes, ma'am.

Miss Simpson. And where did you get the money?

Mrs. Hildebrand. It was only seventy-five cents.

Miss Simpson. Seventy-five cents is a lot when you're being dispossessed and dependent upon charity. I suppose it came out of the money I gave you to buy groceries with?

Mrs. Hildebrand. We always went, Thursday nights, to the pictures when my husband was home.

Miss Simpson. Yes, but your husband isn't home. And as far as anybody knows, he has no intention of coming home.

Kaplan [*leaning forward out of his window*]. Ees dis your conception of cherity?

Shirley. Papa, why do you interfere?

Miss Simpson [to KAPLAN]. You'll please be good enough to mind your own business.

Kaplan. You should go home and read in your Bible de life of Christ.

Mrs. Jones [to MRS. FIORENTINO]. Will you listen to who's talkin' about Christ!

Miss Simpson [turning her back on KAPLAN *and speaking to* MRS. HILDEBRAND]. You may as well understand right now that nobody's going to give you any money to spend on moving-picture shows.

Lippo. Ah, wotsa da matter, lady? [*He thrusts his hand into his pocket and takes out a fistful of coins.*] 'Ere, you taka da mon', you go to da pitcha ever' night. [*He forces the coins into* MRS. HILDEBRAND's *hand.*] An' here's for da bambini. [*He gives each child a nickel.*]

Mrs. Fiorentino [to MRS. JONES]. Dot's why we never have money.

Mrs. Hildebrand [bewildered]. I really oughtn't to take it.

Lippo. Sure! Sure! I got plenta mon'.

Miss Simpson [disgustedly]. We'd better go inside. I can't talk to you here, with all these people.

Mrs. Hildebrand [meekly]. Yes, ma'am. [*She follows* MISS SIMPSON *into the house, her children clinging to her.*]

Mrs. Jones. Wouldn't she give you a pain?

Lippo. I tella you da whola troub'. She's a don' gotta nobody to sleepa wit'. [*The men laugh.*]

Mrs. Jones [to MRS. FIORENTINO]. Ain't he the limit!

Mrs. Fiorentino [greatly pleased]. Tt!

Lippo. Somebody go sleepa wit' her, she's alla right. Meester Jones, 'ow 'bout you?

SHIRLEY, *embarrassed, leaves the window.*

Jones [with a sheepish grin]. Naw, I guess not.

Lippo. Wot'sa matter? You 'fraid you' wife, ha? Meester Maurrant, how 'bout you?

MAURRANT *emits a short laugh.*

Mrs. Fiorentino [delighted]. Lippo, you're joost awful.

Lippo [enjoying himself hugely]. Alla ri'. Ahma gonna go myself! [*He laughs boisterously. The others laugh too.*]

Mrs. Jones [suddenly]. Here's your wife, now, Mr. Maurrant.

A sudden silence falls upon them all as MRS. MAURRANT *approaches at the left. A swift glance apprises her of* MAURRANT's *presence.*

Lippo. 'Allo, Meeses Maurrant. Why you don' come to da concerto?

Mrs. Maurrant. Well, I was waiting for Rose, but she didn't get home. [To MAURRANT, *as she starts to go up the steps.*] Is she home yet, Frank?

Maurrant. No, she ain't. Where you been all this while?

Mrs. Maurrant. Why, I've been out looking for Willie.

Maurrant. I'll give him a good fannin' when I get hold of him.

Mrs. Maurrant. Ah, don't whip him, Frank, please don't. All boys are wild like that, when they're that age.

Jones. Sure! My boy Vincent was the same way. An' look at him today—drivin' his own taxi an' makin' a good livin'.

Lippo [leaning on the balustrade]. Eees jussa same t'ing wit' me. W'en Ahm twelva year, I run away—I don' never see my parent again.

Maurrant. That's all right about that. But it ain't gonna be that way in my family.

Mrs. Maurrant [as MISS SIMPSON *comes out of the house].* Look out, Frank. Let the lady pass.

Miss Simpson. Excuse me.

They make way for her as she comes down the steps. MRS. MAURRANT *seats herself on the stoop.*

Lippo. Meeses Hil'brand, she gotta de tougha luck, ha? Tomorra, dey gonna t'row 'er out in da street, ha?

Miss Simpson [stopping at the right of the stoop and turning toward him]. Yes, they are. And if she has any place to sleep, it will only be because the Charities find her a place. And you'd be doing her a much more neighborly act if you helped her to realize the value of money, instead of encouraging her to throw it away.

Lippo [with a deprecatory shrug]. Ah, lady, no! I give 'er coupla dollar, make 'er feel good, maka me feel good—dat don' 'urt nobody.

Shirley *reappears at the window.*

Miss Simpson. Yes, it does. It's bad for her character.

Kaplan [throwing away his cigarette and laughing aloud]. Ha! You mek me leff!

Miss Simpson [turning angrily]. Nobody's asking your opinion.

Kaplan. Dot's oll right. I'm taling you vit'out esking. You hoid maybe already dot poem:

Orgenized cherity, measured and iced,
In der name of a kushus, stetistical Christ.

Miss Simpson [fiercely]. All the same, you Jews are the first to run to the Charities.

She strides angrily off at the right, Lippo, *affecting a mincing gait pretends to follow her.*

Kaplan [leaning out of the window]. Come back and I'll tal you somet'ing vill maybe do good your kerecter.

Mrs. Fiorentino. Lippo!

Mrs. Jones [highly amused]. Look at him, will ya?

Lippo [laughing and waving his hand]. Gooda-by, lady! *[He comes back to the stoop.]*

Kaplan [to the others]. Dey toin out in de street a mudder vit' two children, and dis female comes and preaches to her bourgeois morelity.

Mrs. Jones [to Mrs. Fiorentino*].* He's shootin' off his face again.

Shirley. Papa, it's time to go to bed!

Kaplan [irritably]. Lat me alone, Shoiley. *[Rising and addressing the others.]* Dees cherities are notting but anudder dewise for popperizing de verking klesses. Ven de lendlords steal from de verkers a million dollars, dey give to de Cherities a t'ousand.

Maurrant. Yeah? Well, who's puttin' her out on the street? What about the lan'lord here? He's a Jew, ain't he?

Mrs. Jones. I'll say he's a Jew! Isaac Cohen!

Kaplan. Jews oder not Jews—vot has dis got to do vit' de quastion? I'm not toking releegion, I'm toking economics. So long as de kepitalist klesses——

Maurrant [interrupting]. I'm talkin' about if you don't pay your rent, you gotta move.

Mrs. Maurrant. It doesn't seem right, though, to put a poor woman out of her home.

Mrs. Fiorentino. And for her husband to run away— dot vos not right either.

Lippo. I betcha 'e's got 'nudder woman. He find a nice blonda chicken, 'e run away.

Mrs. Jones. There ought to be a law against women goin' around stealin' other women's husbands.

Mrs. Fiorentino. Yes, dot's right, Mrs. Jones.

Maurrant. Well, what I'm sayin' is, it ain't the landlord's fault.

Kaplan. Eet's de folt of our economic system. So long as de institution of priwate property exeests, de verkers vill be at de moicy of de property-owning klesses.

Maurrant. That's a lot o' bushwa! I'm a woikin' man, see? I been payin' dues for twenty-two years in the Stage-hands Union. If we're not gettin' what we want, we call a strike, see?—and then we get it.

Lippo. Sure! Ees same wit' me. We gotta Musician Union. We getta pay for da rehears', we getta pay for da overtime——

Shirley. That's all right when you belong to a strong union. But when a union is weak, like the Teachers' Union, it doesn't do you any good.

Mrs. Jones [*to* MRS. FIORENTINO]. Can y' imagine that? Teachers belongin' to a union!

Kaplan [*impatiently*]. Oll dese unions eccomplish notting votever. Oll dis does not toch de fondamental problem. So long as de tuls of industry are in de hands of de ke*pi*talist klesses, ve vill hev exploitation and sloms and——

Maurrant. T' hell wit' all dat hooey! I'm makin' a good livin' an' I'm not doin' any kickin'.

Olsen [*removing his pipe from his mouth*]. Ve got prosperity, dis coontry.

Jones. You said somethin'!

Kaplan. Sure, for de reech is planty prosperity! Mister Morgan rides in his yacht and upstairs dey toin a voman vit' two children in de street.

Maurrant. And if you was to elect a Socialist president tomorra, it would be the same thing.

Mrs. Fiorentino. Yes, dot's right, Mr. Maurrant.

Jones. You're right!

Kaplan. Who's toking about electing presidents? Ve must put de tuls of industry in de hends of de verking klesses, and dis ken be accomplished only by a sushal revolution!

Maurrant. Yeah? Well, we don't want no revolutions in this country, see?

General chorus of assent.

Mrs. Jones. I know all about that stuff—teachin' kids there ain't no Gawd an' that their gran'fathers was monkeys.

Jones [*rising angrily*]. Free love, like they got in Russia, huh?

KAPLAN *makes a gesture of impatient disgust and sinks back into his chair.*

Maurrant. There's too goddam many o' you Bolsheviks runnin' aroun' loose. If you don't like the way things is run here, why in hell don't you go back where you came from?

Shirley. Everybody has a right to his own opinion, Mr. Maurrant.

Maurrant. Not if they're against law and order, they ain't. We don't want no foreigners comin' in, tellin' us how to run things.

Mrs. Fiorentino. It's nothing wrong to be a foreigner. Many good people are foreigners.

Lippo. Sure! Looka Eetalians. Looka Cristoforo Colombo! 'E'sa firs' man discov' America—'e's Eetalian, jussa like me.

Maurrant. I'm not sayin' anythin' about that——

Olsen [*removing his pipe*]. Firs' man is Lief Ericson.

Lippo [*excitedly, going toward* OLSEN]. Wassa dat?

Olsen. Firs' man is Lief Ericson.

Lippo. No! No! Colombo! Cristoforo Colomb'—'e'sa firs' man discov' America—ever'body knowa dat! [*He looks around appealingly.*]

Mrs. Jones. Why, sure, everybody knows that.

Jones. Every kid learns that in school.

Shirley. Ericson was really the first discoverer——

Lippo [*yelling*]. No! Colomb'!

Shirley. But Columbus was the first to open America to settlement.

Lippo [*happily, as he goes back to the stoop*]. Sure, dassa wot Ahm say—Colomb' is firs'.

Olsen. Firs' man is Lief Ericson.

Lippo [*tapping his forehead significantly*]. Looka wot Eetalian do for America—'e build bridge, 'e build railroad, 'e build subway, 'e dig sewer. Wit'out Eetalian, ees no America.

Jones. Like I heard a feller sayin': the Eye-talians built New York, the Irish run it, an' the Jews own it. [*Laughter.*]

Mrs. Fiorentino [*convulsed*]. Oh! Dot's funny!

Jones [*pleased with his success*]. Yep, the Jews own it all right.

Maurrant. Yeah, an' they're the ones that's doin' all the kickin'.

Shirley. It's no disgrace to be a Jew, Mr. Maurrant.

Maurrant. I'm not sayin' it is. All I'm sayin' is, what we need in this country is a little more respect for law an' order. Look at what's happenin' to people's homes, with all this divorce an' one thing an' another. Young girls goin' around smokin' cigarettes an' their skirts up around their necks. An' a lot o' long-haired guys talkin' about free love an' birth control an' breakin' up decent people's homes. I tell you it's time somethin' was done to put the fear o' God into people!

Mrs. Jones. Good for you, Mr. Maurrant!

Jones. You're damn right.

Mrs. Fiorentino. Dot's right, Mr. Maurrant!

Mrs. Maurrant. Sometimes, I think maybe they're only trying to get something out of life.

Maurrant. Get somethin', huh? Somethin' they oughtn't to have, is that it?

Mrs. Maurrant. No; I was only thinking——

Maurrant. Yeah, you were only thinkin', huh?

Kaplan [*rising to his feet again*]. De femily is primerily an economic institution.

Mrs. Jones [*to* Mrs. Fiorentino]. He's in again.

Kaplan. Ven priwate property is ebolished, de femily will no longer hev eny reason to exeest.

Shirley. Can't you keep quiet, Papa?

Maurrant [*belligerently*]. Yeah? Is that so? No reason to exist, huh? Well, it's gonna exist, see? Children respectin' their parents an' doin' what they're told, get me? An' husbands an' wives, lovin' an' honorin' each other, like they said they would when they was spliced—an' any dirty sheeny that says different is li'ble to get his head busted open, see?

Mrs. Maurrant [*springing to her feet*]. Frank!

Shirley [*trying to restrain* KAPLAN]. Papa!

Kaplan. Oll right! I should argue vit' a low-kless gengster.

Maurrant [*raging*]. Who's a gangster? Why, you goddam——! [*He makes for the balustrade.*]

Mrs. Maurrant [*seizing his arm*]. Frank!

Jones [*seizing the other arm*]. Hey! Wait a minute! Wait a minute!

Maurrant. Lemme go!

Shirley [*interposing herself*]. You should be ashamed to talk like that to an old man! [*She slams down the window.*]

Maurrant. Yeah? [*To* MRS. MAURRANT *and* JONES.] All right, lemme go! I ain't gonna do nothin'.

They release him. SHIRLEY *expostulates with* KAPLAN *and leads him away from the window.*

Mrs. Jones [*who has run over to the right of the stoop*]. Maybe if somebody handed him one, he'd shut up with his talk for a while.

Lippo. 'E talka lika dat een Eetaly, Mussolini's gonna geeve 'eem da castor-oil.

Mrs. Jones [*laughing*]. Yeah? Say, that's a funny idea! [*Still chuckling, she goes back to the railing at the left of the stoop.*]

Jones. No kiddin', is that what they do?

Mrs. Fiorentino. Yes, dot's true. My husband read it to me in the Italian paper.

Mrs. Maurrant. Why must people always be hurting and injuring each other? Why can't they live together in peace?

Maurrant [*mockingly*]. Live in peace! You're always talkin' about livin' in peace!

Mrs. Maurrant. Well, it's true, Frank. Why can't people just as well be kind to each other?

Maurrant. Then let 'im go live with his own kind.

Jones [coming down the steps]. Yeah, that's what I say. [*As* MRS. JONES *laughs aloud.*] What's eatin' you?

Mrs. Jones. I was just thinkin' about the castor-oil. [MAURRANT *seats himself on the right balustrade.*]

Lippo. Sure, 'esa funny fell', Mussolini. [*Doubling up in mock pain.*] 'E geeve 'em da pain in da belly, dey no can talk. [*Suddenly.*] Look! 'Eresa da boy. 'Esa walk along da street an' reada da book. Datsa da whola troub': reada too much book.

While LIPPO *is speaking* SAMUEL KAPLAN *appears at the left. He is twenty-one, slender, with dark, unruly hair and a sensitive, mobile face. He is hatless, and his coat is slung over one shoulder. He walks along slowly, absorbed in a book. As he approaches the stoop* SHIRLEY, *in a kimono, appears at the closed window, opens it, and is about to go away again when she sees* SAM.

Shirley [calling]. Sam!

Sam [looking up]. Hello, Shirley.

Shirley. Are you coming in?

Sam. No, not yet. It's too hot to go to bed.

Shirley. Well, I'm tired. And Papa's going to bed too. So don't make a noise when you come in.

Sam. I won't.

Shirley. Good night.

Sam. Good night. [SHIRLEY *goes away from the window.*]

Sam [to the others, as he seats himself on the curb to the right of the stoop]. Good evening!

Several. 'Evening.

Lippo [approaching SAM]. 'Ow you lika da concerto? I see you sittin' in da fronta seat.

Sam. I didn't like it. Why don't they play some real music instead of all those Italian organ-grinder's tunes?

Lippo [excitedly]. Wotsa da matter? You don't lika da Verdi?

Sam. No, I don't. It's not music!

Lippo. Wot you call music—da Tschaikov', ha? [*He hums derisively a few bars from the first movement of the "Symphonie Pathétique."*]

Sam. Yes, Tschaikovsky—and Beethoven. Music that comes from the soul.

Mrs. Maurrant. The one I like is—— [*She hums the opening bars of Mendelssohn's "Spring Song."*]

Lippo. Datsa da "Spreeng Song" from da Mendelson.

Mrs. Maurrant. Yes! I love that. [*She goes on humming softly.*]

Mrs. Fiorentino. And the walzer von Johann Strauss. [*She hums the "Wienerwald Waltz."*]

Mrs. Jones. Well, gimme a good jazz band, every time.

Lippo [*protesting*]. Ah, no! Ees not music, da jazz. Ees breaka your ear. [*He imitates the discordant blaring of a saxophone.*]

Jones [*bored*]. Well, I guess I'll be on me way.

Mrs. Jones. Where are *you* goin'?

Jones. Just around to Callahan's to shoot a little pool. Are you comin' along, Mr. Maurrant?

Maurrant. I'm gonna wait awhile.

A man with a clubfoot appears at the right and crosses the stage.

Mrs. Jones [*as* JONES *goes toward the right*]. Don't be comin' home lit, at all hours o' the mornin'.

Jones [*over his shoulder*]. Aw, lay off dat stuff! I'll be back in a half an hour.   [*He exits at right.*

A Voice [*offstage*]. Char-lie!

Mrs. Jones. Him an' his pool! Tomorra he won't be fit to go to work again.

Sam [*who has been awaiting a chance to interrupt*]. When you hear Beethoven, it expresses the struggles and emotions of the human soul.

Lippo [*waving him aside*]. Ah, ees no good, da Beethoven. Ees alla time sad. Ees wanna maka you cry. I don' wanna cry, I wanna laugh. Eetalian music ees maka you 'appy. Ees maka you feel good. [*He sings several bars of "Donna è mobile."*]

Mrs. Maurrant [*applauding*]. Yes, I like that too.

Lippo. Ah, ees bew-tiful! Ees maka you feela fine. Ees maka you wanna dance. [*He executes several dance steps.*]

Mrs. Fiorentino [*rising*]. Vait, Lippo, I vill give you music. [*She goes away from the window. The lights go on in the Fiorentino apartment.*]

Lippo [*calling after her*]. Playa Puccini, Margherita!

[*He hums an air from* Madame Butterfly. *Then, as* MRS.
FIORENTINO *begins to play the waltz from* La Bohème *on
the piano.*] Ah! *La Bohème!* Bew-tiful! Who'sa gonna
dance wit' me? Meeses Maurrant, 'ow 'bout you?

Mrs. Maurrant [*with an embarrassed laugh*]. Well, I
don't know. [*She looks timidly at* MAURRANT, *who gives no
sign.*]

Lippo. Ah, come on! Dansa wit' me! [*He takes her by the
hand.*]

Mrs. Maurrant. Well, all right, I will.

Lippo. Sure, we hava nica dance. [*They begin to dance
on the sidewalk.*]

Lippo [*to* MAURRANT]. Your wife ees dansa swell.

Mrs. Maurrant [*laughing*]. Oh, go on, Mr. Fiorentino!
But I always loved to dance!

They dance on. SANKEY *appears at the left, carrying a
paper bag from which the neck of a ginger ale bottle protrudes.* MAURRANT *sees him and rises.*

Mrs. Jones [*following* MAURRANT'*s stare and seeing*
SANKEY]. Look out! You're blockin' traffic!

Sankey [*stopping at the left of the stoop*]. I see you're
having a little dance. [MRS. MAURRANT *sees him and stops
dancing.* LIPPO *leans against the right balustrade, panting.
The music goes on.*] Say, go right ahead. Don't let me stop
you.

Mrs. Maurrant. Oh, that's all right. I guess we've danced
about enough. [*She goes up the steps, ill at ease.*]

Sankey. It's a pretty hot night for dancing.

Mrs. Maurrant. Yes, it is.

Sankey [*going toward the right*]. Well, I got to be
going along. Good night, folks.

The Others [*except* MAURRANT]. Good night.

Lippo [*as he seats himself at the left of the stoop*].
Stoppa da music, Margherita!

The music stops. SANKEY *goes off at the right.* MRS. MAUR-
RANT *goes quickly up the steps.*

Maurrant [*stopping her*]. Who's that bird?

Mrs. Maurrant. Why, that's Mr. Sankey. He's the milk
collector.

Maurrant. Oh, he is, is he? Well, what's he hangin' around here for?

Mrs. Maurrant. Well, he lives just down the block some-where.

Mrs. Jones. He's just been down to the drugstore, gettin' some ginger ale for his wife.

Maurrant. Yeah? Well, what I want to know is, why ain't Rose home yet?

Mrs. Maurrant. I told you, Frank——

Maurrant. I know all about what you told me. What I'm sayin' is, you oughta be lookin' after your kids instead of doin' so much dancin'.

Mrs. Maurrant. Why, it's the first time I've danced in I don't know when.

Maurrant. That's all right about that. But I want 'em home instead o' battin' around the streets, hear me?

While he is speaking WILLIE *appears, sobbing, at the left, his clothes torn and his face scratched. He is carrying his skates.*

Mrs. Maurrant [coming down the steps]. Why, Willie, what's the matter? [*Reproachfully, as* WILLIE *comes up to her, sniffling.*] Have you been fighting again?

Willie [with a burst of indignation]. Well, dat big bum ain't gonna say dat to me. I'll knock da stuffin's out o' him, dat's what I'll do!

Maurrant [tensely, as he comes down the steps]. Who's been sayin' things to you?

Willie. Dat big bum Joe Connolly, dat's who! [*Blubbering.*] I'll knock his goddam eye out next time!

Mrs. Maurrant. Willie!

Maurrant [seizing WILLIE'S *arm].* Shut up your swearin', do you hear?—or I'll give you somethin' to bawl for. What did he say to you, huh? What did he say to you?

Willie [struggling]. Ow! Leggo my arm!

Mrs. Maurrant. What difference does it make what a little street loafer like that says?

Maurrant. Nobody's askin' you! [*To* WILLIE.] What did he say? [*He and* MRS. MAURRANT *exchange a swift involuntary look; then* MAURRANT *releases the boy.*] G'wan up to bed now, an' don't let me hear no more out o' you.

[*Raising his hand.*] G'wan now. Beat it! [WILLIE *ducks past* MAURRANT *and hurries up the steps and into the vestibule.*]

Mrs. Maurrant. Wait, Willie, I'll go with you. [*She goes up the steps, then stops and turns.*] Are you coming up, Frank?

Maurrant. No, I ain't. I'm goin' around to Callahan's for a drink, an' if Rose ain't home when I get back, there's gonna be trouble. [*Without another glance or word he goes off at the right.* MRS. MAURRANT *looks after him for a moment with a troubled expression.*]

Mrs. Maurrant [*entering the vestibule*]. Well, good night, all.

The Others. Good night.

SAM *rises. As* MRS. MAURRANT *and* WILLIE *enter the house,* MRS. FIORENTINO *reappears at the window.*

Mrs. Fiorentino. Lippo! [*She sees that something is wrong.*]

Mrs. Jones. Say, you missed it all!

SAM, *about to go up the steps, stops at the right of the stoop.*

Mrs. Fiorentino [*eagerly*]. Vat?

Mrs. Jones [*volubly*]. Well, they was dancin', see? An' who should come along but Sankey?

Mrs. Fiorentino. Tt!

A *light appears in the Maurrant apartment.*

Mrs. Jones. Well, there was the three o' them—Mr. Maurrant lookin' at Sankey as if he was ready to kill him, an' Mrs. Maurrant as white as a sheet, an' Sankey as innocent as the babe unborn.

Mrs. Fiorentino. Did he say something?

Mrs. Jones. No, not till after Sankey was gone. Then he wanted to know who he was an' what he was doin' here. "He's the milk collector," she says.

Mrs. Fiorentino. It's joost awful.

Mrs. Jones. Oh, an' then Willie comes home.

Lippo. Da boy tella 'eem 'is mamma ees a whore an' Weelie leeck 'im.

Mrs. Jones. Well, an' what else is she?

Sam [*unable longer to restrain himself*]. Stop it! Stop it!

Can't you let her alone? Have you no hearts? Why do you tear her to pieces, like a pack of wolves? It's cruel, cruel! [*He chokes back a sob, then dashes abruptly into the house.*]

Lippo [*rising to his feet and yelling after him*]. Wotsa matter you?

Mrs. Jones. Well, listen to him, will you! He must be goin' off his nut too.

Lippo. 'Esa reada too mucha book. Ees bad for you.

Mrs. Fiorentino. I think he is loving the girl.

Mrs. Jones. Yeah? Well, that's all the Maurrants need is to have their daughter get hooked up wit' a Jew. It's a fine house to be livin' in, ain't it, between the Maurrants upstairs an' that bunch o' crazy Jews down here.

A girl appears at the left, glancing apprehensively over her shoulder at a man who is walking down the street behind her. They cross the stage and go off at the right.

Mrs. Jones [*as* Mrs. Olsen *comes up the cellar steps and over to the stoop*]. Well, good night.

Mrs. Fiorentino. Good night, Mrs. Jones.

Lippo. Goo' night, Meeses Jones.

Mrs. Jones. Wait a minute, Mrs. Olsen. I'll go with you.

Mrs. Jones *and* Mrs. Olsen *enter the house.* Olsen *yawns mightily, knocks the ashes from his pipe, and goes down the cellar steps.* Willie Maurrant *leans out of the window and spits into the areaway. Then he leaves the window and turns out the light. A* Policeman *appears at the right and strolls across the stage.*

Lippo [*who has gone up the steps*]. Margherita, eef I ever ketcha you sleepin' wit' da meelkaman, Ahm gonna breaka your neck.

Mrs. Fiorentino [*yawning*]. Stop your foolishness, Lippo, and come to bed!

Lippo *laughs and enters the house.* Mrs. Fiorentino *takes the pillow off the window sill, closes the window, and starts to pull down the shade.* Rose Maurrant *and* Harry Easter *appear at the left.* Rose *is a pretty girl of twenty, cheaply but rather tastefully dressed.* Easter *is about thirty-five, good-looking, and obviously prosperous.*

Mrs. Fiorentino. Good evening, Miss Maurrant.

Rose [*as they pass the window*]. Oh, good evening, Mrs. Fiorentino. [ROSE *and* EASTER *cross to the stoop.* MRS. FIORENTINO *looks at them a moment, then pulls down the shade and turns out the lights.* ROSE *stops at the foot of the steps.*] Well, this is where I live, Mr. Easter. [*She extends her hand.*] I've had a lovely time.

Easter [*taking her hand*]. Why, you're not going to leave me like this, are you? I've hardly had a chance to talk to you.

Rose [*laughing*]. We've been doing nothing but talking since six o'clock. [*She tries gently to extricate her hand.*]

Easter [*still holding it*]. No, we haven't. We've been eating and dancing. And now, just when I want to talk to you—— [*He puts his other arm around her.*] Rose——

Rose [*rather nervously*]. Please don't, Mr. Easter. Please let go. I think there's somebody coming.

She frees herself as the house door opens and MRS. OLSEN *appears in the vestibule. They stand in silence as* MRS. OLSEN *puts the door off the latch, tries it to see that it is locked, dims the light in the vestibule, and comes out on the stoop.*

Mrs. Olsen [*as she comes down the steps*]. Goot evening, Miss Maurrant. [*She darts a swift look at* EASTER *and crosses to the cellar steps.*]

Rose. Good evening, Mrs. Olsen. How's the baby?

Mrs. Olsen. She vas cryin' all the time. I tank she vas gettin' new teet'.

Rose. Oh, the poor little thing! What a shame!

Mrs. Olsen [*as she goes down the steps*]. Yes, ma'am. Goot night, Miss Maurrant.

Rose. Good night, Mrs. Olsen. [*To* EASTER.] She's got the cutest little baby you ever saw.

Easter [*rather peevishly*]. Yeah? That's great. [*Taking* ROSE's *hand again.*] Rose, listen——

Rose. I've really got to go upstairs now, Mr. Easter. It's awfully late.

Easter. Well, can't I come up with you—for a minute?

Rose [*positively*]. No, of course not!

Easter. Why not?

Rose. Why, we'd wake everybody up. Anyhow, my father wouldn't like it.

Easter. Aren't you old enough to do what you like?

Rose. It's not that. Only I think when you're living with people, there's no use doing things you know they don't like. [*Embarrassed.*] Anyhow, there's only the front room and my little brother sleeps there. So good night, Mr. Easter.

Easter [*taking both her hands*]. Rose—I'm crazy about you.

Rose. Please let me go now.

Easter. Kiss me good night.

Rose. No.

Easter. Why not, hm?

Rose. I don't want to.

Easter. Just one kiss.

Rose. No.

Easter. Yes! [*He takes her in his arms and kisses her.* Rose *frees herself and goes to the right of the stoop.*]

Rose [*her bosom heaving*]. It wasn't nice of you to do that.

Easter [*going over to her*]. Why not? Didn't you like it? Hm?

Rose. Oh, it's not that.

Easter. Then what is it, hm?

Rose [*turning and facing him*]. You know very well what it is. You've got a wife, haven't you?

Easter. What of it? I tell you, I'm clean off my nut about you.

Rose [*nervously, as the house door opens*]. Look out! Somebody's coming.

Easter *goes to the other side of the stoop and they fall into a self-conscious silence as* Mrs. Jones *comes out of the house, leading an ill-conditioned dog.*

Mrs. Jones [*as she comes down the steps*]. Oh, good evenin'. [*She stares at* Easter, *then goes toward the right.*]

Rose. Good evening, Mrs. Jones. It's been a terrible day, hasn't it?

Mrs. Jones. Yeah. Awful. [*Stopping.*] I think your father's been kinda worried about you.

Rose. Oh, has he?

Mrs. Jones. Yeah. Well, I gotta give Queenie her

exercise. Good night. [*She stares at* EASTER *again, then goes off at right.*]

Rose. Good night, Mrs. Jones. [*To* EASTER.] I'll soon have all the neighbors talking about me.

Easter [*going over to her again*]. What can they say, hm? That they saw you saying good night to somebody on the front doorstep?

Rose. They can say worse than that—and what's more, they will, too.

Easter. Well, why not snap out of it all?

Rose. Out of what?

Easter [*indicating the house*]. This! The whole business. Living in a dirty old tenement like this; working all day in a real-estate office, for a measly twenty-five a week. You're not going to try to tell me you like living this way, are you?

Rose. No, I can't say that I like it especially. But maybe it won't always be this way. Anyhow, I guess I'm not so much better than anybody else.

Easter [*taking her hand*]. Do you know what's the matter with you? You're not wise to yourself. Why, you've got just about everything, you have. You've got looks and personality and a bean on your shoulders—there's nothing you haven't got. You've got It, I tell you.

Rose. You shouldn't keep looking at me, all the time, at the office. The other girls are beginning to pass hints about it.

Easter [*releasing her hand, genuinely perturbed*]. Is that a fact? You see, that shows you! I never even knew I was looking at you. I guess I just can't keep my eyes off you. Well, we've got to do something about it.

Rose [*nervously snapping the clasp of her handbag*]. I guess the only thing for me to do is to look for another job.

Easter. Yes, that's what I've been thinking too. [*As she is about to demur.*] Wait a minute, honey! I've been doing a little thinking and I've got it all doped out. The first thing you do is throw up your job, see?

Rose. But——

Easter. Then you find yourself a nice, cozy little apartment somewhere. [*As she is about to interrupt again.*] Just a minute, now! Then you get yourself a job on the stage.

Rose. How could I get a job on the stage?

Easter. Why, as easy as walking around the block. I've got three or four friends in show business. Ever hear of Harry Porkins?

Rose. No.

Easter. Well, he's the boy that put on "Mademoiselle Marie" last year. He's an old pal of mine, and all I'd have to say to him is—[*Putting his arm around her shoulder.*] —"Harry, here's a little girl I'm interested in," and he'd sign you up in a minute.

Rose. I don't think I'd be any good on the stage.

Easter. Why, what are you talking about, sweetheart? There's a dozen girls, right now, with their names up in electric lights, that haven't got half your stuff. All you got to do is go about it in the right way—put up a little front, see? Why, half the game is nothing but bluff. Get yourself a classy little apartment, and fill it up with trick furniture, see? Then you doll yourself up in a flock of Paris clothes and you throw a couple or three parties and you're all set. [*Taking her arm.*] Wouldn't you *like* to be on Broadway?

Rose. I don't believe I ever could be.

Easter. Isn't it worth trying? What have you got here, hm? This is no kind of a racket for a girl like you. [*Taking her hand.*] You do like me a little, don't you?

Rose. I don't know if I do or not.

Easter. Why, sure you do. And once you get to know me better, you'd like me even more. I'm no Valentino, but I'm not a bad scout. Why, think of all the good times we could have together—you with a little apartment and all. And maybe we could get us a little car——

Rose. And what about your wife?

Easter [*letting go her hand*]. The way I figure it is, she doesn't have to know anything about it. She stays up there in Bronxville, and there are lots of times when business keeps me in New York. Then, in the summer, she goes to the mountains. Matter of fact, she's going next week and won't be back until September.

Rose [*shaking her head and going toward the stoop*]. I don't think it's the way I'd want things to be.

Easter. Why, there's nothing really wrong about it.

Rose. Maybe there isn't. But it's just the way I feel about it, I guess.

Easter. Why, you'd get over that in no time. There's lots of girls——

Rose. Yes, I know there are. But you've been telling me all along I'm different.

Easter. Sure, you're different. You're in a class by yourself. Why, sweetheart—— [*He tries to take her in his arms.*]

Rose [*pushing him away*]. No. And you mustn't call me sweetheart.

Easter. Why not?

Rose. Because I'm not your sweetheart.

Easter. I want you to be—— [*A sudden yell of pain is heard from upstairs. They both look up, greatly startled.*] My God, what's that—a murder?

Rose. It must be poor Mrs. Buchanan. She's expecting a baby.

Easter. Why does she yell like that? God, I thought somebody was being killed.

Rose. The poor thing! [*With sudden impatience she starts up the steps.*] I've got to go now. Good night.

Easter [*taking her hand*]. But, Rose——

Rose [*freeing her hand quickly*]. No, I've got to go. [*Suddenly.*] Look, there's my father. There'll only be an argument if he sees you.

Easter. All right, I'll go. [*He goes toward the left as* MAURRANT *appears at the right.*]

Rose [*going up to the top step*]. Good night.

Easter. Good night. [EASTER *goes off at the left.* ROSE *begins searching in her handbag for her latchkey.*]

Rose [*as* MAURRANT *approaches*]. Hello, Pop.

Maurrant [*stopping at the foot of the steps*]. Who was that you was talkin' to?

Rose. That's Mr. Easter. He's the manager of the office.

Maurrant. What's he doin' here? You been out wit' him?

Rose. Yes, he took me out to dinner.

Maurrant. Oh, he did, huh?

Rose. Yes, I had to stay late to get out some letters. You see, Pop, the office is closed tomorrow, on account of Mr. Jacobson's funeral——

Maurrant. Yeah, I know all about that. This is a hell of a time to be gettin' home from dinner.

Rose. Well, we danced afterward.

Maurrant. Oh, you danced, huh? With a little pettin' on the side, is that it?

Rose [*rather angrily, as she seats herself on the left balustrade*]. I don't see why you can never talk to me in a nice way.

Maurrant. So you're startin' to go on pettin' parties, are you?

Rose. Who said I was on a petting party?

Maurrant. I suppose he didn't kiss you or nothin', huh?

Rose. No, he didn't! And if he did——

Maurrant. It's your own business, is that it? [*Going up the steps.*] Well, I'm gonna make it my business, see? Is this bird married? [*Rose does not answer.*] I t'ought so! They're all alike, them guys—all after the one thing. Well, get this straight. No married men ain't gonna come nosin' around my family, get me?

Rose [*rising agitatedly as the house door opens*]. Be quiet, Pop! There's somebody coming.

Maurrant. I don't care!

BUCHANAN *hurries out of the house. He is a small and pasty young man—a typical "white-collar slave." He has hastily put on his coat and trousers over his pajamas, and his bare feet are in slippers.*

Buchanan [*as he comes down the steps*]. I think the baby's coming!

Rose [*solicitously*]. Can I do anything, Mr. Buchanan?

Buchanan [*as he hurries toward the left*]. No, I'm just going to phone for the doctor.

Rose [*coming down the steps*]. Let me do it, and you go back to your wife.

Buchanan. Well, if you wouldn't mind. It's Doctor John Wilson. [*Handing her a slip of paper.*] Here's his number. And the other number is her sister, Mrs. Thomas. And here's two nickels. Tell them both to come right away. She's got terrible pains. [*Another scream from upstairs.*] Listen to her! I better go back. [*He dashes up the steps and into the house.*]

Rose. Oh, the poor woman! Pop, tell Ma to go up to her. Hurry!

Maurrant. Aw, all right.

He follows BUCHANAN *into the house.* ROSE *hurries off at the left just as* MAE JONES *and* DICK MCGANN *appear.* MAE *is a vulgar shopgirl of twenty-one;* DICK, *a vacuous youth of about the same age.* MAE *is wearing* DICK'S *straw hat and they are both quite drunk.*

Mae [*to* ROSE]. Hello, Rose. What's your hurry?

Rose [*without stopping*]. It's Mrs. Buchanan. I've got to phone to the doctor.   [*She hurries off.*

Dick [*as they approach the stoop*]. Say, who's your little friend?

Mae. Oh, that's Rose Maurrant. She lives in the house.

Dick. She's kinda cute, ain't she?

Mae [*seating herself on the stoop*]. Say, accordin' to you, anythin' in a skirt is kinda cute—providin' the skirt is short enough.

Dick. Yeah, but they ain't any of 'em as cute as you, Mae.

Mae [*yawning and scratching her leg*]. Yeah?

Dick. Honest, I mean it. How 'bout a little kiss? [*He puts his arms about her and plants a long kiss upon her lips. She submits with an air of intense boredom. Removing his lips.*] Say, you might show a little en-thoosiasm.

Mae [*rouging her lips*]. Say, you seem to think I oughta hang out a flag every time some bozo decides to wipe off his mouth on me.

Dick. De trouble wit' you is you need another little snifter. [*He reaches for his flask.*]

Mae. Nope! I can't swaller any more o' that rotten gin o' yours.

Dick. Why, it ain't so worse. I don't mind it no more since I had that brass linin' put in me stomach. Well, happy days! [*He takes a long drink.*]

Mae [*rising indignantly*]. Hey, for God's sake, what are you doin'—emptyin' the flask?

Dick [*removing the flask from his lips*]. I t'ought you didn't want none.

Mae. Can't you take a joke? [*She snatches the flask from him and drains it, kicking out at* DICK *to prevent his taking it from her.*]

Dick [*snatching the empty flask*]. Say, you wanna watch your step, baby, or you're li'ble to go right up in a puff o' smoke.

Mae [*whistling*]. Phew! Boy! I feel like a t'ree alarm fire! Say, what de hell do dey make dat stuff out of?

Dick. T'ree parts dynamite an' one part Army mule. Dey use it for blastin' out West.

Mae [*bursting raucously into a jazz tune*]. Da-da-da-da-dee! Da-da-da-da-dee! [*She executes some dance steps.*]

Dick. Say, shut up, will ya? You'll be wakin' the whole neighborhood.

Mae [*boisterously*]. What the hell do I care? Da-da-da-da-dee! Da-da-da-da-dee! [*Suddenly amorous, as she turns an unsteady pirouette.*] Kiss me, kid!

Dick. I'll say! [*They lock in a long embrace.* SAM, *coatless, his shirt collar open, appears at the window, watches the pair for a moment, and then turns away, obviously disgusted. They do not see him.* DICK *takes* MAE'S *arm.*] Come on!

Mae. Wait a minute! where y' goin'?

Dick. Come on, I'm tellin' ya! Fred Hennessy gimme de key to his apartment. Dere won't be nobody dere.

Mae [*protesting feebly*]. I oughta go home. [*Her hand to her head.*] Oh, baby! Say, nail down dat sidewalk, will ya?

Dick. Come on!

ROSE *appears at the left.*

Mae. Sweet papa! [*She kisses* DICK *noisily, then bursts into song again.*] Da-da-da-da-dee! Da-da-da-da-dee! [*As they pass* ROSE.] Hello, Rose. How's de milkman?

Dick [*raising his hat with drunken politeness*]. Goo' night, sweetheart.

They go off at the left, MAE'S *snatches of song dying away in the distance.* ROSE *stands still for a moment, choking back her mortification.*

Buchanan's Voice. Miss Maurrant, did you get them?

Rose [*looking up*]. Why, yes, I did. The doctor will be here right away. And Mrs. Thomas said it would take her about an hour.

VINCENT JONES *appears at the right and stops near the stoop. He is a typical New York taxicab driver, in a cap.* ROSE *does not see him.*

Buchanan's Voice. She's got terrible pains. Your mother's up here with her. [MRS. BUCHANAN *is heard calling faintly.*] I think she's calling me.

ROSE *goes toward the stoop and sees* VINCENT.

Vincent. Hello, Rosie.

Rose. Good evening. [*She tries to pass, but he blocks her way.*]

Vincent. What's your hurry?

Rose. It's late.

Vincent. You don' wanna go to bed yet. Come on, I'll take you for a ride in me hack. [*He puts his arm around her.*]

Rose. Please let me pass.

SAM *appears at the window. They do not see him.*

Vincent [*enjoying* ROSE's *struggle to escape*]. You got a lot o' stren'th, ain't you? Say, do you know, you're gettin' fat? [*He passes one hand over her body.*]

Rose. Let me go, you big tough.

Sam [*simultaneously*]. Take your hands off her!

He climbs quickly out of the window and onto the stoop. VINCENT, *surprised, releases* ROSE *and steps to the sidewalk.* ROSE *goes up the steps.* SAM, *trembling with excitement and fear, stands on the top step.* VINCENT *glowers up at him.*

Vincent. Well, look who's here! [*Mockingly.*] Haster gesehn de fish in de Bowery? [*Menacingly.*] What de hell do you want?

Sam [*chokingly*]. You keep your hands off her!

Vincent. Yeah? [*Sawing the air with his hands.*] Oi, Jakie! [*He suddenly lunges forward, seizes* SAM's *arm, pulls him violently by the right hand down the steps and swings him about, so that they stand face to face, to the left of the stoop.* ROSE *comes down between them.*] Now whaddya got t' say?

Rose. Let him alone!

Sam [*inarticulately*]. If you touch her again——

Vincent [*mockingly*]. If I touch her again——! [*Savagely*.] Aw, shut up, you little kike bastard! [*He brushes* ROSE *aside and, putting his open hand against* SAM's *face, sends him sprawling to the pavement.*]

Rose [*her fists clenched*]. You big coward.

Vincent [*standing over* SAM]. Get up, why don't you?

Rose [*crossing to* SAM]. If you hit him again I'll call my father.

Vincent [*as* MRS. JONES *and the dog appear at the right*]. Gee, don't frighten me like dat. I got a weak heart. [*He is sobered, nevertheless.* SAM *picks himself up.* MRS. JONES *approaches.*] Hello, Ma.

Mrs. Jones [*with maternal pride*]. Hello, Vincent. What's goin' on here?

Vincent. Oh, jus' a little friendly argument. Ikey Finkelstein don't like me to say good evenin' to his girl friend.

Rose. You'd better keep your hands to yourself hereafter.

Vincent. Is dat so? Who said so, huh?

Mrs. Jones. Come on, Vincent. Come on upstairs. I saved some stew for you.

Vincent. All right, I'm comin'. [*To* ROSE.] Good night, dearie. [*He makes a feint at* SAM, *who starts back in terror.* VINCENT *laughs.*]

Mrs. Jones. Aw, let 'im alone, Vincent.

Vincent [*as he goes up the steps*]. Who's touchin' him? A little cockroach like dat ain't woit' my time. [*To* ROSE.] Some sheik you picked out for yourself! [*He enters the vestibule and opens the door with his latchkey.*]

Mrs. Jones [*going up the steps*]. You seem to have plenty of admirers, Miss Maurrant. [*Pausing on the top step.*] But I guess you come by it natural.

ROSE *does not reply.* MRS. JONES *follows* VINCENT *into the house.* ROSE *averts her head to keep back the tears.* SAM *stands facing the house, his whole body quivering with emotion. Suddenly he raises his arms, his fists clenched.*

Sam [*hysterically, as he rushes to the foot of the stoop*]. The dirty bum! I'll kill him!

Rose [*turning and going to him*]. It's all right, Sam. Never mind.

Sam [*sobbing*]. I'll kill him! I'll kill him!

He throws himself on the stoop and, burying his head in his arms, sobs hysterically. ROSE *sits beside him and puts her arm around him.*

Rose. It's all right, Sam. Everything's all right. Why should you pay any attention to a big tough like that? [SAM *does not answer.* ROSE *caresses his hair and he grows calmer.*] He's nothing but a loafer, you know that. What do you care what he says?

Sam [*without raising his head*]. I'm a coward.

Rose. Why, no, you're not, Sam.

Sam. Yes, I am. I'm a coward.

Rose. Why, he's not worth your little finger, Sam. You wait and see. Ten years from now, he'll still be driving a taxi and you—why, you'll be so far above him, you won't even remember he's alive.

Sam. I'll never be anything.

Rose. Why, don't talk like that, Sam. A boy with your brains and ability. Graduating from college with honors and all that! Why, if I were half as smart as you, I'd be just so proud of myself!

Sam. What's the good of having brains if nobody ever looks at you—if nobody knows you exist?

Rose [*gently*]. I know you exist, Sam.

Sam. It wouldn't take much to make you forget me.

Rose. I'm not so sure about that. Why do you say that, Sam?

Sam. Because I know. It's different with you. You have beauty—people look at you—you have a place in the world——

Rose. I don't know. It's not always so easy, being a girl —I often wish I were a man. It seems to me that when you're a man, it's so much easier to sort of—be yourself, to kind of be the way you feel. But when you're a girl, it's different. It doesn't seem to matter what you are, or what you're thinking or feeling—all that men seem to care about is just the one thing. And when you're sort of trying to find out just where you're at, it makes it hard. Do you see what I mean? [*Hesitantly.*] Sam, there's something I want to ask you—— [*She stops.*]

Sam [*turning to her*]. What is it, Rose?

Rose. I wouldn't dream of asking anybody but you.

[*With a great effort.*] Sam, do you think it's true—what they're saying about my mother? [SAM *averts his head, without answering. Wretchedly.*] I guess it is, isn't it?

Sam [*agitatedly*]. They were talking here, before—I couldn't stand it any more! [*He clasps his head and, springing to his feet, goes to the right of the stoop.*] Oh, God, why do we go on living in this sewer?

Rose [*appealingly*]. What can I do, Sam? [SAM *makes a helpless gesture.*] You see, my father means well enough, and all that, but he's always been sort of strict and—I don't know—sort of making you freeze up, when you really wanted to be nice and loving. That's the whole trouble, I guess; my mother never had anybody to really love her. She's sort of gay and happy-like—you know, she likes having a good time and all that. But my father is different. Only—the way things are now—everybody talking and making remarks, all the neighbors spying and whispering —it sort of makes me feel—— [*She shudders.*] I don't know——!

Sam [*coming over to her again*]. I wish I could help you, Rose.

Rose. You do help me, Sam—just by being nice and sympathetic and talking things over with me. There's so few people you can really talk to, do you know what I mean? Sometimes, I get the feeling that I'm all alone in the world and that—— [*A scream of pain from* MRS. BUCHANAN. ROSE *springs to her feet.*] Oh, just listen to her!

Sam. Oh, God!

Rose. The poor thing! She must be having terrible pains.

Sam. That's all there is in life—nothing but pain. From before we're born, until we die! Everywhere you look, oppression and cruelty! If it doesn't come from Nature, it comes from humanity—humanity trampling on itself and tearing at its own throat. The whole world is nothing but a bloodstained arena, filled with misery and suffering. It's too high a price to pay for life—life isn't worth it! [*He seats himself despairingly on the stoop.*]

Rose [*putting her hand on his shoulder*]. Oh, I don't know, Sam. I feel blue and discouraged, sometimes, too. And I get a sort of feeling of, oh, what's the use. Like last night. I hardly slept all night, on account of the heat and on account of thinking about—well, all sorts of things. And this morning, when I got up, I felt so miserable. Well, all of a sudden, I decided I'd walk to the office. And when I got to the Park, everything looked so green and fresh, that I got a kind of feeling of, well, maybe it's not so bad, after all. And then, what do you think?—all of a sudden, I saw a big lilac bush, with some flowers still on it. It made me think about the poem you said for me—remember?—the one about the lilacs.

Sam [*quoting*].

When lilacs last in the dooryard bloom'd

And the great star early droop'd in the western sky in the night,

I mourn'd and yet shall mourn, with ever-returning Spring. [*He repeats the last line.*]

I mourn'd and yet shall mourn, with ever-returning Spring! Yes!

Rose. No, not that part. I mean the part about the farmhouse. Say it for me, Sam. [*She sits at his feet.*]

Sam.

In the door-yard, fronting an old farmhouse, near the white-washed palings,

Stands the lilac bush, tall-growing, with heart-shaped leaves of rich green,

With many a pointed blossom, rising delicate, with the perfume strong I love,

With every leaf a miracle—and from this bush in the dooryard,

With delicate-color'd blossoms and heart-shaped leaves of rich green,

A sprig with its flower I break.

Rose [*eagerly*]. Yes, that's it! That's just what I felt like doing—breaking off a little bunch of the flowers. But then I thought, maybe a policeman or somebody would see me, and then I'd get into trouble; so I didn't.

Buchanan's Voice. Miss Maurrant! Miss Maurrant!

SAM *and* ROSE *spring to their feet and look up.*

Rose. Yes?

Buchanan's Voice. Do you mind phoning to the doctor again? She's getting worse.

Rose. Yes, sure I will. [*She starts to go.*] Wait! Maybe this is the doctor now.

Buchanan's Voice [*excitedly as* DR. WILSON, *a seedy, middle-aged man in a crumpled Panama, appears at the left*]. Yes, that's him. Mrs. Maurrant! Tell her the doctor's here! Doctor, I guess you're none too soon.

Dr. Wilson. Plenty of time. Just don't get excited. [*He throws away his cigarette and enters the vestibule. The mechanical clicking of the door latch is heard as he goes into the house.*]

Rose. I hope she won't have to suffer much longer.

Maurrant [*appearing at the window in his undershirt*]. Rose!

Rose [*rather startled*]. Yes, Pop, I'll be right up.

Maurrant. Well, don't be makin' me call you again, d'ya hear?

Rose. I'm coming right away. [MAURRANT *leaves the window.*] I'd better go up now, Sam.

Sam. Do you have to go to bed, when you're told, like a child?

Rose. I know, Sam, but there's so much wrangling goes on, all the time, as it is, what's the use of having any more? Good night, Sam. There was something I wanted to talk to you about, but it will have to be another time. [*She holds out her hand.* SAM *takes it and holds it in his.*]

Sam [*trembling and rising to his feet*]. Rose, will you kiss me?

Rose [*simply*]. Why, of course I will, Sam. [*She offers him her lips. He clasps her in a fervent embrace, to which she submits but does not respond. Freeing herself gently.*] Don't be discouraged about things, Sam. You wait and see—you're going to do big things, some day. I've got lots of confidence in you.

Sam [*turning away his head*]. I wonder if you really have, Rose?

Rose. Why, of course I have! And don't forget it! Good night. I hope it won't be too hot to sleep.

Sam. Good night, Rose.

He watches her, as she opens the door with her latchkey and goes into the house. Then he goes to the stoop and,

seating himself, falls into a reverie. A POLICEMAN *appears
at the right and strolls across, but* SAM *is oblivious to him.
In the distance a homecomer sings drunkenly. A light appears, in the Maurrant hall bedroom, and a moment later*
ROSE *comes to the window and leans out.*

Rose [*calling softly*]. Hoo-hoo! Sam! [SAM *looks up, then
rises.*] Good night, Sam. [*She wafts him a kiss.*]

Sam [*with deep feeling*]. Good night, Rose dear.

She smiles at him. Then she pulls down the shade. SAM *looks
up for a moment, then resumes his seat. A scream from*
MRS. BUCHANAN *makes him shudder. A deep rhythmic
snoring emanates from the Fiorentino apartment. A steam-
boat whistle is heard. The snoring in the Fiorentino apartment continues.* SAM *raises his clenched hands to heaven.
A distant clock begins to strike twelve.* SAM'S *arms and
head drop forward.*

The curtain falls slowly.

ACT TWO

Daybreak, the next morning. It is still quite dark and comparatively quiet. The rhythmic snoring in the Fiorentino apartment is still heard, and now and then a distant El train or speeding automobile. A moment after the rise of the curtain JONES *appears, at the right, on his way home from the speakeasy. He reels slightly but negotiates the steps and entrance door without too much difficulty. It grows lighter—and noisier. The street light goes out. The* OLSEN *baby begins to cry. An alarm clock rings. A dog barks. A canary begins to sing. Voices are heard in the distance. They die out and other voices are heard. The house door opens and* DR. WILSON *comes out, passing* JONES *at the top of the stoop.* DR. WILSON *stands on the steps and yawns the yawn of an overtired man. Then he lights a cigarette and goes toward the left.*

BUCHANAN'S VOICE. Doctor!

Dr. Wilson [*stopping and looking up*]. Well?

Buchanan's Voice. What if she does wake up?

Dr. Wilson [*sharply*]. She won't, I've told you! She's too exhausted. The best thing you can do is lie down and get some sleep yourself.

As he goes off at the left, MAE *and* DICK *appear. They walk slowly and listlessly and far apart.*

Dick [*as they reach the stoop*]. Well, goo' night.

Mae [*with a yawn, as she finds her latchkey*]. Goo' night. [*Going up the steps and looking toward the Fiorentino apartment.*] Aw, shut up, you wop!

Dick [*his dignity wounded*]. How 'bout kissin' me good night?

Mae [*venomously, from the top step*]. For God's sake, ain't you had enough kissin' for one night! [*She enters the vestibule and puts the key in the lock. The ringing of an alarm clock is heard.*]

Dick [*raising his voice*]. Well, say, if that's the way you feel about it——

Mae. Aw, go to hell! [*She enters the house. The alarm clock has stopped ringing.*]

Dick. You dirty little tart!

He stands, muttering to himself for a moment, then goes

109

off at the right, passing the POLICEMAN, *who looks at him suspiciously. The sounds of a Swedish quarrel are heard from the janitor's apartment. The baby is still crying. As the* POLICEMAN *goes left, a* MILKMAN *appears, whistling and carrying a rack of full milk bottles.*

The Policeman. Hello, Louie.

The snoring in the Fiorentino apartment stops.

The Milkman. Hello, Harry. Goin' to be another scorcher.

The Policeman. You said it.   [*He exits at left.*

The MILKMAN *crosses to the cellar steps.* MAE *appears at the hall-bedroom window of the Jones apartment and removes her dress over her head. The* MILKMAN, *about to go down the steps, sees her and stops to watch.* MAE, *about to slip out of her step-in, sees him, throws him an angry look, and pulls down the shade. The* MILKMAN *grins and goes down the cellar steps.* CHARLIE HILDEBRAND *comes out of the house. He is chewing gum and as he comes out to the top of the stoop he scatters the wrappings of the stick of gum on the stoop. Then he jumps down the four steps of the stoop, in one jump, and goes off at the left, pulling the chewing gum out in a long ribbon, and carefully avoiding all the cracks in the pavement. A young* WORKMAN, *carrying a kit of tools and a tin lunch box, appears at the left, extinguishes the red light on the excavation, and, opening the door, goes in. A* TRAMP *comes on at the right and shuffles across. He sees a cigar butt on the pavement, picks it up, and pockets it as he exits at the left.* ROSE, *in her nightgown, appears at the window, yawns slightly, and disappears. It is daylight now. The baby stops crying.* MRS. OLSEN *comes up the cellar steps. She goes up the stoop, turns out the light in the vestibule, and takes the door off the latch. The* MILKMAN *comes up the cellar steps, his rack laden with empty bottles, and goes off, whistling, at the left.* SAM, *coatless, a book in his hand, appears at the window. He looks out for a moment, then climbs out on the stoop, looks up at* ROSE's *window, then seats himself and begins to read.* WILLIE *comes out of the house.*

Willie [*chanting as he comes down the steps*]. Fat, Fat, the water rat, fifty bullets in his hat.

Sam. Hello, Willie. Is Rose up yet?

Willie [*without stopping or looking at him*]. Yeah. I don't know. I guess so.

He turns a somersault and goes off at left, continuing his chanting. SAM *glances up at* ROSE's *window again, then resumes his book.* MRS. JONES *and her dog come out of the house.*

Mrs. Jones [*haughtily, as she comes down the steps*]. Mornin'.

Sam [*scarcely looking up from his book*]. Good morning.

MRS. JONES *and the dog go off at the right. A middle-aged* WORKMAN, *carrying a large coil of wire, appears at the left and goes to the door of the excavation.* MRS. OLSEN *comes out of the house and exits into the basement.*

The Workman [*calling*]. You down there, Eddie?

A Voice [*from the depths*]. Yeah!

The Workman. All right!

He climbs down into the excavation. ROSE *comes to window and pulls up the shade.* WILLIE *and* CHARLIE *can be heard, offstage left, engaged in an earnest conversation.*

Charlie [*offstage*]. He could not!

Willie [*offstage*]. He could so!

They appear at left. Each has under his arm a paper bag from which a loaf of bread protrudes.

Charlie. I'll betcha he couldn't.

Willie. I'll betcha he could.

Charlie. I'll betcha a million dollars he couldn't.

Willie. I'll betcha five million dollars he could. Hold that! [*He hands* CHARLIE *his loaf of bread and turns a cartwheel.*] Bet you can't do it.

Charlie. Bet I can. [*He puts both loaves of bread on the pavement, attempts a cartwheel and fails.*]

Willie [*laughing raucously*]. Haw-haw! Told you you couldn't!

Charlie. Can you do this? [*He turns a back somersault.*]

Willie. Sure—easy! [*He turns a back somersault. They pick up their loaves again.* WILLIE's *drops out of the bag, but he dusts it with his hand and replaces it.*] How many steps can you jump up?

Charlie. Three. [*He jumps up three steps.*]

Willie. I can do four.

Charlie. Let's see you.

WILLIE, *the bread under his arm, jumps up the four steps, undisturbed by* SAM's *presence. He drops the bread and is about to replace it in the bag but gets a better idea. He inflates the bag and explodes it with a blow of his fist.*

    CHARLIE *looks on in admiration and envy.*

Rose [*appearing at the window*]. Willie, we're waiting for the bread.

Willie [*holding it up*]. All right! Cantcha see I got it? [*He enters the house, followed by* CHARLIE.]

Sam [*rising*]. Hello, Rose.

Rose. Hello, Sam.

Sam. Come down.

Rose. I haven't had breakfast yet. [*Calling into the room.*] Yes! He's on his way up.

Miss Cushing [*coming out of the house*]. Good morning. [*She looks inquiringly from* SAM *to* ROSE.]

Sam [*impatiently*]. Good morning.

A *middle-aged* NUN *appears at the right, accompanied by a scrawny* CHILD *of about fourteen. They walk across the stage.*

Rose. Good morning, Miss Cushing. [MISS CUSHING *goes off at the left, glancing back at* ROSE *and* SAM]. I'm going to Mr. Jacobson's funeral. [*Calling into the room.*] Yes, I'm coming. [*To* SAM.] Breakfast's ready. I'll be down as soon as the dishes are done.

She disappears. SAM *looks up at the window for a moment, then begins to read again.* MRS. FIORENTINO *appears at the window, at the extreme left, with a double armful of bedding, which she deposits upon the window sill. Then she goes away again.*

Shirley [*appearing at the window*]. Sam, breakfast is ready.

Sam. I don't want any breakfast.

Shirley. What do you mean, you don't want any breakfast? What kind of a business is that, not to eat breakfast?

Sam. Do I have to eat breakfast if I don't want to?

Shirley. You've got your head so full of that Rose Maurrant upstairs that you don't want to eat or sleep or anything, any more.

Sam. If I don't feel like eating, why should I eat? [*Bursting out.*] You're always telling me: "Eat!" "Don't eat!" "Get up!" "Go to bed!" I know what I want to do, without being told.

Shirley. I don't see, just when you're graduating from college, why you want to get mixed up with a little batzimer like that!

Sam. It's always the same thing over again with you. You never can get over your race prejudice. I've told you a hundred times that the Jews are no better than anybody else.

Shirley. I'm not talking about that! Look at the kind of family she comes from. What's her father? Nothing but an illiterate roughneck. And her mother——

Sam [*indignantly*]. Are you starting too?

Kaplan's Voice. Shoi-ley!

Shirley. Wait a minute, Papa's calling. [*Into the room.*] All right, Papa! [*To* SAM.] Come in, Sam, or Papa will be making long speeches again.

Sam [*impatiently*]. All right! All right! I'll come.

A young SHOPGIRL, *smiling to herself, appears at the right and walks across the stage.* SAM *rises and goes into the house.* SHIRLEY *leaves the window.* BUCHANAN, *emerging from the house, collarless and unshaven, encounters* SAM *in the vestibule.*

Buchanan [*eagerly*]. Good morning!

Sam [*abruptly*]. Good morning.

He enters the house. BUCHANAN *looks back at him, then comes down the steps.* MRS. FIORENTINO *raises the drawn shade and opens the window.*

Mrs. Fiorentino. Good morning, Mr. Buchanan.

Buchanan. Oh, good morning, Mrs. Fiorentino. [*Going over to the left balustrade.*] I guess you know that the baby came last night, don't you?

Mrs. Fiorentino. No! I did not hear a vord about it.

Buchanan. Why, I thought she'd wake up the whole neighborhood, the way she was yelling. Three-thirty this morning the baby came. I been up the whole night.

An old LETTER CARRIER, *coatless, appears at the right.*

Mrs. Fiorentino. A boy, is it?

Buchanan. No, it's a little girl. I guess we'll call her Mary, after my mother.

Letter Carrier [*going up the steps*]. Mornin'.

Mrs. Fiorentino. Good morning. Any letters for me?

Letter Carrier [*from the top of the steps*]. No, not a thing.

Buchanan [*turning toward him*]. I was just telling Mrs. Fiorentino, I had a little addition to my family last night.

Letter Carrier. Your first, is it?

Buchanan [*hastening to explain*]. Well, we've only been married a little over a year.

Letter Carrier. Well, I've had seven, an' I'm still luggin' a mailbag at sixty-two. [*He goes into the vestibule and puts the mail into the letter boxes.*]

Mrs. Fiorentino. How is your wife?

Buchanan. Well, she had a pretty hard time of it. Her sister's up there with her. And Mrs. Maurrant was up, nearly all night. I don't know what we'd have done without her.

Letter Carrier [*coming down the steps*]. It don't pay to let 'em have their own way too much. That's where I made my mistake.

As the LETTER CARRIER *goes off at the left,* LIPPO *appears at the window behind his wife and tickles her.*

Mrs. Fiorentino [*startled*]. Lippo!

Buchanan. Morning. I was just telling your wife——

Mrs. Fiorentino. Lippo, what do you think? Mr. Buchanan has a little girl!

Lippo. Ah, dotsa fine! Margherita, why you don' have da baby, ha?

Mrs. Fiorentino [*abruptly*]. I must go and make the coffee.

She goes away from the window. OLSEN *comes halfway up the steps and leans against the railing, smoking his pipe.*

A Voice [*offstage left*]. Oh-h! Corn! Sweet corn!

Lippo. Ees funny t'ing. You gotta da leetla skeeny wife an' she's hava da baby. My Margherita, she's beeg an' fat an' she no can hava da baby.

Buchanan. Well, that's the way o' the world, I guess.

As he goes off at the left, Mike, *an* Iceman, *appears, trundling a three-wheeled cart filled with ice.*

Lippo. Buon giorno, Mike.
Mike. Buon giorno, signore. Come sta?
Lippo. Benissimo. Fa molto caldo ancora, oggi.
Mike. Si, si, signore. Bisognera abbastanza ghiaccio. Twen'y fi' cent, ha?
Lippo. No, no, e troppo.
Mike. Twen'y cent? Eesa melta fas'.
Lippo. Alla right. Gimme twen'y cent.
Mike. Si, si, signore. Sure.

As he wheels the cart to the cellar entrance and begins to chop a block of ice a Man *in shirtsleeves strides in from the left and stops at the curb, as though seeing someone in a house across the street.*

The Man [*angrily*]. Well, what about it? We've been waiting a half an hour!
A Voice. I'll be right over!
The Man. Yeah? Well, make it snappy!

He strides off at the left, muttering angrily. Rose *comes out of the house and stands in the doorway, looking for* Sam. *Then she comes out on the stoop and peers into the Kaplan apartment. As she turns away she sees* Lippo.

Rose [*crossing to the left of the stoop*]. Good morning.
Lippo. Gooda mornin', Meesa Maurrant.

Mike *goes down into the cellar with a chunk of ice.*

Rose. It's awful hot again, isn't it?
Lippo. You don' like?
Rose. I don't sleep very well when it's so hot.
Lippo. No? Ahm sleepa fine. Een Eetaly, where Ahm born, is much more 'ot like 'ere. Een summer, ees too 'ot for workin'. Ees too 'ot only for sleepin'. W'en Ahm leetla boy, Ahm sleepa, sleepa, whola day. I don' wear no clo's —nawthin' only leetle short pair pants: I lay down on groun' under da lemon tree, Ahm sleepa whola day.
Rose. Under a lemon tree! That must have been nice.
Lippo. Ees smella sweet, lemon tree. Where Ahm born ees t'ousan' lemon tree. Lemon an' olive an' arancia.
Rose. Oh, that must be lovely!

Lippo. Ah, ees bew-tiful! Ees most bewtiful place in whole worl'. You hear about Sorrent', ha?

Rose. No, I don't think I ever did.

Lippo [*incredulously*]. You never hear about Sorrent'?

Rose. No. I don't know much about geography. Is it a big place?

Lippo. Ees not vera beeg—but ever'body know Sorrent'. Sorrento gentile! La bella Sorrento! You hear about Napoli —Baia di Napoli?

Rose. Oh, yes, the Bay of Naples! Is it near there?

Lippo. Sure, ees on Bay of Napoli. Ees bew-tiful! Ees alla blue. Sky blue, water blue, sun ees shine alla time.

Rose. Oh, how lovely!

MIKE *comes up the cellar steps, chops another block of ice, and goes down the cellar steps with it.*

Lippo. An' ees Vesuvio too. You hear about Vesuvio? —ees beeg volcano.

Rose. Oh, yes, sure. I saw a picture once, called *The Last Days of Pompeii*, and it showed Mount Vesuvius, with smoke coming out of the top.

Lippo. Da's right. An' night time, ees fire come out, maka da sky red.

Rose. Didn't it frighten you?

Lippo. Ah no, ees nawthin' to be afraid. Ees jus' volcano.

Rose. I'd love to go to Italy. It must be awfully pretty. But I don't suppose I ever will.

Lippo. W'y sure! Some day you gonna marry reech fella; 'e's taka you Eetaly—ever'where.

Rose. I guess there's not much chance of that. Rich fellows aren't going around looking for girls like me to marry. Anyhow, I don't think money is everything, do you?

Lippo. Ees good to hava money. Da's w'y Ahm come to America. Een Eetaly, ees bewtiful, but ees no money. 'Ere ees not bewtiful, but ees plenty money. Ees better to 'ave money.

An elderly MAN, *in the gray uniform of a special officer, comes out of the house, filling his pipe from a tobacco box.*

The Man. Good mornin'.

Rose. Good morning, Mr. Callahan. [*The man drops the empty tobacco tin on the sidewalk and goes off slowly at the left.*] I don't think I'd be happy, just marrying a man with money, if I didn't care for him too.

Lippo [*laughing*]. Wotsa matter, ha? You lova da leetla kike, ha?

Rose. Why, no, I don't. I don't love anybody—at least I don't think I do. But it's not on account of his being a Jew.

Lippo. No, ees no good—Jew. 'E's only t'ink about money, money—alla time money.

Rose. But Sam isn't like that a bit. He's only interested in poetry and things like that.

MIKE *comes up out of the cellar and trundles off his cart at the right.*

Mrs. Fiorentino [*calling*]. Lippo! Breakfast!

Lippo [*calling*]. Alla right, Margherita! [*To* ROSE.] You marry fella wit' lot o' money. Ees much better.

He goes away from the window as MISS CUSHING *appears at the left, carrying a paper bag.*

Rose. How's your mother today, Miss Cushing?

Miss Cushing. She's not feeling so good today.

Rose. It's too bad she's not feeling well.

Miss Cushing. I'm afraid it's her heart. At her age, you know——!

As she enters the house, two COLLEGE GIRLS *of nineteen appear at the right.*

First Girl [*as they appear*]. I don't understand it.

Second Girl. Convex is this way; and concave is this way.

First Girl. That I know.

Second Girl. When you're nearsighted, they give you convex glasses, and when you're farsighted they give you concave.

First Girl. That I didn't know.

Second Girl. Of course you know it. Didn't we have it in psychology?

First Girl [*as they disappear at the left*]. I don't remember.

WILLIE *comes out of the house, on his way to school. He is hatless and carries his books under his arm.*

Rose [*intercepting him at the top of the stoop*]. Why, Willie, the way you look! Your collar's all open.

Willie. I know it! De button came off.

Rose. Why didn't you ask Ma to sew it on for you?

Willie. She ain't dere. She's up at Buchanan's.

Rose. Well, wait till I see if I have a pin. [*She searches in her handbag.*]

Willie [*starting down the steps*]. Aw, it's all right de way it is.

Rose [*following him to the sidewalk*]. No, it isn't. You can't go to school like that. [*Producing a safety pin.*] Now, hold still, while I fix it.

Willie [*squirming*]. Aw, fer de love o' Mike——!

Rose. You'll get stuck if you don't hold still. There, that looks better now. And you didn't comb your hair either.

Willie [*trying to escape*]. Say, lemme alone, cantcha?

Rose [*taking a comb out of her handbag and combing his hair*]. You can't go to school looking like a little street loafer.

Willie. Aw, you gimme a pain in de——

Rose. You're getting big enough to comb your own hair, without being told. There! Now you look very nice.

Willie. So's your old man! [*He runs toward the left, kicking the empty tobacco tin ahead of him, then stops, turns, and deliberately rumples his hair.*]

Rose [*indignantly, as* WILLIE *runs off*]. Why, Willie! [MRS. JONES *and the dog appear at the right.* OLSEN *knocks the ashes out of his pipe and goes down into the cellar.* MRS. MAURRANT *comes out of the house.*] Hello, Ma.

Mrs. Jones [*at the steps*]. Good mornin'.

Rose and Mrs. Maurrant. Good morning, Mrs. Jones.

Mrs. Jones. How's little Mrs. Buchanan gettin' on?

Mrs. Maurrant. Well, she's sleeping now, poor thing. She was so worn out, she just went off into a sound sleep. I really didn't think, last night, she'd have the strength to pull through it.

Mrs. Jones. Well, it's somethin' we all got to go through. I been through enough with mine, I hope to tell you. Not that they didn't turn out all right.

Mrs. Maurrant. I wouldn't give up having mine for anything in the world.

Mrs. Jones. Well, after all, what more does any woman

want than watchin' her kids grow up an' a husband to look out for her?

Mrs. Maurrant. Yes, that's true.

Mrs. Jones. Yes, and the world would be a whole lot better off, if there was more that lived up to it. [*Starting up the steps.*] Well, I gotta get my Mae up out o' bed. Gawd knows what time she got in this mornin'. [*She enters the vestibule, then stops and turns.*] If you don't mind my bein' so bold, Mrs. Maurrant—an' I don't mind sayin' it in front of your daughter either—I'd think twice before I'd let any child o' mine bring a Jew into the family.

Rose [*with a show of temper*]. I don't see what it has to do with you, Mrs. Jones.

Mrs. Jones. There's no need to get huffy about it. I'm only advisin' you for your own good. I'm sure it don't make no difference to me what you do. Come on, Queenie. [*She goes into the house.*]

Rose. Well, of all the nerve I ever heard in my life! She and those wonderful children of hers!

Mrs. Maurrant [*coming halfway down the steps*]. The best way is not to pay any attention to her. There's lots of people like that in the world—they never seem to be happy unless they're making trouble for somebody. Did Willie go to school?

Rose. Yes, he did. It's awful the way he goes around, looking like a little tough. And the language he uses too.

Mrs. Maurrant. I know. I just don't seem able to manage him any more.

Rose. I sometimes wonder if it wouldn't be better for us all if we moved out to the suburbs somewhere—you know, some place in Jersey or Staten Island.

Mrs. Maurrant. I don't think Pop would do it. [*As* MAURRANT *comes out of the house, carrying a much-battered satchel.*] Are you leaving now, Frank?

Maurrant [*from the top of the stoop*]. Looks like it, don't it. Where you been all this while?

Mrs. Maurrant. Why, you know where I've been, Frank —up to Mrs. Buchanan's.

Maurrant. Yeah? An' where you goin' now?

Mrs. Maurrant. Just around to Kraus's to get a chicken

I thought I'd make her some chicken soup, to give her strength.

Maurrant. Say, how about lookin' after your own home an' lettin' the Buchanans look after theirs.

Mrs. Maurrant. All I'm trying to do is to be a little neighborly. It's the least anybody can do, with the poor thing hardly able to lift her hand.

Maurrant. That's all right about that! [*Coming down the steps.*] A woman's got a right to stay in her own home, lookin' after her husband an' children.

Mrs. Maurrant [*going toward him*]. What else have I been doing all these years, I'd like to know?

Maurrant. Well, just see that you don't forget it, that's all—or there's li'ble to be trouble.

Mrs. Maurrant [*putting her hand on his arm*]. All right, Frank. Don't say any more, please. When will you be back—tomorrow?

Maurrant. I don' know when I'll be back. Whenever I'm t'roo wit' me work—that's when. What are you so anxious to know for, huh?

Mrs. Maurrant. Why, I just asked, that's all.

Maurrant. Oh, you just asked, huh? Just in case somebody wanted to come aroun' callin', is that it?

Mrs. Maurrant. No, it isn't. It isn't anything of the kind. You got no right to talk to me like that, in front of my own daughter. You got no right. No, you haven't! [*She turns away and hurries off, abruptly, at the left.*]

Rose. Ma! [*She starts to run after her mother.*]

Maurrant [*imperiously*]. Come back here, you! [ROSE hesitates.] Come back, hear me? [ROSE *turns and comes slowly back.*] You stay right here. [*He puts down his satchel and takes a flask from his pocket.*]

Rose. Why do you talk to her like that?

Maurrant. Nobody's askin' you.

Rose. If you were only a little nicer to her, maybe everything would be different.

Maurrant. Yeah? Where's she got any kick comin'? Ain't I always been a good husband to her? Ain't I always looked after her? [*He takes a drink.*]

Rose. It's not that, Pop. It's somebody to be sort of nice to her that she wants—sort of nice and gentle, the way she is to you. That's all it is.

Maurrant [*turning to her*]. So she's got you headed the same way, has she? Goin' out nights with married men, huh?

Rose. You don't need to worry about me, Pop. I can take care of myself all right.

Maurrant. No daughter o' mine ain't gonna go that way. I seen too many o' those kind around the theayter.

Rose. Things are different nowadays, Pop. I guess maybe you don't realize that. Girls aren't the way they used to be—sort of soft and helpless. A girl nowadays knows how to look out for herself. But not her, Pop; she needs somebody to look after her.

Maurrant. Aw, can all that talk! You been listenin' to them Bolshevikis, that's the trouble. But I'm gonna keep you straight, by God, or I'll know the reason why.

Rose. I guess I've got a right to think about things for myself.

Maurrant. Yeah? Well, don't let me ketch that other bozo comin' around here either—that's all I got to say.

Rose [*hesitantly going up to him*]. Pop, listen—couldn't we get a little house somewhere—Queens or somewhere like that?

Maurrant. What's the idea?

Rose. Well, I don't know. I sort of thought it would be nice for all of us. And maybe if Ma had a nice little home and some real nice neighbors—do you see what I mean?

Maurrant. This place suits me all right.

Rose. You can get some real nice little houses that don't cost such an awful lot. And I wouldn't mind helping to pay for it. And once we had it all fixed up——

Maurrant. Forget it! I don' know when I'll be back. [*As he starts to go right.*] An' remember what I tol' you, hear?

Mrs. Jones [*appearing at her window with a tin dustpan*]. Good mornin', Mr. Maurrant. You off on a little trip?

Maurrant [*curtly*]. Yeah.

He goes off. Mrs. Jones *empties the dustpan out of the window and goes away.* Kaplan *comes out of the house, a bundle of newspapers under his arm. He walks slowly and painfully with the aid of a heavy stick.*

Kaplan [*at the foot of the steps*]. Vy do you look so sed, hm?

Rose [*turning and sitting on the right balustrade*]. Oh, good morning, Mr. Kaplan.

Kaplan. A young girl, like you, should not look so sed.

Rose. I'm not sad, especially, only——

Kaplan. You got trobles, hm?

Rose. I don't know. It's just sort of everything.

Kaplan. Velt-schmerz you got, hm? Vit' my boy Sem is de same t'ing. Dees vay you feel only ven you are yong. Ven you gat old like me, you tink only: "Moch longer I von't be here."

Rose. Why should things be the way they are, Mr. Kaplan? Why must people always be fighting and having troubles, instead of just sort of being happy together?

Kaplan. My dear yong leddy, ef I could enser dis quastion, I vould be de greatest benefactor thet de verld hes ever known. Dees is som't'ing vich all de philosophers hev been unable to enser. De ones thet believe in God, say de davil is responsible; and de ones thet don't believe in God, say 'uman nature is responsible. It is my opinion thet most unheppiness can be traced to economic cosses and thet——

CHARLIE *and* MARY HILDEBRAND *have come out of the house, carrying their schoolbooks.*

Mary. Hello.

Rose. Hello, Mary. Hello, Charlie.

Charlie. Hello.

Mary [*chattily, as they reach the sidewalk*]. We're going to be dispossessed today.

Rose. What a shame!

Mary. Yes, ma'am. My father went away and so we couldn't pay the rent.

Charlie [*tugging at her arm*]. Aw, come on, Mary.

Rose. Have you another place to live, Mary?

Mary. No, ma'am. But Miss Simpson, from the Charities, says she'll find us a place. She says we must learn to be less extravagant.

Charlie. Come ahead, will you?

Mary. I'm going to school now. Good-by.

Rose. Good-by.   [*The children exit left.*

Kaplan. More trobles!

Rose. I know. Isn't it awful to think of them being turned out in the street like that?

Kaplan. In a ciwilized verld, soch t'ings could not heppen.

Rose. You mean if there were different laws?

Kaplan. Not laws! Ve got already too many laws. Ve must hev ection, not laws. De verking-klesses must t'row off de yoke of kepitalism, and ebolish vage slevery.

Rose. But wouldn't people still be unkind to each other and fight and quarrel among themselves?

Kaplan. My dear young leddy, so long as ve keep men in slevery, dey vill behave like sleves. But wance ve establish a verld based upon 'uman needs and not upon 'uman greed——

Rose. You mean people will begin being nice to each other and making allowances and all?

Kaplan. All dees vill come. Vot ve hev now is a wicious soicle. On de one hend, ve hev a rotten economic system——

Rose. Excuse me, here's my mother.

She goes toward the left as MRS. MAURRANT *approaches, a paper package in her hand.* KAPLAN *goes off at the right.*

Mrs. Maurrant [*as* ROSE *comes up to her*]. Did he go? [*They stop on the pavement, at the left of the stoop.*]

Rose. Yes.

Mrs. Maurrant. I got a little chicken, to make Mrs. Buchanan some soup.

Rose. He had a flask with him, Ma. I hope he doesn't start drinking.

Mrs. Maurrant. What did he say—anything?

Rose. No, only the way he always talks. I tried to talk to him about buying a house somewheres, but he wouldn't listen.

Mrs. Maurrant. No, I knew he wouldn't.

Rose. It doesn't seem to be any use trying to get him to listen to anything.

Mrs. Maurrant. It's always been that way. I've always tried to be a good wife to him, Rose. But it never seemed to make any difference to him.

Rose. I know, Ma.

Mrs. Maurrant. And I've tried to be a good mother too.

Rose. I know, Ma. I know just the way you feel about it.

Mrs. Maurrant [*appealingly*]. Do you, Rose?

Rose. Yes, Ma, I do. Honest I do.

Mrs. Maurrant. I've always tried to make a nice home for him and to do what's right. But it doesn't seem to be any use.

Rose. I know, Ma. [*Hesitantly.*] But it's on account of—— [*She stops.*]

Mrs. Maurrant. Are you going to start too? Are you going to start like all the others? [*She turns away and bursts into tears.*]

Rose [*fondling her*]. Don't, Ma. Please don't.

Mrs. Maurrant. I thought you'd be the one that would feel different.

Rose. I do, Ma—really I do.

Mrs. Maurrant. What's the good of being alive if you can't get a little something out of life? You might just as well be dead.

Rose. Look out, Ma. Somebody's coming.

A smartly dressed girl, with one side of her face covered with cotton and adhesive tape, appears at the left and crosses the stage. At the same time JONES *comes out of the house.* ROSE *and* MRS. MAURRANT *stand in awkward silence as he comes down the stoop and approaches them.*

Jones. Well, is it hot enough for you today?

Rose. It's awful, isn't it?

Jones [*as he goes toward the left*]. You said it. Still, along about January, we'll all be wishin' we had a little o' this weather.

He exits. MRS. MAURRANT *goes toward the stoop.*

Rose. Ma, listen. If I say something, will you listen to me?

Mrs. Maurrant. Yes, sure I will, Rose. I'll listen to anything you say, only——

Rose. Well, what I was thinking was, if he didn't come

around here so much, maybe. Do you see what I mean, Ma?

Mrs. Maurrant [constrainedly]. Yes, Rose.

Rose [putting her arm around her]. It's on account of all that's going around—everybody in the whole house. You see what I mean, don't you, Ma?

Mrs. Maurrant. Every person in the world has to have somebody to talk to. You can't live without somebody to talk to. I'm not saying that I can't talk to you, Rose, but you're only a young girl and it's not the same thing.

Rose. It's only on account of Pop. I'm scared of what he's likely to do, if he starts drinking.

Mrs. Maurrant. Well, I'll see, Rose. Sometimes I think I'd be better off if I was dead.

Rose. If there was only something I could do.

Mrs. Maurrant. There isn't anything anybody could do. It's just the way things are, that's all. [BUCHANAN *appears at the left. They turn and face him as he approaches.*] Oh, Mr. Buchanan, I got a little chicken, so that I could make her some good, nourishing soup.

Buchanan. Well, say, you got to let me pay you for it.

Mrs. Maurrant. Oh, never mind about that. We'll have the chicken for supper tonight. Did you have her medicine made up?

Buchanan. Yes, I got it right here. I called up the office and they told me not to come down today.

Mrs. Maurrant. Well, that's very nice. It'll be a comfort to her to have you around.

Buchanan. Yes, that's what I thought too. Well, I'd better be getting upstairs. [*He goes up the steps.*]

Mrs. Maurrant. I'll be up later, with the soup.

Buchanan. Well, thanks. [*Stopping at the top of the stoop and turning to her.*] You've been a mighty good neighbor, Mrs. Maurrant.   [*He enters the house.*

Mrs. Maurrant. He's an awful nice young feller—so nice and gentle. And he's always trying to be so helpful. It makes you feel sort of sorry for him. [SHIRLEY *comes out of the house, carrying a large wicker bag, which contains her lunch and schoolbooks. She takes a postcard out of the mailbox. Going up the steps.*] Well, I'd better go and start this chicken. Are you coming home for lunch, Rose?

Rose. Yes. I'll be back, as soon as the funeral's over.

Mrs. Maurrant. Oh, all right. [*As she sees* SHIRLEY.] Good morning.

Shirley [*coming out of the vestibule, reading the postcard*]. Good morning.

Rose. Good morning. [MRS. MAURRANT *goes into the house. The shade of* MAE's *window flies up, and she is seen, for an instant, dressed only in her step-in. She yawns noisily and turns away from the window. Seating herself on the stoop.*] It's another awful day, isn't it?

Shirley. Yes, and when you have to keep forty children quiet——! Well, thank goodness, in two weeks, school closes. Otherwise, I think I'd go crazy.

Rose. Well, you get a nice, long vacation anyhow.

Shirley. Not much vacation for me. I'm taking summer courses at Teachers College. [*She looks at* ROSE *a moment, hesitates, and then comes down the steps.*] Miss Maurrant, if you don't mind, I want to talk to you about my brother Sam.

Rose. Why, certainly, Miss Kaplan.

Shirley. I guess you know he's only finishing college, this month——

Rose. Yes, of course I do.

Shirley. Then he has to go three years to law school and pass the bar examination before he can be a full-fledged lawyer.

Rose. Yes, it takes a long time.

Shirley. A long time and lots of money. And before a young lawyer begins to make his own living, that takes a long time too. It will be ten years, maybe, before he's making enough to support himself and a family. [*Looking away.*] Then, it's time enough for him to think about marriage.

Rose. You don't mean me and Sam, Miss Kaplan?

Shirley. Yes, that's just what I mean.

Rose. Why, we're just good friends, that's all.

Shirley. I know how it is with a boy like Sam, Miss Maurrant. He thinks he's a man already; but he's nothing but a boy. If you're such a good friend, you shouldn't take his mind away from his work.

Rose. But I haven't meant to, Miss Kaplan—honest I haven't.

Shirley. I've had to work hard enough to get him as far as he is. And I have my father to take care of too. The few dollars he makes, writing for the radical papers, don't even pay the rent. Believe me, every dollar I make goes.

Rose. I know. Sam's often told me how much he owes to you.

Shirley. He doesn't owe me anything. I don't care about the money. Only he should be thinking about his work and not about other things.

Rose. Yes, he should be thinking about his work. But don't you think there are other things in the world, too, besides just work?

Shirley. Don't you think I know that? I know that just as well as you do. Maybe, you think I'm only an old-maid schoolteacher, without any feelings.

Rose. Oh, I don't—really I don't!

Shirley [*turning her head away*]. Maybe I'm not a movie vamp, with dimples—but I could have had my chances too. Only, I wanted to give Sam an education.

Rose. I haven't tried to vamp Sam, honestly I haven't. We just seemed sort of naturally to like each other.

Shirley. Why must you pick out Sam? You could get other fellows. Anyhow, it's much better to marry with your own kind. When you marry outside your own people, nothing good ever comes of it. You can't mix oil and water.

Rose. I don't know. I think if people really care about each other——

Shirley. He's nothing but a baby. He sees a pretty face and, right away, he forgets about everything else.

Rose [*with a flash of temper*]. I know I haven't as much brains as Sam, or as you either, if that's what you mean.

Shirley [*contritely, going toward her*]. I didn't mean to hurt your feelings. I haven't got anything against you. Only, he's all I've got in the world. What else have I got to live for?

Sam [*appearing at the extreme right window with a cup of coffee and a piece of coffee cake*]. Hello, Rose.

Rose. Hello, Sam.

Shirley [*in a low tone*]. Please don't tell him what I said. [SAM *goes to the other window.*]

Rose. Oh, no, I won't. [SHIRLEY *hurries off at the left. Rising and turning toward* SAM.] Sam——

Sam [*holding out the coffee cake*]. Want some coffee cake?

Rose. No. [*Going up the steps.*] Sam, there's something I want to ask you, before I forget. Is there any special way you have to act in a synagogue?

Sam [*eating throughout*]. In a synagogue?

Rose. Yes. The funeral I'm going to is in a synagogue, and I thought there might be some special thing you have to do. Like in church, you know, a girl is always supposed to keep her hat on.

Sam. I don't know. I've never in my life been in a synagogue.

Rose. Didn't you ever go to Sunday school, or anything like that?

Sam. No.

Rose. That's funny. I thought everybody went, once in a while. How about when your mother died?

Sam. She was cremated. My parents were always rationalists.

Rose. Didn't they believe in God or anything?

Sam. What do you mean by God?

Rose [*puzzled*]. Well—you know what I mean. What anybody means—God. Somebody that sort of loves us and looks after us, when we're in trouble.

Sam [*sitting on the window sill*]. That's nothing but superstition—the lies that people tell themselves, because reality is too terrible for them to face.

Rose. But, Sam, don't you think it's better to believe in something that makes you a little happy, than not to believe in anything and be miserable all the time?

Sam. There's no such thing as happiness. That's an illusion, like all the rest.

Rose. Then what's the use of living?

Sam [*brushing the last crumbs off his hands*]. Yes, what is the use?

Rose. Why, you oughtn't to talk like that, Sam—a

person with all the talent and brains that you've got. I know things aren't just the way you want them to be. But they aren't for anybody. They aren't for me either.

Sam. Then why don't we get out of it, together?

Rose. I don't see just how we could do that, Sam.

Sam. It would be easy enough—ten cents' worth of carbolic acid.

Rose. Why, Sam, you don't mean kill ourselves!

Sam. Is your life so precious to you that you want to cling to it?

Rose. Well, yes. I guess it is.

Sam. Why? Why? What is there in life to compensate for the pain of living?

Rose. There's a lot. Just being alive—breathing and walking around. Just looking at the faces of people you like and hearing them laugh. And seeing the pretty things in the store windows. And roughhousing with your kid brother. And—oh, I don't know—listening to a good band, and dancing. Oh, I'd hate to die! [*Earnestly.*] Sam, promise you won't talk about killing yourself any more.

Sam. What difference would it make to you if I did?

Rose. Don't talk like that, Sam! You're the best friend I've ever had. [*She puts her hand on his.*]

Sam. I can't think of anything but you.

Rose. There's something I want to ask your advice about, Sam. It's about what I started to tell you about, last night. A man I know wants to put me on the stage.

Sam [*releasing her hand and drawing back*]. What man?

Rose. A man that works in the office. He knows a manager and he says he'll help me get started. You see, what I thought was, that if I could only get out of here and have a decent place to live and make a lot of money, maybe everything would be different, not only for me, but for Ma and Pop and Willie.

Sam. But don't you know what he wants, this man?

Rose. Nobody gives you anything for nothing, Sam. If you don't pay for things in one way, you do in another.

Sam. Rose, for God's sake, you mustn't!

VINCENT JONES *comes out of the house.*

Rose [*seeing* VINCENT *in the vestibule*]. Look out, Sam, here's that tough from upstairs. [*She goes over to the left of the stoop.*]

Vincent [*in the doorway*]. Hello, Rosie. Been here all night, talkin' to the little yit? [ROSE *does not answer. Turning to* SAM.] Hello, motzers! Shake! [*He leans over the balustrade and seizes* SAM's *hand in a crushing grip.*]

Sam [*writhing with pain*]. Let me go!

Rose. Let him alone!

VINCENT *gives* SAM's *hand another vicious squeeze and then releases him.* SAM *cowers back in the window, nursing his hand.*

Vincent [*waving his hand about in mock pain*]. Jesus, what a grip dat little kike's got! I'd hate to get into a mix-up wit' him. [*To* ROSE.] Got a date for tonight, kid?

Rose. Yes, I have.

Vincent. Yeah? Gee, ain't dat too bad. I'll give you two dollars if you let me snap your garter.

Rose. Shut up, you! [VINCENT *laughs.* SAM *makes an inarticulate sound.*]

Vincent [*threateningly*]. Whadja say? I t'ought I hoid you say sumpin. [*He makes a threatening gesture.* SAM *shrinks back. With a loud laugh as he goes down the steps.*] Fightin' Kaplan, de pride o' Jerusalem! [*He looks at them both, then laughs again.*] Fer cryin' out loud! [*He exits left.*

Rose. Oh, if there was only some way of getting out of here! [SAM *puts the back of his hand to his forehead and turns away.*] I sometimes think I'd just like to run away.

Sam [*without turning*]. Yes!

Rose. Anywhere—it wouldn't matter where—just to get out of this.

Sam [*turning*]. Why shouldn't we do it?

Rose [*rather startled, coming over to the right balustrade*]. Would you go with me, Sam?

Sam. Yes—anywhere.

Rose. I've heard that people are much nicer and friendlier, when you get outside of New York. There's not so much of a mad rush, other places. And being alone, you could sort of work things out for yourself. [*Suddenly.*] Only, what would you do, Sam?

Sam. I could get a job too.

Rose. And give up your law work?

Sam. I'd give up everything, to be with you.

Rose. No. I wouldn't let you do that, Sam. It's different with me——

EASTER *appears at the right.*

Easter [stopping at the right of the stoop]. Good morning, Miss Maurrant.

Startled, ROSE *turns and sees him for the first time.*

Rose [none too pleased]. Oh, good morning, Mr. Easter. What brings you in this neighborhood?

Easter [not very plausibly]. Well, I just happened to have a little business right around the corner. So, I thought as long as you were going to the funeral, we might just as well go together.

Rose. Well, I hardly expected to see you around here. [*An awkward pause.*] Oh, I'd like you to meet my friend, Mr. Kaplan.

Easter. How do you do, Mr. Kaplan? Glad to know you. [SAM *murmurs something inaudible. An awkward silence.*]

Rose [to SAM*].* Mr. Easter is the manager of the office. [SAM *does not reply. Another silence. To* EASTER.] It's awful hot again, isn't it?

Easter. Worse than yesterday. [*Approaching the stoop.*] Tell you what I was thinking. I was thinking, that after the funeral, we might take a run down to the beach, somewhere, and cool off a little.

Rose. I can't today. I've got a lot of things I want to do.

Easter. Oh, you can do 'em some other day.

Rose. No, really, I can't. [*Looking at her watch.*] Well, I guess it's time we got started. [*She comes down the steps.*]

Easter. Yes, it is. We'll pick up a cab at the corner.

MRS. MAURRANT *appears at her window, looks out, and sees* ROSE *and* EASTER.

Rose. Why, I thought I'd walk. It's not far.

Easter. Too hot, today, for any walking.

Rose [starting to go toward the left]. Not if you keep in the shade.

Easter. Much more comfortable taking a cab.

Rose. I'd rather walk.

Easter. Well, whatever you say. Good morning, Mr. Kaplan. Glad to have met you. [Sᴀᴍ *murmurs an inaudible reply*.]

Rose. Good-by, Sam, I'll see you later. [Sᴀᴍ *does not answer*. Rose *and* Easter *go toward the left in silence.* Sᴀᴍ *watches them intently, trembling with jealousy.* Mrs. Mᴀᴜʀʀᴀɴᴛ, *surprised and disturbed, watches* Rose *and* Easter. *To* Easter, *as they disappear*.] It's a lucky thing my father wasn't around.

Sᴀᴍ *suddenly turns and goes into the room.* Mrs. Mᴀᴜʀ-ʀᴀɴᴛ *remains at the window, looking out, with obvious expectancy.*

A Distant Voice [*offstage left*]. Straw-berries! Straw-berries!

A Mᴜsɪᴄ Sᴛᴜᴅᴇɴᴛ, *an anemic girl of eighteen, with a music roll under her arm, appears at the left. She enters the house and pushes one of the buttons in the vestibule, then goes to the entrance door and waits. A moment later* Mrs. Fɪᴏʀᴇɴᴛɪɴᴏ *appears hastily at the window and whisks away the bedclothes. After another moment the latch clicks and the girl enters the house.*

The Voice [*a little nearer*]. Oh-h! Straw-berries! Straw-berries!

Sᴀɴᴋᴇʏ *appears at the right. He carries a pencil behind his ear, wears a round cap with a metal nameplate and a stiff visor, and carries a large black-covered bill holder. He and* Mrs. Mᴀᴜʀʀᴀɴᴛ *see each other and both become tense with excitement.* Mrs. Mᴀᴜʀʀᴀɴᴛ *beckons to him, and he comes over to the railing under her window.*

Mrs. Maurrant [*in a low, tense voice*]. Come up.
Sankey [*looking about, nervously*]. Now?
Mrs. Maurrant. Yes. I got to talk to you.
Sankey. Is it all right?
Mrs. Maurrant. Yes. He's gone to Stamford.
Sankey. How about later?
Mrs. Maurrant. No. Rose'll be home in a hour. She's not working today.
Sankey. All right.

He looks about again, then goes quickly toward the steps. Sᴀᴍ *appears at the entrance door. He is about to step out*

when he sees SANKEY. *He stops and looks at him.* SANKEY·
sees SAM, *hesitates a moment, then goes quickly into the
house. Meanwhile* MRS. MAURRANT *has closed both windows and pulled down the shades.* SAM *takes a periodical
out of the mailbox, then comes out of the house and down
the steps. He looks up at the Maurrant windows, sees the
drawn shades, and looks around in perturbed perplexity,
not knowing what to do. At last, he sits down on the steps
of the stoop, tears the wrapper off the periodical—The
Nation—and begins to read. The girl in Lippo's apartment
begins playing the piano. This continues throughout the
scene. Two untidy and rather coarse-looking men appear at
the left and approach the stoop:* JAMES HENRY, *a city
marshal, and* FRED CULLEN, *his assistant. They stop in
front of the house.* SAM *pays no attention to them.*

Marshal [*crossing to the left of the stoop and taking a
paper from his pocket*]. Dis is it. [*To* SAM.] Hildebrand
live here?

Sam [*startled*]. What?

Marshal. I'm askin' you if Hildebrand lives here.

Sam. Yes. Fourth floor.

Marshal. Better give de janitor a buzz, Fred. [FRED *goes
up the steps and rings the janitor's bell, then leans over
the left balustrade.*]

Fred [*bawling*]. Hey, janitor.

Olsen [*below*]. Vell?

Fred. Come on out a minute. [OLSEN *appears below.*]
We got a warrant for Hildebrand.

Olsen. Fourt' floor—Hildebrand.

Fred. Yeah, I know. We got a warrant for her.

Marshal. I'm City Marshal Henry. We got a dispossess
warrant.

Olsen [*coming up the steps*]. Oh, sure. You gonna put
'em out?

Marshal. Yeah, dat's it. Has she got anybody to take de
foinicher away?

Olsen [*with a shrug*]. I don' know.

Marshal. Well, we'll have t' dump it on de sidewalk
den. Go ahead, Fred.

They enter the house. OLSEN *leans his elbows on the coping
and smokes his pipe.* SAM *sits on the steps, deep in troubled*

thought. A Grocery Boy *with a full basket appears at the right and goes down the cellar steps.* Mae Jones *comes out of the house. She stands on the top step, yawns noisily, and goes off at left. She and* Sam *do not pay the slightest attention to each other.*

A Voice [*a little nearer*]. Straw-*berries!* Straw-*berries!*

Mrs. Olsen *comes up the cellar steps with a heavy pail of water.* Olsen *leans forward to make room for her. She staggers over to the stoop almost dropping the pail, and goes up the steps into the vestibule.* Olsen *yawns and goes down into the cellar.* Mrs. Jones *appears at the window, her hair wet and stringy, a towel pinned about her shoulders, and leans out to dry her hair.*

Old-Clothes Man [*appearing at left*]. I kesh ko! I kesh ko! [*He wears a battered derby and carries a folded newspaper under his arm.* Mrs. Olsen, *on her knees, begins washing up the vestibule.* Fred *comes out of the house, carrying a worn chair and a large gilt-framed picture, which he deposits on the sidewalk, against the railing, to the left of the stoop. As if to someone across the street.*] Kesh ko? [*To* Sam] Any ol' klose, mister? [Sam *pays no attention to him.* Fred *re-enters the house. To* Mrs. Jones.] Any ol' klose, leddy?

Mrs. Jones. Naw, nawthin'.

Old-Clothes Man. Hets? Shoes? Ol' stockings?

Mrs. Jones. Nawthin', I tell you. [*As the* Old-Clothes Man *goes off at the right,* Maurrant *appears, still carrying his satchel.*] Why, hello, Mr. Maurrant. [Maurrant *looks up without replying and comes over to the stoop.*] I thought you was off to Stamford.

Maurrant. I changed me——

He stops, to the right of the stoop, and looks up at the drawn shades of his apartment. Sam *rises, slowly and rigidly, his eyes glued in fascination upon* Maurrant. Maurrant's *movements take on a lithe and catlike quality. Then, slowly and deliberately, he goes toward the steps, his back arched, like a tiger ready to spring.*

Sam [*suddenly blocking the steps*]. No! No! For God's sake——!

Maurrant [*raging*]. Out o' me way, you goddam little rat!

He flings SAM *violently aside, almost knocking him down.*
MRS. OLSEN, *terrified, rises and shrinks into a corner as*
MAURRANT, *with swift stealthiness, enters the house.* MRS.
JONES *leans out to see what is wrong.* SAM *rushes down the*
steps and stands under the MAURRANT *windows. The*
MARSHAL *comes out of the house, carrying a wash boiler*
filled with pots.

Sam [*hysterically*]. Mrs. Maurrant! Mrs. Maurrant!

Mrs. Jones. What's the matter? [*The* MARSHAL *puts the*
wash boiler on the balustrade and looks on in amazement.]

Sam [*to* MRS. JONES]. Quick! Run and tell her! Quick!

Mrs. Jones. What is it? [*Suddenly.*] Oh, Gawd, is he in
there? [*She leaves the window hastily.*]

Sam. Yes! Mrs. Maurrant! Mrs. Maurrant!

A scream of terror is heard from the MAURRANT *apartment.*

Mrs. Maurrant's Voice. Frank! Frank!

Two shots are heard, in quick succession, and then a heavy
fall. MRS. OLSEN *runs out of the vestibule and down into*
the cellar. SANKEY'S *voice is heard, inarticulate with fear.*
Then one of the shades shoots up, and SANKEY *appears at*
the window, coatless, his face deformed by terror. He tries
to open the window but succeeds only in shattering the pane
with his elbow. MAURRANT *appears behind him and pulls*
him away from the window. Then another shot is heard.

Marshal. For Chris' sake, what's happenin'? Get an ambulance, you!

He pushes SAM *toward the left, then hurries off at the right.*
As SAM *runs off a crowd begins to form.* OLSEN *comes up*
from the cellar, followed by the GROCERY BOY. *The two*
WORKMEN *come up out of the excavation. Two or three of*
the WORKMEN *from the demolished building run on at*
the right.

A Workman. What's happening?

A Man. What is it? A murder?

Still others join the crowd: a HUCKSTER, *a* JANITOR *from a*
neighboring house, a MULATTO GIRL, *six or eight* WOMEN
of the neighborhood, some in street dresses, others in
housedresses or dingy wrappers. Lippo's PUPIL *appears at*
the window, badly frightened. The crowd surges about un-

certainly, not knowing what has happened and buzzing
with questions which nobody can answer. While the crowd
is still forming FRED, *the* MARSHAL'S *assistant, appears at*
the broken window.

Fred [*excitedly*]. Grab dat boid! He's comin' down!
A *Workman.* What boid?
A *Man.* Here he is, now!

The crowd murmurs with excitement and surges about the
stoop as the house door opens and MAURRANT *appears. His*
coat is open and his shirt is torn almost to shreds. His face,
hands, and clothing are covered with blood. He stands in
the doorway for a moment, surveying the crowd, his eyes
glaring.

Fred. Grab him! Don't let him get away!

As the crowd makes a concerted movement toward MAUR-
RANT *he whips out an automatic revolver and levels it. The*
crowd shrinks back. Some of the women scream.

Maurrant. Git back! Git back, all o' you!

The crowd falls back toward the left, to make way for him.
With his back to the balustrade he comes quickly down
the steps and, still leveling his revolver at the crowd, re-
treats backward to the cellar steps. A man, approaching at
the right, comes stealthily up behind him, but MAURRANT
senses his presence in time, wheels quickly, menaces the
man with his revolver, then rushes down the cellar steps.
While all this is happening the other shade in the Maur-
rant apartment flies up and MISS CUSHING *opens the win-*
dow and leans out.

Miss Cushing. Hurry up! Get an ambulance! [*No one*
pays any attention to her as they are all watching MAUR-
RANT. *As* MAURRANT *runs down the cellar steps the crowd*
surges forward to the railing on both sides of the stoop and
leans over. A scream from MRS. OLSEN *is heard from the*
basement. FRED *goes away from the window.*] Get an ambulance, somebody! [*Unable to attract anyone's attention,*
she leaves the window.]

Olsen. Olga! [*He hurries down the cellar steps.*]

A *Man* [*calling*]. Here's a cop! [*The crowd looks to the*
right.] Hey! Hurry up!

A Policeman *runs on from the right.*

Policeman. Where is he?

Voices in the Crowd. He's down the cellar! He ran down the cellar! He went down the steps!

Policeman. Get out of the way! [*The* Policeman *and two men in the crowd go down the cellar steps.*]

Voices in the Crowd. Watch yourself! Look out, he's got a gun! He's a big guy with his shirt torn! [*The rest of the crowd peers over the railing.*]

Miss Cushing [*leaning out of* Rose's *window*]. Hey, don't you hear me? Get an ambulance!

Another Man [*looking up*]. What's de matter? You want de ambulance?

Miss Cushing. Yes! Right away!

Another Man [*to the* Grocery Boy]. Run aroun' de corner to de horspital, Johnny, an' tell 'em to send de ambulance!

Grocery Boy. Sure!

Miss Cushing. Run!

The Grocery Boy *runs off swiftly at the left.* Miss Cushing *leaves the window. Meanwhile, as the* Policeman *and the two men have gone down the cellar steps, the* Marshal *has run on from the right, panting.*

Marshal [*as the* Grocery Boy *runs off*]. Did dey git 'im?

A Man. He beat it down de cellar.

A Workman. De cop's gone after him.

Marshal. Why de hell didn' you stop 'im?

Fred *comes out of the house.*

A Workman. He had a gun.

Fred. Did somebody go for de ambulance?

A Man. Yeah. De kid went.

A Woman. It's only aroun' de corner.

Another Man. Dey'll be here, right away.

The crowd moves over toward Fred.

Marshal [*pushing his way through the crowd and up the steps*]. What de hell happened, Fred?

Fred [*as the crowd moves toward the stoop*]. It's a moider. Dis boid's wife an' some other guy. Jesus, you oughta see de blood. [*Another* Policeman *runs up at the left,*

closely followed by SAM.] Upstairs, officer! Dere's two of
'em got shot.

Second Policeman [*elbowing his way through the crowd*].
Look out o' de way, youse! [*He goes up the stoop and
crosses to the door.*] Where's de guy dat did it?

Voices in the Crowd. Down de cellar! He beat it down
de steps!

Fred. Dere's another cop after 'im. You better look after
dem upstairs. Foist floor.

Sam [*agonized*]. Are they dead? [*No one pays any attention to him.*]

Marshal [*stopping the* POLICEMAN *and exhibiting his
badge*]. I'm City Marshal Henry. Kin I do anythin'?

Second Policeman. Don't let anybody in or out! Hear?

Marshal. Yeah, sure!

The SECOND POLICEMAN *goes quickly into the house.*

Sam. Are they dead? [*No one notices him. The* MARSHAL
takes up his position in the doorway.]

Buchanan [*appearing at the Maurrant window*]. Where's
the ambulance?

Marshal. It'll be here, right away. Dere's a cop on his
way up.

Sam. Mr. Buchanan! Mr. Buchanan! Are they dead?

But BUCHANAN *has already disappeared. The two men who
followed the* FIRST POLICEMAN *into the cellar now come up
the steps. The crowd moves over to the railing, at the right.*

Marshal. Did you get him, boys?

One of the Men. He must be hidin' somewheres. De
cop's lookin' for 'im.

Another Man. Somebody better call de resoives.

Sam runs up the steps and tries to enter the house.

Marshal [*seizing him roughly*]. You can't get in now!
Get back dere! [*He pushes* SAM *back into the crowd at the
foot of the steps.*]

Second Policeman [*appearing at the Maurrant window*].
Hey, call up headquarters an' tell 'em to send the resoives.
Make it quick! [*He goes away from the window.*]

Marshal. You go, Fred.

Fred. Sure!

A Man. Dere's a phone in de warehouse.

An ambulance bell is heard at the left as FRED *goes quickly toward the left. Another spectator hurries on and joins the crowd.*

Voices in the Crowd. Dere it is! Dere's de ambulance now! Here dey come! [*The crowd moves over toward the left.*]

A Man. Dey won't be able to git past.

Second Policeman [*reappearing at the window*]. Is dat de ambulance?

Marshal. Yeah.

BUCHANAN *and* MRS. JONES *crowd to the window behind the* SECOND POLICEMAN, *and, at the other window,* LIPPO, MISS CUSHING, *and* MRS. HILDEBRAND *appear. A* HOSPITAL INTERN *and an* AMBULANCE DRIVER *come on at the left.*

Second Policeman. Hurry up, Doc! She's still breathin'.

Intern [*forcing his way through the crowd*]. All right! Better bring the stretcher, Harry.

Ambulance Driver. Yes, sir.

He hurries off at the left. The INTERN *goes quickly into the house. The crowd attempts to follow, several of its members going up the steps.*

Marshal [*pushing them back*]. Keep back, now! Back off de stoop, everybody!

The crowd forms a compact mass around the foot of the steps. The persons at the Maurrant windows have disappeared. FRED *hurries on at the left.*

Fred [*pushing his way through the crowd and up the steps*]. I got 'em. Dey'll be right up. Anudder cop jes' wen' in t'roo de warehouse cellar.

Marshal. Dey'll git 'im all right. [*Looking at his watch.*] Better git busy wit' dat foinicher, Fred. We got two udder jobs today.

Fred. Yeah, sure, Jimmy.

He enters the house. The AMBULANCE DRIVER *appears at the left, carrying a canvas stretcher.*

Ambulance Driver. Get out o' the way!

Marshal. Git back, can't youse? What de hell's de matter wit' youse? [*He comes down the steps and violently pushes the crowd back. The* AMBULANCE DRIVER *enters the house.*]

Second Policeman [*at the window*]. Are dey bringin' dat stretcher?

Marshal. On de way up! [*To the crowd.*] Keep back!

The POLICEMAN *leaves the window. Lippo's* PUPIL, *her music roll under her arm, appears timidly in the doorway.*

Marshal [*grabbing her arm roughly*]. Where you goin'?

Music Student [*nervously*]. I'm going home.

Marshal. Home? Where do you live?

Music Student. Ninety-first Street.

Marshal. What are you doin' here?

Music Student. I just came for a music lesson, that's all.

Marshal. Yeah? Well, you can't go now.

Music Student [*beginning to whimper*]. I want to go home.

Marshal. You can't go now. Nobody can't leave de house now.

Second Policeman [*coming out of the house*]. Who's dis kid?

Marshal. Says she come here to take a music lesson an' she wants to go home.

Second Policeman [*to the girl*]. Do you know anythin' about this killin'?

Music Student. No, I don't. I just heard some shooting, that's all. My mother will be worried if I don't come home.

Second Policeman. Well, you can't go now. Get inside dere, out o' de way. Dey'll be bringin' her down in a minute. [*He pushes the girl inside the house and comes down the steps.*] Come on, git back from dem steps! Back now, all o' youse! [*He and the* MARSHAL *push the crowd back to the right of the stoop, leaving the steps and the sidewalk in front of them clear. Then he goes up the steps again.*]

Marshal. What did he do? Shoot two of 'em?

Second Policeman. I'll say he did! His wife an' her sweetie. A guy named Sankey. He was dead when I got up dere.

Marshal. I seen him tryin' to climb out t'roo de winder. An' dis guy grabs 'im an' pulls 'im back.

Intern [*from the Maurrant window*]. Officer! Come on up!

He leaves the window as the SECOND POLICEMAN *exits into the house. Suddenly* SAM *utters an exclamation of anguish and, pushing his way out of the crowd, hurries over to the left.*

Marshal. Hey, you! Where you goin'? [SAM *ignores him and hurries on.*]

A Woman. Look! There's the Maurrant girl!

Another Woman. Who?

A Woman. It's her daughter. [*The crowd murmurs excitedly as* ROSE *comes on quickly at the left.*]

ROSE. What's the matter, Sam? What's the ambulance for? Did anybody get hurt?

Sam. Go away, Rose. Go away.

Rose. Who is it, Sam? What's the matter? Is it my mother? It's not my mother, is it? [*Clinging to him.*] Sam, is it?

Sam. There's been an accident. Go away, Rose. [*He tries to force her away.*]

Rose. Tell me what's happened! Tell me!

Miss Cushing [*appearing at the window*]. They're bringing her down!

Rose [*with a cry*]. It *is* my mother!

Miss Cushing [*seeing her*]. Oh, my God, there's Rose!

MRS. FIORENTINO, MRS. JONES, MRS. HILDEBRAND, LIPPO, *and* BUCHANAN *crowd to the Maurrant windows.*

Sam. Rose! Go away!

She pays no attention to him but stands watching the door, transfixed. The INTERN *comes briskly out of the house.*

Intern [*to the* MARSHAL]. Hold the door open, will you? [*He comes down the steps.*]

Marshal. Sure, Doc! [*He hurries into the vestibule.*]

Intern [*to the crowd*]. Keep back now!

Rose [*seizing the* INTERN'*s arm*]. Doctor! Is she dead?

Intern. Who are you? Her daughter?

Rose. Yes, sir. I'm her daughter.

Intern. She's pretty badly hurt. Step aside now!

They step aside as the AMBULANCE DRIVER *and the* SECOND

POLICEMAN *come out of the house, carrying* MRS. MAUR-
RANT *on the stretcher. There is a low murmur from the
crowd.*

Ambulance Driver. Easy now.

Second Policeman. All right. [*They come down the steps
and go toward the left.*]

Rose [*running forward and gripping the side of the
stretcher*]. Mother! Mother!

Mrs. Maurrant [*opening her eyes feebly*]. Rose! [*She tries
to lift her hand, but it falls back.*]

Intern [*pulling* ROSE *back*]. You mustn't talk to her
now.

SAM *takes her around the shoulders. They and the* INTERN
*follow the stretcher off at the left. The crowd swarms after
them.* FRED *comes out of the house, carrying one end of
an iron bedstead.*

Curtain.

ACT THREE

Midafternoon of the same day. At the left of the stoop is a large roll of bedding. Before the rise of the curtain, and continuing faintly thereafter, a woman can be heard singing scales. OLSEN, *pipe in mouth, is leaning against the railing. Two men, furniture movers, appear at the left.*

ONE OF THE MEN [*picking up the bedding*]. All right. Dat's all, Charlie!

The men exit left. A POLICEMAN *comes out of the house, carrying the bloodstained dress of* MRS. MAURRANT *and* SANKEY's *coat, cap, and bill holder. He comes down the steps and exits at the right. At the left two young* NURSE-MAIDS *in smart uniforms appear, each wheeling a de luxe baby carriage.*

First Nursemaid [*seeing the house number*]. This must be the place, right here—three forty-six. [*They stop under the Maurrant windows.*]

Second Nursemaid. Yes, I guess it is.

First Nursemaid. Yes, this is it, all right. [*Looking up.*] Must be right up there, on the first floor, see?

Second Nursemaid. Yes, sure. [*Excitedly.*] Say, look! You can see where the glass is out of the window. That's where this feller What's-his-name tried to climb out.

First Nursemaid. Oh, yes, I see it! Say, what do you know about that!

Second Nursemaid [*taking a pink tabloid newspaper from under the hood of the baby buggy*]. Wait! There's a picture of it somewhere. [*Turning the pages.*] Here it is. [*They excitedly examine it together, as she reads.*] "Composograph showing Sankey, scantily clad, in a last vain attempt to escape the vengeance of the jealousy-crazed husband, whose home he had destroyed." And there's Maurrant pulling him back. And Mrs. Maurrant trying to get the pistol away from him, see? Look at the blood running down her face, will you?

First Nursemaid. It's worse than awful! Can you *imagine* what those two must have felt like, when he walked in on them like that?

Second Nursemaid. Well, he just happened to be one of the ones that finds out! Believe me, there's lots and lots of

143

husbands that don't know the half of what goes on uptown, while they're downtown making a living.

First Nursemaid. Say, you're not telling me, are you? If I was to spill all I know, there'd be many a happy home busted up. I wonder if they caught him?

Second Nursemaid [*as her baby begins a thin wailing*]. Oh, God, he's in again! [*To the unseen baby.*] Shut up a little while, can't you? [*She shakes the carriage.*]

Policeman [*appearing at the Maurrant windows, a tabloid in his hand*]. Keep movin', ladies. No loiterin' aroun' here.

First Nursemaid [*eagerly*]. Say, have they caught him yet?

Policeman. Why, ain't you hoid? He was last seen flyin' over Nova Scotia, on his way to Paris.

First Nursemaid. Who are you trying to string anyhow?

Second Nursemaid [*coquettishly*]. Say, will you let us come up and look around?

Policeman. Why, sure, sure! Bring de babies too. De commissioner is soivin' tea up here at four-thoity.

Second Nursemaid. You're awful smart, aren't you?

Policeman. Yeah, dat's why dey put me on de entertainment committee. I'm Handsome Harry Moiphy, de boy comedian o' Brooklyn.

First Nursemaid [*looking at her watch*]. Oh, say, I ought to be getting back. [*Turning her carriage.*] Clarice darling would throw a duck fit if she knew I brought her precious Dumplings to a neighborhood like this.

Second Nursemaid [*turning her carriage*]. There's not so much to see anyhow. It's nothing but a cheap, common dump. [*They go toward the left.*]

Policeman. Over de river, goils. See you in de funny paper.

Second Nursemaid. Don't you get so fresh.

Policeman. Drop in again when you're in de neighborhood. An' tell Mrs. Vanderbilt Harry was askin' for her.

As the NURSEMAIDS *go off at the left,* EASTER *hurries on at the right, several folded newspapers under his arm.*

Easter [*to the Policeman, going to the left of the stoop*]. Is Miss Maurrant up there, Officer?

Policeman. No. There ain't nobody up here but me.

Easter. You don't happen to know where she is, do you?

Policeman. No, I don't. Are you a reporter?

Easter. Who, me? I'm just a friend of hers. I've got to see her.

Policeman. Well, I ain't seen her since she went off to the horspital this mornin'. She ain't been back since. [*He starts to leave the window.*]

Easter. Oh, Officer!

Policeman. Yeah?

Easter. Have they caught him yet?

Policeman. Naw, not yet. But we'll get 'im all right!

He leaves the window. EASTER *remains at the left of the stoop, uncertain whether to go or not.* MRS. JONES *appears at the right, carrying several newspapers.*

Mrs. Jones [*to* OLSEN]. Have they caught him yet?

OLSEN [*shaking his head*]. No.

Mrs. Jones. I been down at Police Headquarters all this while—— [*Breaking off, as she notices* EASTER.] Say, what's he want here? [OLSEN *shrugs his shoulders.*]

Easter [*approaching them*]. Pardon me, but maybe you can tell me where I can find Miss Maurrant? [OLSEN *shakes his head.*]

Mrs. Jones. Why, no, I can't. I jus' this minute got back from Police Headquarters. Maybe she's aroun' at the horspital.

Easter. No, I just came from there.

Mrs. Jones. Well, I really couldn't say where she is. Was there somethin' special you wanted to see her about?

Easter. I'm a friend of hers——

Mrs. Jones. Yeah, I noticed you talkin' to her, last night, when I took the dog out. [*Staring at him.*] Well, I guess she'll need all the friends she's got now. Imagine a thing like that happenin' right here in this house, at ten o'clock in the mornin'! Everythin' goin' on just as usual, and then, all of a sudden, before you know it, there's two people murdered.

Olsen. I tal everybody someday he kill her.

Mrs. Jones. Well, I ain't sayin' it's right to kill anybody, but if anybody had a reason, he certainly had. You oughta heard some o' the questions they was askin' me down at the Police. I could feel myself gettin' redder an' redder. "Say,"

I says, "how do you expect me to know things like that?" [*Suddenly, as she looks left.*] Here's Rose now!

Easter. Where? [*He turns quickly and hurries to the left as* Rose *appears, carrying four or five packages.*]

Mrs. Jones [*to* Olsen]. He seems to take a pretty friendly interest in her. [Olsen *nods.*]

Rose [*anxiously, as she comes up to* Easter *at the left of the stoop*]. Have they caught him yet?

Easter. Why, no, they haven't. I just asked the officer upstairs.

Rose. Oh, I hope he got away! If they get him, there's no telling what they'll do to him. And what would be the good of that? He never would have done it if he'd been in his right mind.

Easter. I only heard about it a little while ago. So I went right around to the hospital. But they said you'd left.

Rose [*going to the steps*]. She never opened her eyes again. They did everything they could for her, but it didn't help.

Easter. Here, let me take your bundles.

Rose. No, it's all right. I think I'll just sit down for a minute. [*She sits on the stoop and puts the packages beside her.*]

Easter. Can't I get you something? A drink or something?

Rose. No, I'm all right. It's so hot. [*She puts her hand to her head.*] And all those people asking me a lot of questions.

Mrs. Jones [*approaching the stoop*]. Are you feelin' dizzy or anythin'?

Rose. No, I'll be all right in a minute.

Mrs. Jones. Well, I was gonna say, if you want to go up to my flat an' lay down for a minute——

Rose. No, thanks; I don't want to lie down. I've got to go upstairs to get some things.

Easter. Why, say, you don't want to go up there!

Rose. I've got to; there's some things I need.

Easter. Well, let me get them for you. Or this lady here.

Mrs. Jones. Yeah, sure. The place is a sight up there. You're li'ble to go into a faint or somethin'.

Rose. I guess nothing can be any worse than what's happened already. [*Indicating the bundles.*] I got to change my dress. I bought a white dress for her. And white silk stockings. I want her to look pretty.

Mrs. Jones. Yeah, white is the nicest.

Rose. She looks so quiet and natural. You'd think she was asleep.

Mrs. Jones. It was the same way with my mother. You'd of thought she was gonna get up the next minute. [*Starting to go up the steps.*] Well, I gotta go up an' get me some lunch. Between everythin' happenin' an' goin' down to Police Headquarters an' all, I ain't had a bite to eat since breakfast. [*Stopping on the top step and looking from* Rose *to* Easter.] Well, you certainly never know, when you get up in the mornin', what the day is gonna bring. [*She enters the house.*]

Rose [*rising*]. Well, I'd better be going up too. There's a lot of things to attend to.

Easter. You better let me come up with you.

Rose. Why, thanks, Mr. Easter. But I'd rather go alone, if you don't mind.

Easter. But, listen here—you can't go through all this alone—a kid like you. That's why I came around. I knew you'd be needing a helping hand.

Rose. That's awfully nice of you, Mr. Easter. But I don't need any help, honest I don't. [*She opens one of the packages.*]

Easter. Why, you can't handle everything yourself! What about a place to live and all that?

Rose [*taking a rosette of black crape out of the package*]. Well, I don't exactly know yet. I'll have to find some place where Willie and I can live. I'd like it to be some place where he wouldn't be running around the streets all the time. You see, there's nobody but me to look out for him now. [Olsen *crosses to the cellar.* Mrs. Jones *appears at her window and furtively peeps out at* Rose *and* Easter. *As* Rose *sees that* Olsen *is about to descend the cellar steps.*] Oh, Mr. Olsen!

Olsen [*stopping*]. Yes, ma'am.

Rose. Would you mind lending me a hammer and some tacks? I want to put up this crape.

Olsen. Yes, ma'am; I bring 'em right away. [*He goes down into the cellar.* Mrs. Jones *leaves the window.*]

Easter [*insistently*]. But why won't you let me help you out?

Rose. It's terribly nice of you, Mr. Easter. But I'll be able to manage alone, really I will. It isn't as if I wasn't young and strong and able to take care of myself. But as it is, I'd sort of rather not be under obligations.

Easter. Why, you wouldn't be under any obligations. I just mean it in a friendly way, that's all.

Rose. You've been very nice to me and all that, Mr. Easter. But—well, I've been sort of thinking things over —you know, about what we talked about last night and all. And I honestly don't think I'd care about going on the stage.

Easter. Say, you've got me all wrong, Rose! Just forget all about that, will you? I just want to help you out, that's all. [*Taking a step toward her.*] I think you're one swell kid, and I want to do something for you. I'm not trying to put anything over on you.

Shirley *appears at the left, carrying her schoolbag, from which a newspaper protrudes.*

Rose. Well, that's nice and friendly of you, Mr. Easter. And if I ever do need any help——

Shirley [*catching sight of* Rose]. Rose! You poor thing! [*She runs up to* Rose *and throws her arms around her.*] It's terrible—terrible!

Rose. Yes, it is. But I sort of had a feeling, all along, that something terrible was going to happen.

Olsen *comes up the steps with a hammer and a box of tacks.*

Shirley. How could he do such a thing! I couldn't believe it when I read it.

Rose. He was out of his mind when he did it. Oh, I only hope he got away! [*As* Olsen *approaches.*] Oh, thanks, Mr. Olsen.

Olsen. I do it.

Rose [*giving him the crape*]. Oh, would you, please? Right up there, I think. [*She indicates the left of the door-way.*]

Olsen [*going up the steps*]. Sure.

Rose [*going to* EASTER *and extending her hand*]. Thanks
for coming around, Mr. Easter. I don't know when I'll be
able to get back to the office.

Easter. Why, that's all right about that. Only, in the
meantime, I wish——

Rose. If I need any help, I'll let you know. [*With a
tone of finality in her voice.*] Good-by.

Easter. All right; but don't forget. [*He hesitates, then
decides to go.*] Well, good-by.   [*He exits at left.*

Rose. I've got to go up and get some things that Willie
and I need. Sam went to call for him at school and take
him around to my aunt's. You see I didn't want him coming back here. He's only a little kid, after all.

Shirley. Oh, it's such a terrible thing! I can't believe it
yet.

Olsen [*holding up the crape*]. Dis vay?

Rose. Yes, like that. [*Hesitantly, as she picks up her
bundles.*] Miss Kaplan, it's sort of silly of me, I guess. But
I'm kind of afraid to go up there alone. I wonder if you'd
mind coming up with me.

OLSEN *tacks up the crape.*

Shirley. Anything I can do for you, poor child! [*She and*
ROSE *go up the steps.*]

Rose. Thanks ever so much. [*To* OLSEN.] Thanks, Mr.
Olsen. It's awfully nice of you.

She and SHIRLEY *enter the house.* OLSEN *exits down the
cellar steps.* KAPLAN *appears at his window and, seating
himself, begins to read a newspaper. An undersized man
and a tall, athletic woman appear at the right. They are
dressed for tennis and carry tennis rackets.*

The Man [*as they cross*]. He *would* say that.

The Woman. So I just looked at him for a moment, without saying anything. And then I said, "My dear boy," I
said. "What do you expect anyhow, in this day and age?"
I said, "Why even Frankl has to do a black bathroom occa-
sionally," I said.

The Man [*as they disappear at the left*]. Exactly! And
what did he say to that?

BUCHANAN *comes out of the house and, seeing* KAPLAN
at the window, stops at the right balustrade.

Buchanan. Well, there's been *some* excitement around
here today.

Kaplan [*looking up from his paper*]. Dees is a terrible
t'ing vich hes heppened.

Buchanan. I'll say it is! You know, the way I look at it,
he didn't have a right to kill the both of them like that.
Of course I'm not saying what she did was right either.

Kaplan. How ken ve call ourselves ciwilized, ven ve see
thet sax jealousy hes de power to avaken in us de primitive
pessions of de sevege?

Buchanan [*rather bewildered by this*]. Yes, that's true
too. Of course, you can't expect a man to stand by and see
his home broken up. But murdering them, like that, is going a little too far. Well, I got to go and phone the doctor.
This thing's given my wife a kind of a relapse. She thought
a lot of Mrs. Maurrant. [*He goes down the steps and off at
the left as* LIPPO *appears at the right.*]

Lippo [*stopping in front of* KAPLAN's *window*]. Dey don'
ketcha Maurrant, ha?

Kaplan. I hevn't hoid anyt'ing foider.

Lippo. He'sa gonna gat da 'lectrica-chair, ha?

Kaplan. De blood lust of our enlightened population
must be setisfied! De Chreestian state vill kerry out to de
last letter de Mosaic law.

Lippo. Eef Ahm ketcha my wife sleepin' wit' 'nudder
man, Ahm gonna keela 'er too.

SAM *hurries on at the left.*

Kaplan. So you t'ink thet merriage should give to de
hosband de power of life and det' and thet——

Sam [*going up the steps*]. Papa, is there any news of
Maurrant?

Kaplan. I hev heard notting.

Sam. The police are going to make me testify against
him. What can I do, Papa?

Kaplan. You ken do notting.

Sam. How can I send a man to the electric chair? How
can I? I tried to stop him, Papa. I tried to warn her——
[*He stops short as several shots are heard offstage at the
left.*] What's that?

Lippo [*excitedly*]. Dey finda 'im!

He runs off at the left, followed by SAM. KAPLAN *leans out of the window. At the same moment* MRS. JONES *leans out of her window and, a moment later,* MRS. FIORENTINO *out of hers. In the Maurrant apartment the* POLICEMAN *leans out and* ROSE *and* SHIRLEY *appear in the hall-bedroom window.* ROSE *is wearing a mourning dress.* OLSEN *comes up the cellar steps and runs off at the left.* MRS. OLSEN *comes up the steps. Several men and women appear at the right and run off at the left.*

Rose [*agitatedly*]. Is that him?

Policeman. Must be!

Voices are heard shouting in the distance, and then another shot. The POLICEMAN *leaves the window.*

Rose. Oh, God! They wouldn't shoot him, would they? [*She leaves the window.*]

Shirley [*following her*]. Rose!

Two or three more persons appear at the right and run off at the left. The POLICEMAN *runs out of the house as* BUCHANAN *appears at the left.*

Buchanan [*excitedly*]. They got him!

The POLICEMAN *runs off at the left.* SHIRLEY *reappears at the Maurrant window.*

Mrs. Jones [*calling*]. Have they got him?

Buchanan. Yes! He was hiding in the furnace, down at three twenty-two. [*As* ROSE *comes out of the house.*] They found him, Miss Maurrant!

Rose [*her hand to her heart*]. Oh! Is he hurt?

Buchanan. I don't know. He fired at the cops and they fired back at him. I was just passing the house when it happened.

Mrs. Jones [*leaning far out*]. Here they come! [*She leaves the window. The low murmur of the approaching crowd can be heard offstage left.*]

Rose. Where? [*She comes down the stoop and looks off, at the left.*] Oh! [*She covers her eyes and turns away.*]

Mrs. Fiorentino. You better come inside.

Shirley. Come up, Rose.

Buchanan. Yes, you better. [*He takes her by the arm.*]

Rose [*resisting*]. No. No. Please let me alone. I want to see him. [*She leans against the railing. Meanwhile the murmur and tramp of the approaching crowd has grown nearer and nearer.*]

Mrs. Fiorentino. Look at him, vill you!

Miss Cushing *comes out of the house and stands on the stoop, followed a moment later by* Mrs. Jones. Maurrant *appears at the left, between two* Policemen. Behind *him a third* Policeman *holds back a swarming crowd, which includes* Sam *and* Lippo. Maurrant's *clothes are torn, and his right arm is in a crude sling. Sweat, blood, and grime have made him almost unrecognizable. The* Policemen *too show evidences of a struggle.*

Rose [*running forward*]. Pop! Are you hurt?

Maurrant [*seeing her for the first time*]. Rose!

First Policeman [*to whom* Maurrant *is manacled*]. Keep back, Miss!

Maurrant. It's me daughter! Fer Chris' sake, boys, lemme talk to me daughter! Maybe I'll never be seein' her again!

Second Policeman. Give 'im a woid wit' her. [*He is the officer who was on duty in the Maurrant apartment.*]

First Policeman [*after a moment's hesitation*]. Well, all right. [*Savagely to* Maurrant.] But don't try to pull nothin', hear?

There is a forward movement in the crowd.

Second Policeman [*to the crowd*]. Keep back, youse!

Maurrant. Rose! You're wearin' a black dress, Rose!

Rose. Oh, Pop, why did you do it? Why did you?

Maurrant. I must o' been out o' me head, Rose. Did she say anythin'?

Rose. She never opened her eyes again.

Maurrant. I'd been drinkin', Rose—see what I mean?—an' all the talk that was goin' around. I just went clean off me nut, that's all.

Rose. What'll they do to you, Pop?

Maurrant. It's the chair for me, I guess. But I don't care—let 'em give me the chair. I deserve it all right. But it's her I'm thinkin' of, Rose—the way she looked at me. I oughtn't to done it, Rose.

Rose. She was always so good and sweet.

Maurrant. Don't I know it? I ain't no murderer—you

ought to be the one to know that, Rose. I just went out o' me head, that's all it was.

First Policeman. All right, that's all now. Come on!

Maurrant. Gimme a minute, can't you? She's me daughter. Gimme a chance, can't you? What's gonna happen to you, Rose?

Rose. I'll be all right, Pop. You don't need to worry about me.

Maurrant. I ain't been a very good father, have I?

Rose. Don't worry about that, Pop.

Maurrant. It ain't that I ain't meant to be. It's just the way things happened to turn out, that's all. Keep your eye on Willie, Rose. Don't let Willie grow up to be a murderer, like his Pop.

Rose. I'm going to do all I can for him, Pop.

Maurrant. You're a good girl, Rose. You was always a good girl.

Rose [*breaking down*]. Oh, Pop! [*She throws her arms around his neck and buries her head against him.* MAURRANT *sobs hoarsely.*]

Second Policeman [*gently*]. Come on, now, Miss. [*He and* SAM *take* ROSE *away from* MAURRANT.]

First Policeman. All right. Come on, Charlie.

They go toward the right, the crowd swarming behind them. Straggling along at the very end of the crowd is an unkempt woman wheeling a ramshackle baby carriage. MRS. JONES *and* MISS CUSHING *fall in with the crowd.* ROSE *gradually recovers her self-control and stands at the stoop with* SAM *beside her. The others watch the receding crowd for a moment. Then* KAPLAN *and* MRS. FIORENTINO *leave their windows. The* SECOND POLICEMAN *enters the house, followed by* LIPPO. MRS. OLSEN *goes to the cellar.* SHIRLEY *looks down at* ROSE *and* SAM *for a moment, then abruptly leaves the window.*

Sam [*taking* ROSE *by the arm*]. Rose, you better come inside.

Rose. No, I'm all right again, Sam—honestly I am. [*Trying to regain her self-composure.*] What about Willie, Sam?

Sam. I told him an accident had happened.

Rose. It's better to break it to him that way. But I'll have to tell him, I guess. He'd only find it out himself, tomorrow, with the papers all full of it. I saw Mrs. Sankey down at Police Headquarters. It's terrible for her, with her two little children.

Shirley [*appearing at the Maurrant window, a covered pot in her hand*]. Rose!

Rose [*looking up*]. Yes, Miss Kaplan?

Shirley. There's a chicken here that I found on the gas stove.

Rose. A chicken?

Shirley. Yes. The policeman says he smelled it cooking this morning, so he turned out the gas.

Rose. Oh, I remember now. My mother said she was going to make some soup for poor Mrs. Buchanan upstairs.

Shirley. It won't keep long, in this weather.

Rose. No. I really think Mrs. Buchanan ought to have the good of it.

Shirley. All right. I'll take it up to her.

Rose. Thanks ever so much, Miss Kaplan. [SHIRLEY *leaves the window.*] It's only a few hours ago that she was standing right here, telling me about the chicken. And then she went upstairs, and the next I saw of her, they were carrying her out. [*Abruptly, as she starts to go up the steps.*] Well, I've got to go up and get my things.

Sam. I must talk to you! What are you going to do, Rose?

Rose. Well, I haven't really had any time to do much thinking. But I really think the best thing I could do would be to get out of New York. You know, like we were saying, this morning—how things might be different if you only had a chance to breathe and spread out a little. Only when I said it, I never dreamed it would be this way.

Sam. If you go, I'll go with you.

Rose. But, Sam dear——

Sam. I don't care anything about my career. It's you—you—I care about. Do you think I can stay here, stifling to death in this slum, and never seeing you? Do you think my life means anything to me without you?

Rose. But, Sam, we've got to be practical about it. How would we manage?

Sam. I don't care what I do. I'll be a day laborer; I'll dig sewers—anything. [*Taking her passionately in his arms.*] Rose, don't leave me!

Rose. I like you so much, Sam. I like you better than anybody I know.

Sam. I love you, Rose. Let me go with you!

Rose. It would be so nice to be with you. You're different from anybody I know. But I'm just wondering how it would work out.

Sam. If we have each other, that's the vital thing, isn't it? What else matters but that?

Rose. Lots of things, Sam. There's lots of things to be considered. Suppose something was to happen—well, suppose I was to have a baby, say. That sometimes happens even when you don't want it to. What would we do then? We'd be tied down then, for life, just like all the other people around here. They all start out loving each other and thinking that everything is going to be fine—and before you know it, they find out they haven't got anything and they wish they could do it all over again—only it's too late.

Sam. It's to escape all that, that we must be together. It's only because we love each other, and belong to each other, that we can find the strength to escape.

Rose [*shaking her head*]. No, Sam.

Sam. Why do you say no?

Rose. It's what you said just now—about people belonging to each other. I don't think people ought to belong to anybody but themselves. I was thinking, that if my mother had really belonged to herself, and that if my father had really belonged to himself, it never would have happened. It was only because they were always depending on somebody else, for what they ought to have had inside themselves. Do you see what I mean, Sam? That's why I don't want to belong to anybody, and why I don't want anybody to belong to me.

Sam. You want to go through life alone?—never loving anyone, never having anyone love you?

Rose. Why, of course not, Sam! I want love more than anything else in the world. But loving and belonging aren't the same thing. [*Putting her arms around him.*] Sam dear, listen. If we say good-by now, it doesn't mean that it has to be forever. Maybe someday, when we're older and wiser, things will be different. Don't look as if it was the end of the world, Sam!

Sam. It *is* the end of my world.

Rose. It isn't, Sam! If you'd only believe in yourself a little more, things wouldn't look nearly so bad. Because once you're sure of yourself, the things that happen to you aren't so important. The way I look at it, it's not what you do that matters so much; it's what you are. [*Warmly.*] I'm so fond of you, Sam. And I've got such a lot of confidence in you. [*Impulsively.*] Give me a nice kiss! [SAM *takes her in his arms and kisses her passionately. A gawky* GIRL *of seventeen, one of* LIPPO's *pupils, appears at the left and looks at them, scandalized. Then she goes into the vestibule and rings the bell. The door clicks and she enters the house as* SHIRLEY *comes out, carrying a wicker suitcase.* SHIRLEY *looks at* SAM *and* ROSE. *To* SHIRLEY.] I was just telling Sam that I think I'll soon be going away from New York.

SAM *looks at her for a moment in agony, then goes abruptly into the house.*

Shirley. I put your things in this suitcase.

She comes down to the pavement. The GIRL *in the Fiorentino apartment begins tuning her violin.*

Rose [*taking the suitcase*]. You've been awfully nice to me. Don't worry about Sam, Miss Kaplan. Everything will be all right with him.

Shirley. I hope so.

From the Fiorentino apartment come the strains of Dvořák's "Humoresque," jerkily played on a violin.

Rose. Oh, I just know it will! [*Extending her hand.*] Good-by, Miss Kaplan.

Shirley. Good-by, Rose. [*Impulsively.*] You're a sweet girl! [*She hugs and kisses her.*]

Rose. I hope I'll see you again.

Shirley [*crying*]. I hope so, Rose.

ROSE *takes up the suitcase and goes off at the left.* SHIRLEY *stands watching her.*

Kaplan [reappearing at his window]. Shoiley, vot's de metter again vit Sem? He's crying on de bed.

Shirley. Let him alone, Papa, can't you?

She turns and enters the house. KAPLAN *sighs and, seating himself at the window, opens a newspaper. A shabby, middle-aged couple appear at the right and approach the stoop.*

The Man [reading the To Let sign]. Here's a place. Six rooms. Want to take a look at it?

A group of children, offstage left, begin singing "The Farmer in the Dell." This continues until after the curtain is down.

The Woman. All right. No harm lookin'. Ring for the janitor. [*The* MAN *goes up the stoop and rings the janitor's bell.*] Somebody must o' just died.

The Man. Yeah, maybe that's why they're movin' out. [*Wiping his face with a handkerchief.*] Phoo! Seems to be gettin' hotter every minute.

MRS. FIORENTINO *seats herself at her window, a sewing basket in her lap.* MRS. JONES *and* MISS CUSHING *appear at the right, busily engaged in conversation.*

Miss Cushing. The poor little thing!

Mrs. Jones [as they go up the steps]. Well, you never can tell with them quiet ones. It wouldn't surprise me a bit if she turned out the same way as her mother. She's got a gentleman friend that I guess ain't hangin' around for nothin'. I seen him, late last night, and this afternoon, when I come home from the police—— [*She is still talking, as they enter the house.*]

MRS. OLSEN *comes up the cellar steps. A sailor appears at the left with two girls, an arm around the waist of each. They stroll slowly across.*

Curtain.

DREAM GIRL

A Comedy in Two Acts

(Originally presented at the Coronet Theatre, New York City,
December 14, 1945)

CHARACTERS

GEORGINA ALLERTON
LUCY ALLERTON
RADIO ANNOUNCER
DR. J. GILMORE PERCIVAL
GEORGE ALLERTON
MIRIAM ALLERTON LUCAS
OBSTETRICIAN
NURSE
JIM LUCAS
CLAIRE BLAKELY
STOUT WOMAN
DOCTOR
CLARK REDFIELD
POLICEMAN
JUDGE
DISTRICT ATTORNEY
GEORGE HAND
BERT
MEXICAN
TWO OTHER MEXICANS
WAITER
ARABELLA
LUIGI
USHER
MISS DELEHANTY
ANTONIO
SALARINO
THEATER MANAGER
HEADWAITER
WAITER
JUSTICE OF THE PEACE BILLINGS
CHAUFFEUR

DREAM GIRL

ACT ONE

As the curtain rises on a dark stage, a deep-toned, distant bell is striking the hour of eight. On the eighth stroke an alarm clock begins its incessant clamor, and as the lights go up, slowly and dimly at center, a bed glides into view. Beside it is a night table on which are a lamp, the alarm clock, and a small radio. In the bed a girl, struggling against the rude awakening, turns and twists, then sits bolt upright. She is GEORGINA ALLERTON, *young, slender, and pretty. She shakes her head and rubs her closed eyes with her fists. The alarm clock is still ringing.*

GEORGINA [*yawning heavily*]. Ohhhh! [*Then, angrily, to the alarm clock.*] For heaven's sake, will you please shut up? [*She shuts off the alarm clock, then leans over and pulls up an imaginary window shade. The bed is flooded with morning sunlight.* GEORGINA *moans, shakes her head, and stretches her arms.*] Oh, dear! Another day! How awful! Who was it that said, "Must we have another day?" Dorothy Parker, I suppose. I wonder if she really says all those things. [*With a sigh.*] Well, time to get up, I guess. [*She plumps herself down again and snuggles her head in the pillow.*]

Mrs. Allerton [*off right*]. Georgina! It's time to get up!

Georgina [*calling*]. Yes, I know. I've been up for hours! [*Indignantly.*] Goodness, you'd think sleep was some sort of a crime. [*Gloomily, as she looks toward the window.*] Yes, another day. And what a day! Beautiful sunshine. Not a cloud in the sky. How wonderful it must be to be able to enjoy it. [*She sighs, then says firmly.*] Well, come on, Georgina, snap out of it, and get yourself up out of bed! [*She switches on the radio and an orchestra is heard softly playing "Paris in the Spring."*] I wonder how long a person can go on like this without developing a psychosis or something. For all I know, I may have a psychosis already. Good grief, what a thought! I wish I could remember that awful nightmare I had last night. Still, they say it's awfully hard to make anything out of your own dreams. That damned little psychic censor gets in your way. And besides,

161

I really don't know very much about dream symbols. Just the obvious ones, like Maypoles and church steeples—and I never seem to dream about them. Oh, well, to hell with it! [*She throws back the covers, swings her legs out of bed, and gets into her slippers and negligee. The music stops, and the voice of a radio announcer is heard.*]

Announcer's Voice. And so we bring to a close our half-hour of recorded music. And friends, don't forget your date tonight at eight-thirty, with your counselor on human relations, Dr. J. Gilmore Percival, brought to you through the courtesy of Kellogg's Kidney Capsules. If you are maladjusted, if you are worried about some emotional problem, come and tell your troubles to Dr. Percival, whose wise and kindly counsel has helped hundreds to solve——

Georgina [*switching off the radio indignantly*]. How ridiculous! As though that little quack could really solve people's emotional problems for them! Still, I suppose the poor deluded people who go to him get a kind of relief just from spilling their troubles to somebody. After all, that's what psychiatry is—only on a scientific basis, of course. [*She sits musing on the bed, her chin in her palm.*] Maybe I should try psychiatry. Only what's the use when I know so well what's the matter with me? Except that the right psychiatrist might help me to forget Jim. But do I want to forget Jim? And suppose it isn't just Jim that's the matter with me! What if it all goes back to something that's lurking deep in my unconscious, quietly festering away? [*Sharply.*] How absurd! In the first place, it costs a fortune. And besides, what do I need a psychiatrist for? I'm a perfectly healthy, normal person. All that's the matter with me is that I'm in love with the wrong man. But that's plenty! Anyhow, how do I know I'm really normal? Is anybody? [*Angrily.*] Honestly, it's disgraceful that they allow charlatans like that Dr. Percival on the air! Imagine standing up in front of a microphone and revealing the things that—— [*As she sits musing, the radio lights up again and the vioce of the* ANNOUNCER *is heard.*]

Announcer's Voice. And remember, folks, it's the kidneys that are the key to your health. And now here is Dr. Percival.

Percival's Voice. Good evening, friends. Tonight we begin with the problem of Miss G. A. Now, miss, just step right up to the microphone and tell me what is troubling you.

Georgina [*picking up the bedside lamp and speaking low into it, as though it were a microphone*]. Well, I——

Percival's Voice. A little louder, please, so that we can all hear you. There's nothing to be nervous about.

Georgina. I'm not nervous. It's just—well, it's just that it's a little hard to discuss your personal problems with several million people listening in.

Percival's Voice. I can't help you, unless you——

Georgina. I know. Well, you see, I'm in love with a man named Jim——

Percival's Voice. No names, please! No one's identity is ever revealed on this program.

Georgina. Oh, I'm sorry! I——

Percival's Voice. Go on, please. You are in love with a man named J. And he does not reciprocate your feeling for him, is that it?

Georgina. Oh, that's not the point! It's that he—he——

Percival's Voice. Well, what?

Georgina. Well, he happens to be my brother-in-law.

Percival's Voice. One moment, please! Do I understand you to say that you are in love with your brother-in-law?

Georgina. Yes. Yes, I am. I have been, for years and years.

Percival's Voice. This is really quite an extraordinary case. And, if I understand you correctly, he is not in love with you.

Georgina. Well, I used to think he was. And then suddenly he married Miriam and——

Percival's Voice. No names, please!

Georgina. Sorry! He married my sister, two years ago, and that was just about the end of everything for me.

Percival's Voice. And is he aware of your feeling for him?

Georgina [*indignantly*]. Certainly not! What kind of a girl do you think I am? Why, I'd die rather than let him know. Nobody knows or even suspects. [*Weepily.*] But I just can't keep it bottled up any longer. That's why I thought I'd——

Percival's Voice. Yes. You have a feeling of guilt about it, haven't you?

Georgina. In a way, I suppose. Being in love with your own brother-in-law—well, it seems just a little—a little incestuous.

Percival's Voice [*hastily*]. One moment, Miss A. That is not a word that is acceptable on the air.

Georgina. I'm terribly sorry, I——

Percival's Voice. Well, young woman, if you want my advice, you'll put this brother-in-law completely out of your mind and——

Georgina. Yes, that's easy to say. I've tried and tried. In fact, there's a man I'm having lunch with, a Mr.——

Percival's Voice. Careful!

Georgina. Well, I've been careful, up to now. Oh, you mean about his name. Well, he's a Mr. H.

Percival's Voice. And this Mr. H. is interested in you?

Georgina. Well, when a man keeps asking a girl out all the time—especially a married man——

Percival's Voice. Your involvements seem to be exclusively with married men.

Georgina. I know.

Percival's Voice. Miss A., I think your situation is a very serious one, indeed. It is hard for me——

Mrs. Allerton [*off right*]. Georgina! Are you daydreaming again in there? It's almost nine!

Georgina [*leaping up*]. All right, Mother. I'm practically dressed. [*The lights fade on the scene and come up, at the left, on* GEORGINA's *bathroom, which she enters, talking all the while.*] Maybe your mother is right, Georgina. Maybe it's time you cut out the daydreaming—time you stopped mooning around and imagining yourself to be this extraordinary creature with a strange and fascinating psychological life. [*She has removed her negligee and donned a bathing cap; and she now goes around behind the bathroom, invisible but still audible. The sound of a shower is heard.*] Oh, damn it! Cold as ice! There, that's better! [*She sings "Night and Day" lustily. Then the shower is turned off, and she reappears wrapped in a large bath towel and stands, her back to the audience, rubbing herself vigorously.*] Still, to be honest, I must admit that, compared to the average girl you meet, I'm really quite complex. Intelligent and well informed too; and a good conversationalist. [*Indignantly, as over her shoulder, she sees someone looking in at her.*] Well, for heaven's sake! Honestly, some people! [*She pulls down an imaginary window shade and the scene is blacked out, her voice coming out of the darkness.*] And my looks are nothing to be ashamed of either. I have a neat little figure and my legs are really very nice. Of course, my nose is sort of funny, but my face definitely has character—not just one of those magazine-cover deadpans. [*With a yawn.*] Oh, I never seem to get enough sleep! [*The lights come up as she raises the imaginary shade. She is dressed now in her shoes, stockings, and slip. She seats herself at her dressing table, facing the audience, and brushes her hair.*] If I could only stop lying awake for hours, dreaming up all the exciting things that could happen but never do. Well, maybe this is the day when things really will begin to happen to me. Maybe Wentworth and Jones will accept my novel. They've had it over a month now, and all the other publishers turned it down in less than two weeks. It certainly looks promising. And especially with Jim's recommendation. Wouldn't that be wonderful! With a published novel, I'd really be somebody. Reviews in all the book sections; royalty checks coming in; women nudging each other at Schrafft's and whispering, "Don't look now, but that girl over there—the one with the smart hat—that's Georgina Allerton, the novelist." [*Going to the washbasin.*] Gee, that would be thrilling! To feel that I'd accomplished something. To feel that I had a purpose in life. To feel that—— [*She busies herself with a toothbrush, becoming momentarily unintelligible.*] Ubble-ba-glub-ab-lub-mum. Only it wouldn't make up for Jim. [*Going back to the dressing table.*] Fifty novels wouldn't make up for Jim. If Miriam only appreciated him. But she doesn't. She doesn't understand him. All his fine sensitive qualities— they're completely lost on her. It's really ironic. [*Baring her teeth.*] Gosh, my teeth could certainly stand a good cleaning. It's awful the way I put off going to the dentist. Maybe that's psychopathic too. What to do? What to do? Here I am twenty-three years old—no, let's face it, twenty-four next month! And that's practically thirty. Thirty years old—and nothing to show for it. Suppose nothing ever does happen to me. That's a frightening thought! Just to go on and on like this, on through middle age, on to senility, never experiencing anything—what a prospect! [*Putting on her make-up.*] Of course I suppose that up to a certain point there's nothing abnormal about virginity. But the question is, how can you ever be sure you haven't passed that point? Heavens, is that a gray hair? No, thank goodness. What a scare! Still, there must be a lot of women who go right on being virgins until the very day they die. It can be done, I guess. Doesn't sound like much fun though. [*She rises and gets into her dress.*] Well, that brings me right smack back to George Hand. Maybe I shouldn't have accepted his invitation for today. He really is rushing me. Of course, he may not have any intentions at all. No, he's too busy a man to keep on dating up a girl, without having something on his mind. So that puts it squarely up to me. Well, anyhow, if I'm going to play with fire, I may as well look my best. So here goes.

Mrs. Allerton [*off right*]. Georgina, I'm getting tired of keeping the coffee hot.

Georgina. Coming! Coming! [*As she quickly crosses the stage the light fades out on the bathroom and comes up at the right on a breakfast table at which her parents are seated. MRS. ALLERTON is a stoutish, good-looking woman in a negligee; MR. ALLERTON is a pleasant round-faced man in a business suit. He is busy with the morning's mail. Briskly, as she takes her place at the table.*] Morning, Mother. Morning, Dad.

Allerton [*looking up from the letter he is reading*]. Oh, good morning, Georgie.

Mrs. Allerton. Don't tell me you're wearing that new dress to work.

Georgina. I have a lunch date.

Mrs. Allerton [*with lively interest*]. Oh?

Georgina. No, Mother, he is *not* a matrimonial prospect. We just happen to be going to a swanky place so——

Mrs. Allerton. I didn't say—I didn't say—[*suppressing a sneeze.*]—a single—solitary—word. [*The sneeze bursts forth.*] Excuse me!

Georgina. Goodness, Mother, have you got a cold?

Mrs. Allerton. Well, what does it sound like—appendicitis?

Georgina. I told you not to put your fur coat in storage yet.

Mrs. Allerton [*sharply*]. That has nothing—nothing whatever—nothing whatever to do with it. [*Another sneeze.*] Oh, damn it! I hate colds.

Georgina. Some aspirin might do it good.

Mrs. Allerton. Nothing does a cold any good. And if you want to know how I got it, I got it from sleeping next to an open window. Your father, after consulting the calendar, decided that spring is here, so of course up went the window all the way.

Allerton [*mildly*]. I offered to change beds with you, Lucy.

Mrs. Allerton. That would have only meant your getting a cold, and I'd have not only had to nurse you but would have caught it myself. It was much simpler to catch my own cold in the first place.

Georgina [*pouring herself some coffee*]. But why didn't you close the window?

Mrs. Allerton. Well, we discussed the pros and cons of that at some length, but, in the middle of your father's second rebuttal, I fell asleep, with the result that—— [*A sneeze.*]

Allerton. Some butter, Georgie?

Georgina. Dad, aren't you ever going to learn that I don't take butter?

Mrs. Allerton. How can you swallow that dry toast?

Georgina. You get used to it.

Mrs. Allerton. I would never get used to it. Has it ever occurred to you that if nature had intended our skeletons to be visible it would have put them—on the outside— on the outside of our bodies? [*A sneeze.*]

Allerton. Oh, there's a letter for you, Georgie. [*He hands it to her.*]

Georgina. From Wentworth and Jones! [*She tears it open eagerly, then registers deep disappointment.*] Oh, damn! They've turned down my novel.

Allerton. Too bad! But you mustn't be discouraged.

Georgina. Well, I am! I was sure they were going to accept it. Especially after Jim recommended it for publication.

Mrs. Allerton. Sounds to me like an excellent reason for turning it down.

Georgina. I don't see why you're always picking on poor Jim.

Mrs. Allerton. Well, I'm fed up with poor Jim. I think a fellow his age shouldn't just be sitting around reading manuscripts at thirty-five dollars a week.

Allerton. Oh, give the boy a chance, my dear. He hasn't found himself yet.

Georgina. That's exactly it!

Mrs. Allerton. Well, I'm sick and tired of financing the search. First, I had to see him through law school. Then——

Georgina. Don't go all over that again, Mother. Just because he's too sensitive to bring himself——

Allerton. Yes. Law, as it's practiced today, is hardly the profession for an idealist.

Mrs. Allerton. Well, *you* should know! What *is* this case you're going to Washington on?

Allerton. It's the Sons of Solomon case.

Georgina. Who are they, Dad?

Allerton. A religious sect in Montana that's being prosecuted for advocating polygamy. We've lost all along the line, but I'm very hopeful of winning in the Supreme Court.

Mrs. Allerton. And that will mean a whopping fee, I'm sure.

Allerton [*rising*]. No fee at all, win or lose. I'm handling the case as a matter of principle. Free speech, freedom of religion.

Georgina. But, Dad, do you believe in polygamy?

Allerton. Personally speaking, no.

Mrs. Allerton. And a lot of good it would do him if he did!

Allerton. But I can say with Voltaire: I disapprove of what you say, but I will defend to the death your right to say it.

Georgina. Oh, did Voltaire say that?

Mrs. Allerton [*interrupting*]. George, doesn't anybody ever walk into your office who's been run over by a millionaire's limousine or who's robbed a bank and is willing to give you—to give you half—to get him—get him out of it? [*A sneeze.*]

Georgina. Why, Mother, aren't there enough ambulance-chasers and police-court shysters without Dad becoming one?

Allerton. Thank you, Georgie. [*He kisses her.*] Good-by, dear. [*About to kiss* MRS. ALLERTON.] Good-by, Lucy.

Mrs. Allerton [*drawing back*]. Don't kiss me, or you'll have the entire Supreme Court sneezing their heads off.

Allerton [*solicitously*]. I'm worried about you. Maybe a little aspirin——

Mrs. Allerton. If aspirin is mentioned again—I'll—I'll—I'll—— [*A sneeze.*] Sometimes I think that even monogamy is going too far.

Allerton. I'll be back late tonight. Don't be downcast about the novel, Georgie. These things take time.

Georgina. Yes, it certainly looks that way.

[ALLERTON *exits.*

Mrs. Allerton. Do you have to encourage him?

Georgina. Well, I admire him for sticking unselfishly to his principles, instead of just practicing law on a sordid, commercial basis.

Mrs. Allerton. Yes, there is certainly no taint of commercialism upon this family, including the connections by marriage. And it's a fortunate coincidence that I am able to foot the bills on the income from Grandpa's sordid commercial estate.

Georgina. Well, I have every intention of contributing my share, just as soon as—— [MRS. ALLERTON *sneezes.*]

Mrs. Allerton. Excuse me. How much did the bookshop lose last month?

Georgina. Only a hundred and eighteen dollars. Claire says it's the best month we've had yet.

Mrs. Allerton [*rising*]. Why, you're right on the highroad to success. [*She sneezes.*] Well, I'm going to go and suffer in solitude.

Georgina. Good-by, Mother. I do hope——

MRS. ALLERTON *has gone off right.* GEORGINA *sighs as*

MIRIAM LUCAS, *a young attractive woman, enters at left.*

Miriam. 'Lo, Sis.

Georgina. Why, Miriam!

Miriam. Why, look at you, all dressed up to kill.

Georgina. Well, I'm lunching at the Canard Rouge, so I thought I'd——

Miriam. Oh-oh!

Georgina. Nothing like that. Just somebody who's in the book trade. Since when do you get up at daybreak?

Miriam. I had a date with a doctor. Where are Mother and Dad?

Georgina. Dad's gone to Washington, and Mother's got an awful cold.

Miriam. That's good. I mean, I'd rather not spring this on the whole family at once. I hate collective reactions.

Georgina. Is anything wrong?

Miriam. That's a matter of opinion. It seems that the old medico went into a huddle with some mouse or rabbit that he keeps around and they've decided that you're about to become an aunt.

Georgina. But, Miriam, how exciting! When's it going to be?

Miriam. Oh, not for a hell of a while—a good five or six months. All those engineers, with their blueprints, knocking hours off the transcontinental flying time, but not one day do they save us mothers. Well, I guess I'll go break the news to Mother.

Georgina. I'll bet Jim is happy about it.

Miriam. He doesn't know it yet. I saw no point in getting him into an interesting condition until I was really sure myself. [*Vehemently.*] And to come right out with it, I don't care a hoot whether he's happy about it or not.

Georgina [*greatly embarrassed*]. Well, I know it's going to make all the difference in the world for you both. Gee, I certainly envy you.

Miriam. And may I say that I certainly envy you. Here am I, a seething mass of unpleasant symptoms, and there are you, fit as a fiddle, and positively suffused with the soft glow of vicarious maternity.

Georgina. I just wish I could change places with you, that's all.

Miriam. It's a deal. I'll send my agent around after lunch. And I hope you have a boy.

Georgina. Maybe it'll be twins.

Miriam. Don't say things like that! You never know who's listening.

She exits at right. GEORGINA *sits looking dreamily after* MIRIAM. *Then, as the light fades on the scene, a chorus of female voices sings "Sleep, Baby, Sleep." The stage is in darkness for a few moments, then the singing dies out and merges into a chorus of wailing infants. The lights come up slowly at the center, revealing a hospital bed, completely surrounded by flowers, in which* GEORGINA *sits propped up. She wears a silk jacket and holds a large doll in each arm, one wrapped in a blue blanket, the other in pink. At one side of the bed stands an* OBSTETRICIAN, *who looks like* ALLERTON; *at the other side, a* NURSE, *who looks like* MRS. ALLERTON.

Obstetrician. Well, my dear, you've come through wonderfully.

Georgina. All thanks to you, Doctor. You've been like a father to me.

Obstetrician. In all my years, I've never known a harder confinement or a braver patient. Yes, you're a plucky little woman.

Georgina. A lucky one, you mean! [*Smiling down at the babies.*] Just look at my little darlings!

Obstetrician. I've never seen two finer ones.

Nurse. You're the envy of every mother in the hospital.

Georgina [*beaming*]. Well, what's a little suffering compared to that? Besides, pain is a part of life, and to live fully we must taste every form of human experience.

Nurse. Oh, that's beautifully expressed!

Georgina. And, Doctor, I definitely *don't* want them to go on the bottle. It's such a joy!

Obstetrician [*patting her head*]. Good girl!

As the OBSTETRICIAN *exits,* JIM LUCAS *enters. He is an attractive young man with a face and manner that are almost too sensitive.*

Jim. Georgina, darling!

Georgina. Oh, Jim!

Nurse. Not too long, Mr. Lucas. We mustn't tire her.

Jim. No, no. I understand. [*As the* NURSE *exits he goes to* GEORGINA.]

Georgina. Oh, Jim, isn't it wonderful?

Jim. Yes, wonderful! Birth, the most universal experience, and yet the greatest of all miracles. Are you happy, darling?

Georgina. Just look at me! I've waited so long for this, afraid it was never going to happen. I'm a new woman, Jim.

Jim. And I'm a new man—with someone to understand me, someone to have faith in me.

Georgina. And a new world to build for ourselves—and for them: Gerald and Geraldine.

Miriam [*entering at right, smoking a cigarette*]. Hand them over quick, Georgina. I'm parked in front of a fire plug.

Georgina [*clinging to the babies*]. No, you shan't have them! They're mine.

Miriam [*coming to the bed*]. Yours? Look, darling, it wasn't my idea to have a baby! But having produced a couple of brats in the customary, antiquated manner, I don't think I'm unreasonable in contending that they're mine.

Jim. Only in the crudest physiological sense.

Miriam. Oh, forgive me! Is there some other sense?

Georgina. There is indeed!

Jim. You wouldn't have to be told that, Miriam, if you had any feeling for the deeper values of life. There's no real marriage between you and me—no love, no understanding, no spiritual communion. The children of my body may be yours, but the children of my spirit will always be Georgina's.

Miriam. All right. I'll settle for that. [*Calling.*] Nurse!

Nurse. Coming!

Miriam [*snatching one baby and pointing to the other*]. Here, you take that one. And hurry up before I get a ticket. [*The* NURSE *takes the other baby from* GEORGINA *and follows* MIRIAM *off, sneezing into the baby's face.*]

Miriam [*as she exits*]. And watch that sneezing!

Jim [*taking a step after her*]. Miriam, I——

Georgina [as the scene fades out]. Jim! Jim! Don't leave me! Don't leave me!

Jim [stretching his arms toward the disappearing GEORGINA]. I'm sorry, Georgina! I know it isn't right! I know it shouldn't be this way! Georgina! Georgina! Georgina!
[*He exits.*

Mrs. Allerton [off right]. Georgina! Georgina, are you still there?

The lights come up right on GEORGINA *as she sits at the breakfast table, as before.*

Georgina [startled]. What? Yes. Yes, I am. [*She hastily wipes her eyes as* MRS. ALLERTON *enters.*]

Mrs. Allerton. You'll be late again at the shop. What on earth are you moping about now?

Georgina. Just happy about Miriam. And a little wistful at the prospect of being a maiden aunt. Don't you feel sort of——

Mrs. Allerton. I'm much too furious to feel sort of anything.

Georgina. Why? What's the matter?

Mrs. Allerton. Didn't Miriam tell you about Jim?

Georgina [anxiously]. No, what about him?

Mrs. Allerton. He's out of a job again.

Georgina. He's left Wentworth and Jones?

Mrs. Allerton. Well, that's one way of putting it. In less diplomatic language, they fired him.

Georgina. So that's why she was so upset. Poor Jim!

Mrs. Allerton. What do you mean, poor Jim! What about poor Miriam?

Georgina. It's much worse for him. He's just had nothing but hard luck.

Mrs. Allerton. Why, the way you stand up for him, anybody would think you were madly in love with him.

Georgina [angrily]. Don't talk such nonsense! Just because I happen to feel some sympathy for a boy who——

Mrs. Allerton. All right, you can feel all the sympathy you like for him. But, in my opinion, the sooner Miriam gets herself unattached from that balmy dreamer, the better off she'll be.

Georgina. Well, I hope you don't tell her anything like that.

Mrs. Allerton. I just this minute—just this minute—finished telling her! [*A sneeze.*]

Georgina. How *could* you, just when she's going to have a baby?

Mrs. Allerton. That's just exactly it. She'd be a fool to hang on to him, now that he's accomplished what will probably be the only affirmative act of his life.

Georgina. But it's just the time when a woman needs her husband most!

Mrs. Allerton. You read too many serious books. What on earth does she need him for now?

Georgina. I don't see how you can be so cynical about your daughter's happiness.

Mrs. Allerton. I'm not the least bit cynical. If she gets rid of that piece of excess baggage, she has a chance to make a fresh start. Otherwise, she's just stuck with him. Everybody else seems to fire him. Why shouldn't she?

Georgina. Well, I trust and pray that Miriam won't pay any attention to you. In fact, I'm going to call her up and tell her so.

Mrs. Allerton. You keep out of this. If Miriam had wanted your advice, she'd have asked for it. And if that unemployed Galahad comes crying to you, I wish you'd tell him for me that—that—that—— [*She sneezes.*] For goodness' sake, will you run along to work now, before I use language unbecoming a grandmother?

Georgina. All right, good-by, then. And, for heaven's sake, take care of yourself.

Mrs. Allerton [*as* GEORGINA *exits*]. If you—if I—if anybody——

The lights fade on the scene and come up, at the left, on a corner of a small bookshop. The telephone is ringing. On the third ring CLAIRE BLAKELY, *a brisk young woman about* GEORGINA's *age, enters and answers it.*

Claire. Mermaid Bookshop. No, madam, I'm terribly sorry. This is not the Bide-a-wee Home. You must have the wrong number. [*A stout woman enters and* CLAIRE *turns to her.*] Good morning. Can I help you?

Woman. I was just wondering if you happen to have a copy of *Always Opal?*

Claire. No, I'm afraid not at the moment.

Woman. Oh, dear. This is about the fifth shop I've been to.

Claire. We have a dozen copies but they're all out. And a waiting list of at least fifty. But here's something you might like. Mary Myrtle Miven's latest, *My Heart Is Like a Trumpet.* It's a sort of idyllic love story about two horses. Very tender and poetic.

Woman. No, I really don't think——

Claire. Well, how about *The Dnieper Goes Rolling Along?* It's that new Soviet novel about the electrification of collective farms. Very stark and powerful.

Woman. No, what I really want is *Always Opal.* You see, all my friends are reading it, and I feel so out of it. I understand it's very—very——

Claire. Well, it certainly doesn't leave much to the imagination in the way of——

Woman. Yes, so I understand. [*As she starts to go.*] Oh, I wonder if you happen to have a three-cent stamp.

Claire. Yes, I think so. [*She opens a tin cashbox on the desk.*]

Woman [*fumbling in her handbag*]. Oh, dear, I'm afraid the smallest I have is a five-dollar bill. Could you possibly——?

Claire. I guess I can make it. One, and four is five.

Woman. Oh, thank you so much.

Claire. Not a bit. Stop in again.

Woman. Indeed I will! [*She goes out at the right as* GEORGINA *enters.*]

Georgina. Hello, Claire. Sorry I'm late again. Have you had a busy morning?

Claire. You betcha. I directed two people to Oppenheim Collins, one gal wanted to look at the phone book, another had to go to the john, and I just made a cash sale of a three-cent stamp.

Georgina. It's discouraging.

Claire. Oh, I knew there was something else. Frank McClellan called up to say that that asthma of his has got completely out of hand and the doctor has ordered him to Arizona, pronto.

Georgina. Oh, the poor guy! But what about his book-shop?

Claire. Well, he thought we might like to take it over.

Georgina [*excitedly*]. But, Claire, how wonderful! Why, compared to this dinky little——

Claire. You can spare me the comparison. He says he clears five or six hundred a month.

Georgina. Why, we lost nearly that much one month.

Claire. Yes, dear.

Georgina. Well, let's tell him yes, before he changes his mind.

Claire. He wants ten thousand dollars for the business.

Georgina. Ten thousand dollars! For heaven's sake!

Claire. Did you think he wanted to make us a present of it? You don't happen to know where we could dig up ten thousand, do you?

Georgina. Who, me?

Claire. No, I guess not. Well, it's too bad. [*With firmness.*] Georgie, I don't think you and I are cut out for business. I think the best thing for us to do is board up this hole in the wall and call it a day.

Georgina. What, give up the business, when we've put so much into it?

Claire. We could have had sables on what we've put into it.

Georgina. But we're not interested in sables.

Claire. We're not?

Georgina. Well, what I mean is, we're not the frivolous type that's willing just to gad around and fritter our time away.

Claire. But what type are we? And what are we good for? What can we do?

Georgina. Well, we could go to secretarial school.

Claire. Back to school at twenty-four? Listen, darling, beginning with play school at three, I went to school—let me see now—sixteen, seventeen, eighteen, nineteen——! My God, nineteen consecutive years! Nineteen years, thousands of dollars, and the efforts of hundreds of specially trained people have been spent in making us not want to do all the useful things we don't know how to do.

Georgina. And I'm getting terribly discouraged about my novel too. Wentworth and Jones have just turned it down. And after Jim Lucas recommended it. I'm beginning to think that maybe I'm not a novelist.

Claire. Oh, don't take that attitude. William DeMorgan had his first novel published at sixty-six.

Georgina. But he must have had something to keep him occupied in the meantime. I still have one teeny hope. Jim Lucas said he'd give the manuscript to Clark Redfield. You know—the book reviewer.

Claire. Oh, yes.

Georgina. If he turns thumbs down, I'll just——! Oh, well, no use brooding over it. By the way, speaking of Jim Lucas, Miriam is going to have a baby.

Claire. Congratulations! Well, that's something that even we would be capable of, I suppose.

Georgina. They say it takes two.

Claire. Yes, that's the hell of it. We're choosy too. Well, let's not be defeatist about things. Can't you think of some way we could raise that ten thousand? How about your grandfather's estate? It's a perfectly safe investment——

Georgina. Not a chance of that. It's all tied up in a trust fund with some bank, as long as my mother lives.

Claire. And I suppose she's good for another twenty-five years.

Georgina. Why, what a thing to say!

Claire. Oh, I didn't mean it that way. It's just that— oh, you know—always some dead hand, holding us back. Oh, well, I've got to get out this month's bills. [*She starts to go.*] Don't take any more reservations for *Always Opal.* Our lease will be up by the time we fill all we have now.

She exits behind the bookshelves. GEORGINA sighs, lights a cigarette, gets up and walks about the shop, lost in thought. Suddenly the telephone rings.

Georgina [*without going near the telephone*]. Hello? Yes, this is she. What? Oh, no, I can't believe it! Yes! Yes! I'll be right there. [*As she hurries to the center, the lights come up, revealing a* MAN *in a surgeon's uniform with a stethoscope about his neck.*] Oh, Doctor, Doctor, it can't be true about my mother!

Doctor. Yes, my dear, I'm afraid it is.

Georgina. What was it—her heart?

Doctor. That—and other things. It happens that way sometimes. We tried to save her, but it was hopeless.

Georgina. Did you try sodium pentathol?

Doctor. Yes, my dear. Everything was done that medical science can do. But there are still some things we haven't mastered. And now I shall leave you with your father. He needs you, my dear.

He recedes into the darkness as ALLERTON *comes forward.*

Georgina [*in his arms*]. Dad!

Allerton. I'm all alone now, Georgie—except for you!

Georgina. You have Miriam too, Dad.

Allerton [*shaking his head*]. She has Jim to look out for. And a baby coming soon. So there's only you.

Georgina. You can depend on me, Dad. I'll never leave you. You're all I have in the world too.

Allerton. You're a rich girl now, Georgie. Anything that your heart desires——

Georgina. Oh, I don't care about the money, Dad. If I do use any of it, it will only be so that Claire and I——

CLARK REDFIELD, *a young man of twenty-eight, enters at the left. He staggers under the load of a double armful of books. He goes to the desk, plumps down the books, looks toward the center, and coughs tentatively. As* GEORGINA *turns and sees him the lights fade quickly on* ALLERTON.

Clark. Good morning, Miss Allerton.

Georgina [*approaching* REDFIELD]. Oh! Good morning, Mr. Redfield.

Clark. You seem preoccupied. I hope I haven't derailed some train of cosmic thought.

Georgina [*somewhat flustered*]. Of course not. I was just—— [*Seeing the books.*] Goodness! More review copies?

Clark. You betcha! I've got——

Georgina [*preoccupied*]. Do you mind waiting a minute

while I call my mother? She wasn't feeling well this morning and——

Clark. Nothing serious, I hope!

Georgina. Well, I think it's only a cold, but you know
how these respiratory disorders flare up sometimes.

*She dials a number. A telephone rings at the right and the
lights go up on* MRS. ALLERTON. *She is seated on a chaise
longue, dressed as before, and reading a book. The telephone is beside her and she answers it.*

Mrs. Allerton. Hello!

Georgina. This is me, Mother. How are you feeling?

Mrs. Allerton. What do you mean, how am I feeling?
I'm feeling—feeling fine. [*She sneezes.*]

Georgina. You sound awful.

Mrs. Allerton. I've got a cold in the head and every now
and then—I—I—I—have to sneeze. What are you calling
up for?

Georgina. To find out how you are, of course. I've been
worried about you.

Mrs. Allerton. You mean to say you called up just to
ask about my sneezes? You certainly must have very little
on your mind.

Georgina. Well, you might at least appreciate my——

Mrs. Allerton. I was appreciating Opal's hot affair with
Monseigneur de Montrouget and you interrupted me just as
they were about to—to—— [*She sneezes and hangs up.*]

Georgina [*as the lights fade on* MRS. ALLERTON]. All
right. I'm just glad you—— [*She hangs up.*]

Clark. Is she all right?

Georgina. She seems all right. Just sneezing and very
cranky.

Clark. The typical American mother. [*Rubbing his
hands.*] Well, are you ready to do business now?

Georgina. What have you there?

Clark. A fine mixed bag. Three whodunits, a couple of
epics of the soil, a survey of the natural resources of Bolivia,
and a volume called *Fun with a Chafing Dish.* And here
is the prize of the lot: Professor Oglethorpe's two-volume
Life of Napoleon, with the pages still uncut.

Georgina. You mean you haven't read it?

Clark. Do I look like a boy who, six years out of college, would wade through eleven hundred pages on Napoleon?

Georgina. But I read your review of it in the *Globe.*

Clark. I didn't say I didn't review it. I said I didn't read it.

Georgina. How could you review it without reading it?

Clark. Easy. First I quoted liberally from the introduction and quarreled with the author's approach. Next, I leafed quickly through and called attention to three typographical errors. Then I praised the illustrations, grumbled about the footnotes, and intimated that the book added little to what had already been written. Result, a scholarly column and all done in exactly fifty-seven minutes.

Georgina. Is that your idea of literary criticism?

Clark. Look, I'm a working newspaperman and a member of the Newspaper Guild, whose contract guarantees me a minimum wage for a maximum working week. There's nothing in it that requires me to ruin my eyesight and addle my brain in the interests of a Corsican upstart.

Georgina. Well, I've often heard that newspapermen are cynical, but I wouldn't have believed that a man who is entrusted with reviewing books could have so little sense of responsibility.

Clark. You make me feel like a great big brute.

Georgina. I don't see anything funny about it. I think it's disgraceful.

Clark. Don't twist the sword, Miss Allerton. Just give me the price of my shame and let me go in peace. Well, what do you say? How much am I bid for the lot?

Georgina [*examining the books*]. Most of these aren't much use to us. How about five dollars?

Clark. Like all idealists, you drive a hard bargain. But I'm not going to lug these damned things any further, so they're yours.

Georgina. Well, I don't want you to feel I'm taking advantage of you. I'll make it six dollars.

Clark [*holding up his hand*]. No, no! Even a cynical newspaperman has his pride. Give!

Georgina [*handing him a bill*]. You don't have to be so sarcastic about it. We really don't need your secondhand books. Maybe, hereafter, you'd better take them somewhere else.

Clark. Unfortunately, I'm a creature of habit, Miss Aller·ton. Let me but tuck a review copy under my arm, and immediately there is set in motion a whole series of muscular reflexes that takes me straight to your door.

Georgina. If reviewing books is so distasteful to you, why do you do it?

Clark. Well, you see, I have a periodic rendezvous with my stomach. And I find that reviewing books requires less leg work than covering the police courts. And, not to withhold anything from you, I'm sitting in a very pretty spot for the first opening on the sports page.

Georgina [*in amazement*]. You mean you'd rather be a sportswriter than a literary critic?

Clark. I'm afraid you don't grasp the practical realities of journalism. What you euphemistically call a literary critic is only a miserable penny-a-liner, whereas a sportswriter nestles snugly in the upper brackets.

Georgina. I wasn't thinking about the money——

Clark. Pardon the indelicacy. So you think that writing about books is on a higher level than writing about sports?

Georgina. I just think there's no comparison.

Clark. You're right; there isn't. Any young squirt, fresh out of college, can write book reviews. Just as any beginner in the theater can play Polonius. In fact, the technique is much the same. You put on false whiskers and spout platitudes in a high, squeaky voice. But to go in there and play Hamlet and follow all the sinuous twists and turnings of that tortured soul; or, on the other hand, to analyze the strategy of an intricate football formation or judge a fast ten-round bout on points—that's something else again. To do that, you really have to know your stuff.

Georgina. Oh, yes, you're very clever and paradoxical, aren't you?

Clark. Thank you for the compliment, tinged though it is with a certain asperity. But you see, getting on the sports page is only what might be called a primary objective. For to a really good sportswriter, every door is open: literature, movies, radio, politics, anything. Look at Ring Lardner.

Look at Heywood Broun. Look at John Kieran. Look—
if you can bear it—at Westbrook Pegler. In my daydreams,
I write a story about the deciding game of the World Series
that stampedes the Democratic Convention and lands me
in the White House. And on my tentative cabinet slate,
you're down for Secretary of Labor. Ta-ta, Madam Allerton, I'll see you in Washington.

Georgina [*as he is about to go*]. Oh, just a minute. Did
Jim Lucas ever give you——

Clark. Did I hear you aright? Did you mention the name
of Jim Lucas?

Georgina. Have you got something sarcastic to say about
him too?

Clark. Not sarcastic, my dear young woman. Sarcasm
would be a wholly inadequate instrument for a commentary
on that epic character. But perhaps you haven't heard the
news about Jim?

Georgina. I've heard that he's parted company with
Wentworth and Jones, if that's what you mean.

Clark. Parted company, did you say? Really, Miss Allerton, you have a gift for hyperbolic understatement. The impact of Jim's violent expulsion has rocked Publisher's Row
to its foundations. Would you mind telling an inquiring
reporter, Miss Allerton, how it feels to be the sister-in-law
of the man who sent back the manuscript of *Always Opal*
without even turning in a report on it?

Georgina. Is that really true? Did Jim do that?

Clark. Oh, so you haven't heard. An enterprising book
peddler like you should get around more. This Lucas is a
celebrity, the greatest bonehead player since Fred Merkle
forgot to touch second base.

Georgina. Well, that book deserved to be turned down.
It's nothing but a lot of dressed-up smut, atrociously written, and all in very bad taste, if you ask me.

Clark. Wait a minute, Carrie Nation. The verdict of history is already in. Don't try to alibi Jim, or folks will get the
impression that you take more than a sisterly-in-law interest
in him.

Georgina [*flaring up*]. That's an uncalled-for and highly
impertinent remark.

Clark. Or is it just a case of one hand washing the other?

Georgina. And what is that supposed to mean?

Clark. Well, I got the impression that Jim thinks rather highly of that novel of yours that he asked me to read.

Georgina [*eager for his verdict*]. Oh, then he did give it to you?

Clark. Yes, he did.

Georgina. And I suppose, following your usual practice, you haven't read it.

Clark. No, you're wrong. I have read it. All of it—well, almost all.

Georgina [*after a pause*]. Well?

Clark. You mean you want my opinion of it?

Georgina. Well, why do you suppose I let Jim give it to you?

Clark. I wasn't sure. Well, to put the thing as delicately as possible, I think it stinks.

Georgina [*enraged*]. Oh, you do, do you?

Clark. Yes, I do. [*Contemplatively.*] Yes, that really is a malodorous morsel. In the first place——

Georgina [*almost in tears*]. Never mind! I'm not interested in what you have to say.

Clark. Oh, then you really *didn't* want my opinion. That's what I thought.

Georgina. I don't call that an opinion. Just a nasty, insulting——

Clark. I see! You only wanted a favorable opinion.

Georgina. Nobody wants criticism that's just destructive. I say if a critic can't be constructive——

Clark. You mean you want the critic to do the creative job that you failed to do? If that's his function, we might as well dispense with the writer in the first place. Now, if you'll let me give a piece of friendly advice——

Georgina. I don't want your advice. I'd never have let Jim give you the manuscript if I had known that you're just a hockey fan.

Clark. There's a good hockey match at the Garden Saturday night. Want to go?

Georgina. No, I don't! And if you'll excuse me now, I have a lot of work to do.

Clark. You haven't a damn thing to do. You just sit

around this shop all day to give yourself the illusion that you're doing something.

Georgina. Will you please get out of here?

Clark. Sore as a boil, aren't you?

Georgina. Not in the least. It just happens that I find you very unpleasant. I think you're not only lazy and dishonest, but sadistic and vulgar.

Clark. Well, I'm glad you're not sore. And I think that novel of yours is just about the most terrific thing I've read since *War and Peace*.

Georgina. And another thing. I wish you would not ever come here again.

Clark. I'll try to remember that. 'By, now. And thanks for the five bucks.   [*He exits right.*

Georgina [*with tears of anger*]. You great big ape!

She stands looking after him for a moment, trembling with rage and humiliation. Then she begins threshing about in uncontrollable fury. She strides to the desk and violently pushes CLARK's *books to the floor. Then she stands with clenched fists glaring in the direction that* CLARK *has gone and with sudden resolution strides center into the darkness. There is a flash of lightning and a peal of thunder. The lights fade on the bookshop and come up at the right. The pitiful meowing of a cat is heard.* CLARK, *in his shirtsleeves and wearing a green eyeshade, is seated before a typewriter at an untidy table, piled high with books. Beside him on the floor is a stuffed cat whose tail he is twisting. The meowing is heard again.* CLARK *laughs fiendishly, pours himself a stiff drink of whisky, gulps it down, and begins pecking at the typewriter. Again lightning and thunder, followed by a sharp knocking.*

Clark. Who the hell is that? [*He leans over and twists the cat's tail again. There is a wail of pain as* GEORGINA *enters, wearing a hooded cloak. Sneeringly.*] Oh, it's you, is it?

Georgina. Yes, it's me. I mean it's I.

Clark. I'm just having a little fun with kitty.

Georgina [*grimly*]. And I'm going to have a little fun with you! [*She takes a revolver from beneath her cloak and levels it at him.*]

Clark [*cowering in terror*]. No! No! Not that!

GEORGINA *fires two shots.* CLARK *shrieks and slumps to the floor. A* POLICEMAN *rushes on at the right and seizes* GEORGINA *roughly.*

Policeman. Come along, you!

Georgina [*with quiet dignity*]. All right. You needn't be rough about it. I did it and I'm willing to take the consequences.

As the POLICEMAN *takes her off the lights fade. A tumult of voices and the thumping of a gavel is heard. The lights come up at the center. A* JUDGE, *who resembles* ALLERTON, *is seated at the bench, beside which, in the witness chair,* GEORGINA *sits. The* DISTRICT ATTORNEY *and* JIM LUCAS *are seated at the counsel table.*

Judge [*banging his gavel*]. Order! Order! If there are any more demonstrations, I'll have the courtroom cleared. [*As quiet is restored.*] Proceed with your examination, Mr. District Attorney.

District Attorney [*pointing an accusing finger*]. Then you admit that you went there with the deliberate intention of killing Clark Redfield?

Georgina. Yes, I admit it. But I had every justification. He was a savage brute, a man without——

District Attorney. I object!

Judge [*banging his gavel*]. Objection sustained!

Jim [*jumping up*]. Your Honor, I protest. This young woman is on trial for her life. Is she to be railroaded to the chair without even an opportunity to speak in her own defense?

Judge. The point is well taken. Proceed, Miss Allerton.

Georgina. Well, let me just ask you this. If he had attacked me, wouldn't you all agree that I had a right——

Judge. One moment! Are we to understand that Clark Redfield attempted to——

Georgina. No, he didn't. But compared to what he did to me, it would have been easy to submit to—to—— Well, not easy, but almost preferable. He struck at my dignity, humiliated me, trampled my pride in the dust. And if you men think that an injury to a woman's body is a greater provocation to murder than an injury to her spirit, then you know nothing about feminine nature. That's all! That's my case! [*She glares about defiantly.*]

District Attorney. Your Honor, the people of the State of New York demand the death penalty!

Judge. Counsel for the defense will now address the jury. Proceed, Mr. Lucas.

Jim [*rising and addressing the unseen jury*]. Ladies and gentlemen of the jury. I speak to you not merely as counsel for Georgina Allerton but as her brother. And by that I do not refer to my accidental marital relationship to her sister, but to the deep, spiritual, fraternal bond that has long existed between the defendant and myself. I can say, in all honesty, that no one understands her as I do; no other living being has plumbed so profoundly the depths of that tender, sensitive soul. And, in the light of my knowledge and understanding, I say to you that when she struck down Clark Redfield it was no act of murder, but a simple, human gesture of self-defense. [*A murmur from the unseen jurors.*] Yes, ladies and gentlemen, self-defense! For what was this novel of hers that Clark Redfield sought to annihilate with the cruel strokes of his sharp-edged tongue and stabbing wit? It was her baby, ladies and gentlemen, the child of her spirit, as real to her and as dear to her as though it had been, indeed, the flesh-and-blood creation of her body. For it was conceived in the beautiful ecstasy of spiritual passion, nurtured for long months in the dark, secret recesses of her soul, brought forth in an agony of travail. And as it lay nestling in her bosom, so to speak, Clark Redfield struck at it with his lethal weapons! And with the noble, unerring instinct of outraged maternity, she struck back—struck back at the would-be assassin of her baby. Could any mother, could any woman, do less? I leave the answer to you. [*He sits down amid cheers and applause.*]

Judge [*pounding for order*]. What is your verdict, ladies and gentlemen of the jury?

Chorus of Unseen Jurors. Not guilty!

        The DISTRICT ATTORNEY *leaves in a huff.*

Judge. The defendant is dismissed.

Georgina [*shaking hands with him*]. Thank you, Your Honor.

Judge [*as he leaves the bench*]. Not at all. But just a word of fatherly advice, Miss Allerton. In the future, try to avoid the use of firearms.

Georgina [*earnestly*]. I will, Your Honor. [*Turning to* JIM, *as the* JUDGE *exits.*] Oh, Jim, darling, I knew I could depend on you! [*She walks toward* JIM, *but as the telephone rings in the bookshop she ignores his outstretched arms and hurries to answer it. The lights fade on the courtroom and come up, at the left, on the bookshop.*] Mermaid Bookshop. No, madam, I'm sorry; we're all out of *Always Opal*. You're welcome.

Claire [*who has entered*]. Why, what's the matter with you? You look as though you were ready to commit murder.

Georgina. Oh, it's nothing. I'm just mad at myself for losing my temper.

Claire. Who did what to you?

Georgina. It's too trivial to talk about. It's just that that Clark Redfield was in and began shooting off his face about a lot of—— Honestly, of all the brash, egotistical fools I ever met!

Claire. Well, I've only met him once or twice, but I had an idea he was kind of nice. How did he like your novel?

Georgina. Oh, I really don't know. I didn't even bother to ask him.

Claire. Sorry. Excuse it, please.

She exits. As GEORGINA *picks up the scattered books* JIM LUCAS *enters at the right.*

Jim. Hello, Georgina.

Georgina. Oh, hello, Jim.

Jim. Are you busy?

Georgina. Well, I have a lunch date at one-thirty and——

Jim. Oh, you've got lots of time.

Georgina. I was going to stop at Colette's first, to pick up a new hat she's making for me. But it doesn't matter. Sit down.

Jim [*complying*]. I have something to tell you. But maybe you heard it already from Miriam.

Georgina. You mean about your leaving Wentworth and Jones?

Jim. Oh, that, yes! Trust Miriam to waste no time in spreading it around.

Georgina. It wasn't from Miriam I heard it. Clark Redfield was just in——

Jim. Good old Clark! Always the reporter. I suppose he told you why they fired me.

Georgina. Well, he did mention something about *Always Opal*——

Jim. You don't have to be tactful. I'm not in the least bit sensitive about it. If I had it to do over again, I'd still turn that book down. It's just a piece of trash.

Georgina. Well, that's exactly what I said to Redfield.

Jim. Good for you! But what I came in to tell you is that Miriam and I are splitting up.

Georgina. Oh, no, Jim. You mustn't do that! Just because you've had some silly quarrel about losing your job——

Jim. It goes much deeper than that. We never were right for each other. She's much too down to earth for me, and I'm much too undependable for her.

Georgina. It just doesn't seem right to me. And when you get to thinking it over——

Jim. There's nothing more to think over. It's all settled, and Miriam is just as relieved about it as I am. I haven't felt so free and so hopeful in years. Well, you'd better run along to your lunch date. I just wanted to give you my version of the situation, before you heard about it from the other side of the family.

Georgina. Well, I'm glad you did.

Jim [going to her]. So am I! It's wonderful to be able to talk to somebody who has some idea of what you're getting at. One of the things I want most, Georgina, is for you and me to get back on our old footing again. I've felt a kind of restraint in you these past two years and I——

Georgina [greatly troubled]. Well, I——

Jim. Yes, it was natural enough, I suppose. But it doesn't have to be that way any more. Now we can be friends as we used to be. [*Taking her hand.*] Good-by, Georgina. I'll see you soon.

Georgina. Yes, Jim.

JIM *exits quickly.* GEORGINA, *on the verge of tears, stands looking after him.*

Claire [*entering*]. Didn't you say something about a lunch date?

Georgina [*startled*]. What? Oh, yes! [*Looking at her watch.*] Heavens, I'm going to keep him waiting again!

Claire. Somebody interesting?

Georgina [*with attempted nonchalance*]. Just George Hand.

Claire. George Hand is taking you to lunch again?

Georgina. Well, what's wrong about that? He's a book jobber and we run a bookshop——

Claire. Where do you get that "we"? Am I in on this lunch date?

Georgina. What a mind you have! Just because Mr. Hand and I happened to discover that we have a few things in common——

Claire. Which he hopes will eventually include a bed.

Georgina. Claire, will you please stop! You'll make me so self-conscious that I won't know what to say to him.

Claire. Well, if you can't think of anything else, you can always say no.

Georgina. Maybe I should phone the Canard Rouge and tell him I'm not coming. I'm terribly upset and in no mood for one of those fencing matches.

Claire. Goodness, does a little tiff with Clark Redfield make you——

Georgina. Certainly not! I've even forgotten Clark Redfield's existence. Jim Lucas was just in to tell me that he and Miriam are divorcing. Isn't that dreadful?

Claire. People do it every day, with the greatest of ease. And from where I sit, Miriam is well rid of that Jim.

Georgina. That seems to be a general opinion with which I disagree. Oh, well, I may as well have lunch with George Hand and get it over with. I'll be back as soon as I can.

Claire [*as* GEORGINA *exits at the right*]. Don't hurry! And don't say no, until after the liqueurs. [*The telephone rings.*] Mermaid Bookshop—— No, madam, I'm sorry, we're all out of *Always Opal*—— Well, we're expecting——

Her voice and the scene fade out. The lights come up at right on a semicircular upholstered booth in a corner of the Canard Rouge, a chichi midtown restaurant. GEORGINA *and* GEORGE HAND *are seated over their coffee and brandy.* HAND *is a brisk, good-looking man, getting on to forty.*
GEORGINA *is wearing a gay, plumed hat.*

Hand. Think you could manage another brandy?

Georgina. I definitely could not manage one other thing. Except maybe a cigarette.

Hand [*giving her one and lighting it for her*]. Oh, sure! What made you go on the wagon?

Georgina. Two cocktails and two brandies for lunch! Is that your idea of being on the wagon?

Hand. I used to know a girl who took three Cuba libres with breakfast.

Georgina. What interesting people you know! Did she work?

Hand. Well, not in the daytime, I guess. She was a night telephone operator. Is that bookshop keeping you busy?

Georgina. Afraid not. In fact, we've about decided to close it.

Hand. That's a good idea. What astrologer advised you to pick that grim location?

Georgina. I guess we didn't use very good judgment, did we?

Hand. I don't think you're cut out for a business career.

Georgina. That's what my partner says. But what career *am* I cut out for?

Hand. Have you tried love?

Georgina. You won't take me seriously, will you?

Hand. Sure, if I can't have you any other way.

Georgina. No, I mean it!

Hand. Well, what would be the point of both of us taking you seriously? No sense in overdoing the thing.

Georgina. You think I take myself too seriously?

Hand. Well, let's say seriously enough.

Georgina. I suppose I do. And that's bad, isn't it?

Hand. Terrible.

Georgina. Why?

Hand. Think of all the fun you miss.

Georgina. Yes, maybe I do. I've often wished that I could be just—well, just completely reckless and irresponsible, like—like—oh, I don't know who.

Hand. Like Opal?

Georgina. Well, yes, now that you mention it! Is that why everybody is so mad to read that silly book?

Hand. What are you being so snooty about? Why, that book is positively a boon to womankind! For two-fifty flat or three cents a day any Hausfrau in the land can identify herself with the most luscious yes-woman in all literature.

Georgina. Is that really what every woman wants?

Hand. All I can go by is the sales figures.

Georgina. So you think we're all harlots at heart?

Hand. Well, I wouldn't want to run for Congress on that platform.

Georgina. Still, even if you're right, there seems to be an awful lot of women who manage not to——

Hand. I know. That's what makes life so difficult for a man.

Georgina. Oh, poor Mr. Hand! Do we make things difficult for you?

Hand. Very. But I don't complain. No victory without labor, my Sunday-school teacher used to say. And, by the way, my name is George.

Georgina. Yes, George.

Hand. That's better. George and Georgina. We sound like a team of adagio dancers. I consider that very auspicious.

Georgina. I was named after my father. He's George too.

Hand. Now, don't tell me you're attracted to me because I remind you of your father.

Georgina. You don't remind me in the least of my father. And who told you that I'm attracted to you?

Hand. You know, I am really beginning to go for you in a big way. [*Shaking his head.*] I can't figure this out.

Georgina. You mean there's really something you can't figure out?

Hand. Uh-huh. Just one thing. You!

Georgina. Oh, so I'm an enigma! What fun!

Hand. No fooling, how does a girl who has all that you have happen to be so unattached?

Georgina. Maybe my virtues—no, that isn't the word! Maybe my charms aren't as apparent to everyone as they are to you.

Hand. I don't believe that! Or are you one of those girls who think they're only interested in marriage?

Georgina. I'm not in the least interested in marriage.

Hand. You're not? Why?

Georgina. Because from what I've seen of it, I think the odds are all against you.

Hand. You're so right! Well, that makes everything much simpler.

Georgina. For whom?

Hand. For you, of course. It doesn't cramp your style, doesn't limit the range of your experiences.

Georgina. Why, that's true, isn't it? You have a wonderful gift for clarifying things.

Hand. Don't be coy, Georgina. You'll never get me to believe that a sophisticated girl like you has never had any experiences.

Georgina. Well, it would be hard to believe that a sophisticated girl could get to be twenty-two without having had *some* experiences.

Hand. Then what the hell? Or does your aversion to marriage extend to men who are already married?

Georgina. I often wonder how I'd feel if I were the man's wife. Or is that very unsophisticated?

Hand. Not a bit. Does credit to your upbringing. Only Mollie isn't a bit like that. We get along fine together except when she has a drink too many and then we really go to town. Otherwise, I don't interfere with her and she doesn't interfere with me.

Georgina. That's what I mean about marriage.

Hand. I agreed with you, didn't I? But you'll admit I'm not one of the lads who comes crying for sympathy because he's so misunderstood.

Georgina. No, that's true. I knew there was *something* about you that was different.

Hand. No flattery, please! Tell me, have you ever been to Mexico?

Georgina. Thanks for changing the subject. No, I haven't been to Mexico. But I've always wanted to go.

Hand. Wonderful! But I haven't changed the subject. I have to go down next month and I've been thinking what fun it would be if you and I could sort of meet up there.

Georgina. Oh, have you?

Hand. It's a great country. I've been there before and I know my way around. We'd take in jai-alai matches and bullfights——

Georgina. I should say not!

Hand. All right, we'll stay away from bullfights. Anyhow, we'd find some village fiestas, look at the Rivera frescoes, and drift along on the flower boats at Xochimilco. And talk about food! Have you ever eaten mole?

Georgina. No, I don't think I have.

Hand. It's turkey with a sauce made of chocolate and about fifteen different kinds of pepper. Sounds revolting, doesn't it?

Georgina. It certainly does!

Hand. I'm telling you it's tops. Especially when washed down with a bottle of tequila. You've heard of Taxco, haven't you?

Georgina. Yes, of course.

Hand. Well, a friend of mine has a house there that he hardly ever uses. Up on a terraced hill, looking down onto the little village plaza. We'd have dinner in the patio and the local folks would come up and serenade us. Why, I can just see you, done up in a rebozo and——

Georgina. You *are* a salesman, aren't you?

Before HAND *can reply, a* MAN *enters at the left and goes to the right.*

Man [*as he passes the table*]. Hi, George! How are you doing? [*He waves and goes out at the right.*]

Hand. Why, hello, Bert! [*Excitedly to* GEORGINA.] This is really from the gods! You know who that is? Bert Glover, the fellow who owns the house in Taxco. [*Jumping up.*] Excuse me! I'll be right back!

Georgina. No, wait, please!

Hand. I won't be a minute!

He exits quickly at right. GEORGINA *looks after him for a moment, considerably agitated, then sits back dreamily, lost in her imaginings. As the lights fade slowly on the scene*

*the sound of singing is heard, center. The lights come up
on a corner of an exotic patio bathed in moonlight. A trio
of musical-comedy Mexicans are strumming guitars and
singing a sentimental Spanish love song. The leader of the
trio, a tall, good-looking young man, has the face of* CLARK
REDFIELD. *After a moment* GEORGINA *and* HAND *stroll on
at the right,* GEORGINA *wearing a mantilla and a bright
shawl and carrying a fan. He has his arm about her. They
stand listening to the music. The song ends, and the serenaders cover their hearts with their sombreros and bow low.*

Georgina [*clapping her hands*]. Oh, lovely, lovely! Buena!
Buena! Muchas gracias!

Hand. That was great! [*Reaching into his pocket.*]
Here's something for you, boys. [*The* LEADER *comes forward, holding out his sombrero.* HAND *drops a fistful of
coins into it.*]

Leader. Gracias, señor! Muchas gracias! Buenas noches,
señor! Buenas noches, señorita! [*He bend over* GEORGINA's
hand, and kisses it.]

Georgina. Buenas noches! Hasta la vista, caballero!

Leader. Hasta la vista, señorita! Viva los Americanos!
[*Bowing and smiling, the serenaders exit.*]

Georgina. Viva Mé-hi-co! Oh, this is really heavenly.
That wonderful moon, this clear cool air, filled with the
scent of flowers, and that charming song——

Hand. What about that charming singer? Good thing
I'm broad-minded. That young man seemed to take quite
a fancy to you.

Georgina. It's strange. There's something so familiar
about him. And yet I can't think of whom he reminds me.
[*She fans herself throughout.*]

Hand. Well, don't bother. You're supposed to be concentrating on me, you know. By the way, where did you
pick up all that Spanish? Why, you talk it like a native!

Georgina [*modestly*]. Oh, don't be silly. But I was
always good at languages, and Señor Gonzales at Berlitz
did tell me I have a good accent.

Hand. Next time you see him, you can tell him I said
you're an all-around good girl.

Georgina. Well, I'm glad you think so. Oh, that exquisite

food! Who would have believed that turkey with chocolate sauce could taste like that!

Hand. I was right about it, wasn't I?

Georgina. Indeed you were! You were right about lots of things. Only—well, I can't help thinking that tomorrow all this will end.

Hand. Georgina, there's something I want to say to you. I knew darned well that when you finally agreed to this it was only because you thought maybe I could help you forget somebody it made you unhappy to think about. It's true, isn't it?

Georgina. Yes, it's true. I was trying to escape, desperately running away from a situation I didn't know how to cope with.

Hand. Then tell me something else. Have I helped you forget?

Georgina. Yes, George, you have. That's why it's so hard— No, I won't say it!

Hand. You've said all you need to say, all I wanted to know. Georgina, I thought I had nothing more to learn about women, but I was wrong. I don't want this to be the end, but just the beginning.

Georgina. Why do you say such things, when you know it's impossible?

Hand. No, it's not impossible. In fact it's all arranged. While you were at the market this afternoon, I called up my wife. I told her I want a divorce and——

Georgina. No, I won't hear of it! I'm not one of those girls that breaks up marriages. That's one reason I've said no to every married man who——

Hand. Wait a minute! You're not breaking up any marriage. My wife jumped at the suggestion. It seems she's interested in some band leader and she had just about made up her mind to ask me for a divorce.

Georgina. Are you telling me the truth?

Hand. I couldn't lie to you. I respect you too much, and anyhow I know you're too smart for me to get away with it. Georgina, this is really from the gods! You *can't* say no!

Georgina. I—I don't know, George. You've got to give me time to think—— [*As they move right and the lights fade on the scene.*] I must have time to think! [*The lights come up slowly at the right.* GEORGINA *is seated at the table as before, lost in her dreams and fanning herself with the luncheon check. She does not see* HAND *as he hurries on at the right.*]

Hand [*coming up to the table*]. Well, we're in great luck. Everything is——

Georgina [*almost jumping out of her seat*]. Oh! Goodness, you nearly frightened me out of my wits!

Hand. Sorry! You look as though you'd been a million miles away. [*Sitting beside her.*] Listen, Georgina, I've fixed it all up with Bert.

Georgina. Bert?

Hand. Yes, about the house in Taxco. He just was down there and won't be going again for months. It's just sitting there waiting for us. Well, what do you say?

Georgina. Well, goodness, I can't give you an answer just like that!

Hand. Yes, you can! Never fight your impulses. Take it from me, the things we really regret in life are not those we do, but those we don't do.

Georgina. I've got to have time to make up my mind.

Hand. All right. How much time do you want—two days, a week?

Georgina. Do you have to pin me down like that?

Hand. Sure I do! Because when a gay time is lost, it's lost forever.

Georgina. Well, I'll—I'll think it over. [*Looking at her watch.*] Goodness, it's nearly three o'clock. I've got to get back to the shop. [*She rises.*]

Hand [*signing the check*]. And I've got a deskful of work. Can I drop you?

Georgina. No, you run along. I want to powder my nose. [*Extending her hand.*] Thanks for a marvelous lunch.

Hand [*holding her hand*]. Remember what the voice of experience is saying to you; Don't resist your impulses. Good-by! I won't leave you in peace for long!

Georgina [*as he goes off*]. Well——! [*She stands looking after him, greatly flustered. A* WAITER *enters, picks up the check, and starts to clear the table.*] Oh, do you think I could have another brandy?

Waiter. Certainly, madam. The imported?

Georgina. What? Oh, yes, the imported, by all means.

Waiter. Yes, madam. [*He goes.* GEORGINA *sits at the table.*]

Georgina [*gloomily*]. So now you're taking to drink, are you? Just like all the other misfits who can't face their problems and try to make alcohol a substitute for character. Oh, Georgina, Georgina, my girl, you're really in a bad way!

She shakes her head dolefully as the lights fade and the curtain falls.

Curtain.

ACT TWO

As the curtain rises the lights come up on the bookshop, at the left, as in Act One. CLAIRE *is straightening books on the shelves. A moment later* GEORGINA *enters, considerably exhilarated.*

GEORGINA. I'm back.

Claire. I was just about to call the Juvenile Delinquents' Court. [*Seeing* GEORGINA's *new hat.*] Well, for heaven's sake! [*She examines it at close range.*] Colette has really outdone herself.

Georgina. Like it?

Claire. I'm green with envy. How did Mr. Hand react to it?

Georgina. He was very polite about it.

Claire. Now, don't hold out on me. Come on, tell Auntie Claire everything that happened.

Georgina. Well, we ate and ate, and drank and drank, and talked and talked.

Claire. What did you talk about?

Georgina. Oh, all sorts of things. You were right about his intentions. He wants me to go to Mexico with him.

Claire. Just like that? Well, he's obviously not a man who lets the grass grow under his feet.

Georgina. No, he isn't. He's been to Mexico and knows all the places to go. Besides that, a friend of his has a house in Taxco and we could have the use of it.

Claire. But how romantic!

Georgina. It is sort of. And I've always wanted to go to Mexico.

Claire. Yes, they say that travel broadens the mind. And *he* certainly sounds like a broad-minded boy.

Georgina. Well, I must say he was nice and frank about the whole thing. He didn't try to give me any line or pretend a lot of things. He just frankly put it up to me.

Claire. Uh-huh! The direct frontal attack or appeal to the intelligence. After all, we're living in the twentieth century. Let's be modern about this thing. Very flattering.

Georgina [*removing her hat*]. I suppose so. But I prefer it to the usual line of flattery. If I'm going into something like this, I'd rather go in with my eyes open.

Claire. And are you going into it?

198

Georgina. I promised him I'd think it over.

Claire. Why, Georgina Allerton!

Georgina. Does that shock you?

Claire. Well, it just doesn't sound like you. Tell me, are you in love with him?

Georgina. Well, he's a clever, successful, good-looking man. And I am attracted to him. He's not making any demand of me, or pretending he's in love with me. If it's all right for him, why isn't it for me?

Claire. You're desperately logical about it.

Georgina. Why do men have to have a monopoly on logic?

Claire. I don't know. But somehow, when a woman falls back on logic——

Georgina. That's just a hangover from the days when women led sheltered lives. It's time we stopped being a lot of fluttery, scatterbrained little ninnies, who have to rely on something called intuition. Why can't we work out our own problems, just as men do, by using our intelligence?

Claire. It really looks as though Mr. Hand *has* been using the right technique!

Georgina. He's not fooling me with any technique. I'm thinking very clearly about the whole thing, and entirely from my own point of view. After all, what would be the harm in it? It's not so unusual these days for a girl to——

Claire. Oh, I don't think it's likely that you'd be put in the stocks and branded with a large, scarlet capital A.

Georgina. You mean I might be hurt emotionally? All right, suppose I did get hurt a little! It might be the best thing in the world for me—just what I need maybe. If I don't begin to have some experiences soon, when will I begin?

Claire. And yet I never met a girl who seemed less eager to go off on a toot with George Hand.

Georgina. He thinks I'm puritanical, and I'm afraid he may be right.

Claire. Afraid?

Georgina. Well, after all, what is a puritan? Just somebody with such strong desires that she doesn't dare let herself cut loose.

Claire. Oh, so that's what you're afraid of! You think if

you say yes to him it will just be your first step on the road to hell?

Georgina. That *would* be pretty awful, wouldn't it?

Claire. It would indeed! Well, darling, I think I'll pop out and do some shopping. Think you can look after the trade by yourself?

Georgina. Oh, damn it! I wish you'd be a little helpful.

Claire. No, my pet! This is between you and your guardian angel—and I can't wait to see who wins!

Georgina [*as* Claire *exits*]. Neither can I!

She sits lost in thought as the lights fade slowly on the scene. To the music of "Poor Butterfly," the lights come up at the center on a red fire-alarm lamppost. In the background is an illuminated sign bearing the legend "Joyland." Georgina *enters and swaggers to the lamppost. She wears a cheap red coat with a ratty fur collar and a gaudy hat perched on a tousled blond wig.* George Hand, *accompanied by a girl who resembles* Miriam, *emerges from the darkness, at the right.*

Hand [*as they cross*]. Well, Arabella, if you've never eaten at Antoine's in New Orleans, you really don't know what food is.

Arabella. Yes, so I've heard.

Hand [*glancing at* Georgina *as he passes her*]. We'd start with oysters Rockefeller, which Ford Madox Ford, who was a great epicure, describes as swimming in a kind of green scum. [*Stopping at left.*] Excuse me a moment! [*He turns and goes back to* Georgina, *who starts to go as she sees him approaching. Detaining her.*] Just a minute, please!

Georgina [*in a rough voice*]. Hands off, you!

Hand [*turning her around*]. Why, I was right! It's Georgina Allerton.

Georgina. Well, what's it *to* you?

Hand. What are you doing here, hanging around a street corner?

Georgina. Looking after my trade, that's what!

Hand. But—a girl like you! What's brought you to this?

Georgina. It would give you a kick, wouldn't it, to hear all about it? You're all like that!

Hand. But in Mexico you were such a gay, proud girl,

full of the joy of living; and dreaming of all the things you were going to do.

Georgina [*harshly*]. I didn't know how easy it would be to say yes, the next time someone asked me. And the next time after that, it was easier still. Then they stopped asking me—and I began asking them. Now you know all about it. So, go ahead and scram.

Hand. Georgina, if there's anything I can——

Georgina. To hell with that! I don't want your pity.

Hand. Well, let me, at least—— [*He takes a bill from his pocket and offers it to her.* GEORGINA *snatches it and tears it up.*]

Georgina. Go on, now! Beat it! Your girl friend is waiting for you! [HAND *sighs, shakes his head, and goes left.*]

Arabella [*as he rejoins her*]. For heaven's sake, what was that all about?

Hand [*as they exit*]. It's tragic. I used to know that girl, years ago. And believe it or not, she was a sweet, modest little——

His voice trails off. The tune changes to "Broadway Rose." GEORGINA *buries her face in her hands and sobs, then as she hears a man whistling off right, she straightens up and resumes her place at the lamppost.* CLARK REDFIELD *strides on, whistling merrily. He glances quickly at* GEORGINA *as he passes her.*

Georgina. Got a date for tonight, dearie?

Clark. Sorry, baby, but I've got a little wife waiting for me. [*He is about to exit, then stops and turns.*] Say, haven't I seen you somewhere before?

Georgina [*brazenly*]. Have you?

Clark. Why, sure enough! You're that girl who used to run that crummy little bookshop on East——! Well, I'll be dammed!

Georgina [*savagely*]. What the hell's so funny about it?

Clark. Why, who'd have thought it? Little Miss—whatever your name is! The budding literary genius, the highly cultivated young college grad, who lectured me about my manners and thought sportswriting was vulgar. Well, it looks like you're doing a little in the sporting line yourself.

Georgina. Shut up, you great big ape! [*She slaps his face.*]

Clark [*in a rage*]. Oh, that's how you feel about it, is it? Well, I'll show you! There's a place for tramps like you. [*He goes left.*] Officer! Officer!

He disappears in the darkness. GEORGINA *looks about in terror, then opens her handbag, takes out a small bottle, and drains it. The tune changes to "Hearts and Flowers."*

Jim [*off right*]. Georgina! Stop! For God's sake, stop! [*He rushes on.*]

Georgina [*with a wan smile, as she throws the bottle away*]. You're too late, Jim. Nothing can save me, now.

Jim. Why have you done this, Georgina? Why didn't you come to me? I would have——

Georgina. No, Jim, I couldn't do that. You have Miriam and those three lovely children. Once I brought you two together again, there was no place for me in your life. There's no place for me anywhere. [*She totters.*] Hold me, Jim, hold me! I'm—— [*She collapses into his arms.*]

Jim. Georgina, I——

Georgina [*faintly*]. Don't say anything, Jim. Just hold me. I wanted to live in your arms, but it wasn't meant to be. So let me die in them. It's the only happiness I'll ever know now. Good-by, Jim. Kiss Mother and Dad for me. And ask them to forgive me. And try not to forget me, Jim. There was never anybody for me but you——

Jim. I'll never forget you—never!

Georgina. Thank you, Jim. Good-by, darling. [*Standing erect for a moment.*] It is a far, far better thing that I do than I have ever done. It is a far, far better rest I go to than I have ever known. [*She clasps her abdomen in agony, pivots on her heels, and falls inert.*]

Jim [*kneeling beside her*]. Georgina! Georgina, my darling!

CLARK *reappears at left, accompanied by a* POLICEMAN.

Policeman. Is that her?

Clark. Yes, she accosted me! She's nothing but a common—— My God, what's happened to her?

Jim [*looking up*]. She's gone where no one can harm her now.

Clark [*removing his hat*]. You mean she's——?

Jim. Yes, Clark Redfield, she is.

Clark [*with an agonized cry*]. Oh, no! Oh, why did I do it? If only I'd been a little human to her! [*Turning to the* POLICEMAN.] Officer, arrest me! Take me away!

Policeman. What for?

Clark. I'm a murderer. I killed that girl as surely as though I had stabbed her to the heart.

Policeman. Then come along!

He snaps handcuffs on CLARK *as the light fades on the scene and the clanging of a patrol-wagon bell is heard. The sound merges into that of a ringing telephone. The lights come up left on the bookshop.* GEORGINA, *seated moodily, is startled by the ringing of the telephone. She hurries to it and answers it.*

Georgina [*greatly flustered*]. Hello! Mermaid Bookshop!

As she speaks, the lights come up, stage right, on a telephone booth in which CLARK REDFIELD *is standing.*

Clark. Is Miss Allerton there?

Georgina. This is she.

Clark. Oh, I didn't recognize your voice. You sound scared to death.

Georgina [*sharply*]. Who is this, please?

Clark. Clark Redfield.

Georgina [*who knew it all along*]. Oh, it's you, is it? Well, what is it?

Clark. I want to ask you to——

Georgina. I don't care to hear any apologies. The whole thing is of no consequence whatever. I was foolish to let my temper get the better of me. And, as far as I'm concerned, the whole incident is closed.

Clark. Yes, you have got a temper, haven't you? But are you under the impression that I called up to apologize for something?

Georgina. Well, I guess that's foolish too—to expect you to have that much graciousness. Look, I'm quite busy and if you don't mind——

Clark. I'll bet you haven't done a thing all afternoon.

Georgina. If you'll excuse me, Mr. Redfield——

Clark. Whoa! Wait a minute! Don't hang up on me! I'm calling to ask you——

Georgina. Well, what? Please get to the point, will you?

Clark. I've got a pair of tickets for a show tonight and I thought you might like to——

Georgina. Well, of all the unmitigated——! You really *have* got the hide of an elephant. What makes you think I'd consider——

Clark. Well, it's the opening of *The Merchant of Venice,* with James Zerney as Shylock. And I thought that might appeal to a lover of the classics.

Georgina. Well, under ordinary circumstances, it certainly would. Especially with Hilda Vincent playing Portia; but I'm afraid——

Clark. Is she a favorite of yours?

Georgina. It just happens that we went to college together and——

Clark. Good! Then it's a date!

Georgina [*indignantly*]. It certainly is *not* a date! But thank you all the same, though I can't imagine why you——

Clark. I can't either. It was just an impulse and I——

Georgina. You don't strike me as the impulsive type. I should rather think of you as decidedly calculating.

Clark. All right. What do you say we settle for a calculated impulse? [*As the operator cuts in.*] All right, just a minute!

Georgina. What's that?

Clark [*fishing in his pockets*]. The operator wants another nickel.

Georgina. Well, there's no necessity for prolonging——

Clark. No, wait a minute, Georgina! No, I'm not talking to you, operator. Listen, I haven't got a nickel, operator. [*Flourishing a bill.*] Can you change five dollars for me? Well, where's all that service you people do so much advertising about? Just a second! Look, Georgina, call me back, will you?

Georgina. I have nothing further to——

Clark. No, call me back! The number is Circle 5-7933. Hello! Hello! Oh, damn it! [*He bangs down the receiver, leans back in the booth, and lights a cigarette.*]

Georgina. I tell you I—hello! [*She hangs up and slowly jots down the number on a pad. Then she sits staring at the telephone. She raises her forefinger as though to dial,*

then lowers it again. The phone rings and she jumps. Pick-ing up the phone.] I thought you didn't have another——
The lights come up quickly at the center on GEORGE HAND, *seated at his desk, and talking into the telephone. Through-out,* CLARK *keeps looking at his telephone, waiting for it to ring.*

Hand. Hello? Is that you, Georgina?

Georgina. Yes. Who is this? [*Knowing full well.*]

Hand. This is George. Anything wrong? You sound jumpy.

Georgina. It must be all those brandies. I'm not used to——

Hand. Why, I'll have to put you back in training. Look, honey, a business dinner date just blew up on me, so I thought maybe you'd take pity on a poor guy with an evening on his hands and——

Georgina [*nervously*]. Oh, I really don't think I can tonight, George—— [CLARK *is beginning to get impatient.*]

Hand. We can take our time over a nice dinner some-where and then go dancing—or to a show, if you'd rather.

Georgina. I only wish I could. If you'd only called up a half-hour sooner! I just promised somebody I'd go to the theater.

Hand. Tough luck! But I called the minute I knew I'd be free. Why don't you get out of it?

Georgina. I don't see how, after just saying yes ten minutes ago.

Hand. Well, then, how about cocktails and dinner? Or a drink after the show?

Georgina. I'm afraid that's all included.

Hand. Say, who is this monopolist? I'll sic the Attorney General on him!

Georgina. It's nothing like that. Just one of those things that you get into and can't get out of.

Hand. Well, try to get out of at least some part of it. I do want to see you.

Georgina. All right, I'll try my best.

Hand. Shall I call you back?

Georgina. No, I'm just leaving. If I can fix it, I'll call you. [CLARK *leaves the booth and starts to exit, then changes his mind and comes back.*]

Hand. Well, I'll keep my fingers crossed. Because I've got you very much on my mind. And if I do lose tonight, I'll owe you lunch tomorrow—yes?

Georgina. All right! Good-by, George. And thanks.

Hand. Good-by, dear.

He hangs up and the lights fade out quickly on him. GEORGINA *hangs up and leans back with a deep sigh. Then she stares at the telephone number, hesitates a moment, then starts slowly to dial.*

Clark [*with sudden anger*]. Oh, to hell with it! [*He leaves the booth and strides off right. The phone in the booth rings, then again and once again.* GEORGINA, *very much annoyed, is about to hang up, but* CLARK *comes tearing back and picks up the phone in the booth just in time.*] Hello! Is that you?

Georgina. Well, you certainly took your time about answering.

Clark. I fell asleep waiting for you to call. What's the matter, have you got telephone operator's cramp or something?

Georgina. I happened to have another call. You seem to forget I'm running a business.

Clark. Running conveys an idea of activity.

Georgina. The only reason I called back is that I don't want you to have the false impression that I'm sufficiently interested in anything you may have said, this morning or at any other time, to make me feel the slightest bit of resentment.

Clark [*whistling*]. Phew! I was afraid you were never going to get to the end of that one! Now, to get back to *The Merchant of Venice*——

Georgina. Yes, exactly. In the first place, I have no interest whatever in being taken to the theater by you. But I *would* like to see Hilda Vincent play Portia, so——

Clark. Right! So you'll go.

Georgina. Will you please let me finish?

Clark. If you think you can by eight-forty.

Georgina. What I started to say is that I'll consider it only on a strictly business basis.

Clark. I have a feeling that neither of us knows what you're talking about.

Georgina. What I mean is that if you have an extra ticket on your hands, I'll be glad to buy it from you.

Clark. Can't be done. These are press seats.

Georgina [*interestedly*]. Oh, are you going to review the play?

Clark. I am not. I got them from our movie critic. His mother is getting married tonight and he has to give her away.

Georgina. Do the movie critics get tickets for plays too?

Clark. Look, Georgina, this is one of those phones where you have to stand up. How about meeting me at——

Georgina. Are you dressing?

Clark. Certainly not! Nobody dresses for Shakespeare, unless Bea Lillie happens to be in it.

Georgina. Then I'll meet you in the lobby at eight-thirty. Unless you want to leave the ticket with the ticket-taker.

Clark. No, I don't! How about dinner?

Georgina. I'll have dinner somewhere.

Clark. You're a resourceful girl. I think I'll do likewise. Maybe we could have it at the same place—purely by coincidence, of course.

Georgina. Thank you, but I don't care to——

Clark. Look, one of the things I don't like to do is eat alone. It makes me feel so unwanted. You don't have to say a word. I'll do all the talking. And you can read a book or sulk in your beer or whatever you like.

Georgina. Well—only if it's clearly understood that we go Dutch.

Clark. I was thinking of going Italian. Do you know Emilio's?

Georgina. No, I don't.

Clark. Well, it's just a spaghetti and red ink joint, but what would be called, in France, a serious house. They have——

Georgina. There's no reason why you should take me to dinner and I——

Clark. There are two reasons—both valid from my point of view. The first is that that five bucks I got from you is burning a hole in my pocket. And the second is that I have something to celebrate.

Georgina. Well, I'm afraid I haven't.

Clark. All right then, you can watch *me* celebrate. Listen, I'm getting acute claustrophobia. Emilio's at seven.

Georgina. I don't know why I'm doing this.

Clark. Good! That will give you something to brood over at dinner while I talk. I'm hanging up now.

Georgina. Just a minute! Where is this Emilio's?

Clark. Oh, yes, you may as well know *that.* Forty-seventh, just west of Eighth. Good-by!

Georgina. Oh, just one other thing—— [*Then, hastily, as* JIM *enters.*] All right, Emilio's at seven. [*She hangs up. The light fades quickly on* CLARK. *Flustered.*] Oh, hello, Jim!

Jim. Yes, here I am, back again. But only to ask you if you can have dinner with me.

Georgina. Oh, I'm sorry, Jim! I just this minute made a date. Maybe I can break it—only I'm not sure that I know where to——

Jim. That's too bad. I was hoping we could——

Georgina. How about lunch tomorrow? I have a sort of tentative date, but I guess I can get out of it.

Jim. I won't be here tomorrow. I'm leaving for Reno tonight.

Georgina. You're going to Reno? But I thought you said Miriam——

Jim. Yes, I've had another session with Miriam. She made a great to-do about being separated from her obstetrician, so I said I'd go. Georgina, I've got something very important to say to you, and since I have only these few minutes, you'll forgive me if I seem blunt about it.

Georgina. Well, what is it?

Jim. Well, I came here this morning, without knowing why; it was sheer impulse. But now I do know why. It was because it's you I've always wanted, because unconsciously I've always been reaching out for you.

Georgina [*greatly agitated*]. You're just imagining all that. It's the way people always behave when they're going through an emotional crisis.

Jim. Yes, I knew you'd say that. You think I'm just turning to you on the bounce. But it isn't so, and I know

now that you're the answer to everything I want and need. Does that make you unhappy?

Georgina. Oh, no, Jim. Not unhappy. It's just that this is the last thing in the world I was expecting.

Jim. Well, if it disturbs you so, it must mean that you have some deep feeling for me too. Does it, Georgina? Please be honest with me.

Georgina. All right! I will be honest! Yes, I do care for you. I always have, ever since I've known you.

Jim. Then why are you so troubled about it?

Georgina. Because I'm afraid you may feel quite differently about it, sitting out there in Reno for six weeks with plenty of time to think it over. Why don't we wait and see if you still feel the same way when you come back to New York?

Jim. I'm not coming back to New York. I've had enough of cities and the treadmill life you have to lead in them. I want to be able to breathe for once. I'm going to find myself a place where I can see the stars and smell the earth.

Georgina. Yes, I've often dreamed of that. Just running off somewhere, anywhere—and with you too!

Jim. Then why don't you get on that plane with me tonight?

Georgina. It's not as simple as all that, Jim. People daydream about all sorts of things. But when you're faced with actuality, you have to stop and think. If a man and woman are going to spend their lives together, they must have some plan, some way of living.

Jim. Of course they do. But why can't it be a simple one? Why can't we get ourselves a little farm, or a ranch? We'll work the land together, and work at other things too. I've always wanted to paint, and you have your writing——

Georgina. No, I don't think I want to go on with that. Clark Redfield says my novel is a piece of tripe.

Jim. Why do you pay any attention to him? I'll back my judgment of that book to the limit. It expresses all the things that you and I believe in, and beautifully too. Georgina, if you feel that you'd rather not go with me now, promise me at least that you'll come out and join me when I've got my decree.

Georgina. It all means too much to me, Jim, to be able to say yes, just like that. First, I want to be absolutely sure that this is right for both of us.

Jim. Well, I'm completely confident about your decision, because I know that this is meant to be. Well, I've got to run along now and pick up my ticket. I wish I could see you again, before I leave, if only for a moment.

Georgina. So do I. But I'm afraid I won't be free until after the theater.

Jim. Well, my plane doesn't leave until one. Why don't you meet me at the air terminal about twelve and ride out to the airport with me? [*The telephone rings.*]

Georgina [*going to the telephone*]. Excuse me, Jim. Mermaid Bookshop.

As she answers the telephone the lights go up at right on Mrs. Allerton, *seated at the telephone in her negligee, as in Act One. A book is beside her.*

Mrs. Allerton. I have some news for you, Georgina.

Georgina. Oh, just a minute, please. [*Covering the transmitter.*] All right, Jim. I'll be at the air terminal at twelve.

Jim. Thank you, Georgina. [*He presses her free hand and exits.*]

Georgina. I'm sorry, Mother. I had to get rid of a customer.

Mrs. Allerton. That's right. Don't encourage them. Tell me, have you heard from Miriam?

Georgina. No, I haven't.

Mrs. Allerton. Jim either?

Georgina. No, why? Is anything wrong?

Mrs. Allerton. On the contrary. They're divorcing. Jim is leaving for Reno tonight. Miriam didn't want to go, and since Jim is at leisure again, we decided to ship him out. Of course, I'm footing the bills; but this is one expenditure poor old Grandpa would certainly have approved of.

Georgina. Well, I don't approve. I think it's awful.

Mrs. Allerton. I expected you would. That's why I'm calling you—to warn you not to try to upset things, in case Jim comes crying to you.

Georgina. What makes you think he has any intention of doing that?

Mrs. Allerton. Just a hunch. I suspect that it's you he's always been in love with. [*She sneezes.*]

Georgina. Why, Mother, how can you say things like that!

Mrs. Allerton. Well, maybe it's just this irritation of my mucous membrane that makes me think so. But, if he does turn up, be careful not to say anything that will keep him off that plane. I only hope and pray that he's subject to airsickness. [*A sneeze.*] Well, now that everything is settled I can get back to Opal. I certainly do envy that girl.

Georgina. Really, Mother!

Mrs. Allerton. I just don't understand how she can spend so much time without any clothes on and not catch her death of cold. Well, good-by.

Georgina. Oh, I won't be home till late. I'm having dinner out and going to the opening of *The Merchant of Venice*—and somewhere else afterward.

Mrs. Allerton. Oh, I hope there's a promising male involved.

Georgina. No, there isn't. It's just a boorish, conceited newspaperman in whom nobody could have the slightest interest.

Mrs. Allerton. Sounds like a charming evening.

Georgina. Well, I haven't been to a first night in years. Besides, Hilda Vincent is playing Portia and I want to see her.

Mrs. Allerton. What is there in it for the young man?

Georgina. I don't know. I haven't any idea why he asked me, except that he's sadistic and is planning to spend the evening making me feel uncomfortable.

Mrs. Allerton. Well, it certainly looks as though Mr. Right had come along at last. Well, have fun.

As she hangs up the lights fade on her. GEORGINA *hangs up. She sits for a moment, steeped in gloom, then rises and picks up her hat.*

Georgina [*looking at the hat*]. No, not for that uncouth person.

She replaces the hat on the desk and exits. The lights fade on the scene and come up at the center, on CLARK, *seated at a table in Emilio's, a modest Italian restaurant. He is munching a bread stick and listening to a Caruso record.*

Georgina [*entering as the record comes to an end*]. Sorry to be late.

Clark [*half rising*]. Okay. I was just listening to Caruso and wondering if you'd decided to stand me up.

Georgina [*sitting at the table*]. That doesn't happen to be my way of doing things.

Clark. All right. Let's not start fighting right away. We have the whole evening ahead of us. [*Calling.*] Oh, Luigi!

Luigi [*entering*]. Yes, Meester Redfield.

Clark. I think we'll order now. [*To* GEORGINA.] How about a drink first?

Georgina. I'd like a Martini.

Clark. Not with good Italian food. Look, do you mind if I do the ordering?

Georgina. Of course not! You know what I want much better than I do.

Clark. Now you're talking sense! All right, Luigi, we'll have a mixed Vermouth to start with—two parts dry and one part sweet, frappéed and with a slice of lemon peel.

Luigi. Okay, Meester Redfield. And some antipasto?

Clark. No, not all that miscellaneous stuff. Just those little bitter olives and some prosciutto.

Luigi. Then a little minestrone?

Georgina. Not for me, thanks. I'm on a diet and I had a huge lunch.

Clark [*to* LUIGI]. Yes, let's have minestrone. Then some spaghetti.

Luigi. Marinara?

Clark. No, Bolognese. And then how about a nice scallopini à la Parmigiana?

Luigi. Ees very good!

Clark. No, wait a minute! Let's have the scallopini à la Marsala. And eggplant Parmigiana with it.

Luigi. Okay.

Georgina. I hope you're not ordering all this for me, because I really——

Clark [*ignoring her*]. And a mixed green salad. Any zuppe Inglese tonight?

Luigi. I think so.

Clark. Well, save a couple portions for us.

Georgina [*tartly*]. You already ordered soup!

Clark. Soup? Oh, you mean zuppe Inglese. Yes, literally English soup, but actually a kind of rum cake. What they call trifle in England. Depend on the English to make any kind of food sound unappetizing.

Luigi. And about the wine. Some Chianti? Or maybe Lacrime Cristi?

Clark. Have you got any of that Falerno left?

Luigi. I guess we got a few bottles.

Clark. Let's have that. All right, I think that's all for the present.

Luigi. Okay, Meester Redfield. [*He exits.*

Georgina. What are we going to do with all that when it comes?

Clark. Eat it. I'm not sure that the Falerno is better than the Lacrime Cristi, but it gives me a kick to drink a wine that is a lineal descendant of the Falernian of ancient Rome. Attica nectareum turbatis mella Falernum. Honey of Attica make thick the nectar-like Falernian. I forget who said it. Do you know?

Georgina. No, I don't. I went in for modern languages. Spanish and——

Clark. I tried that once, thickening the wine with honey. But maybe I had the wrong formula. Or maybe the Romans had different tastes. So you're a friend of Hilda Vincent's?

Georgina. Well, not a friend, exactly. We just happened to be at college together. So, naturally, I've always been interested in her work.

Clark. I know, the old school tie.

Georgina. Besides, I once played Portia.

Clark. You what?

Georgina. It was our high-school graduation play. Of course, it was only an amateur production, but I don't think I did too badly. I still know the whole thing by heart. At that time I wanted very much to become an actress.

Clark. Well, why didn't you?

Georgina. Oh, I don't know. My father wanted me to be a lawyer, so I just went along with that for a while. I even tried one semester at law school. [*Sighing.*] And now, of course, it's too late to do anything about acting.

Clark. So you turned to literature?

Georgina. Let's keep off that subject, if you don't mind.

Clark. Which reminds me that I've brought back your novel. [*He produces a large envelope from under the table.*]

Georgina [*tartly*]. That's very thoughtful of you, I'm sure. But it might have been a little more practical to have brought it back tomorrow, instead of lugging it all through dinner and theater.

Clark. Aren't you forgetting that you told me never to enter your shop again?

Georgina [*tight-lipped*]. You could have mailed it.

Clark [*weighing the envelope in his hand*]. A heck of a lot of postage. And suppose some little postal inspector had peeped into it? Those poor devils have a hard enough life as it is.

Georgina. You said you were celebrating something tonight. Did some friend of yours die?

Clark. Well, it's almost as good as that. Oliver Quinn is leaving the paper.

Georgina. I suppose I *should* know who Oliver Quinn is.

Clark. Yes, you certainly should. He writes one of the three best sports columns in the country.

Georgina. Excuse my ignorance. But I never read the sports page——

Clark. Yes, so you told me. But several million other people do. Of course, most of them are not important people, but still, as you'll hear Portia say, later in the evening, God made them, so therefore let them pass for men. Well, anyhow, Oliver is leaving the paper to take the chair of Icelandic literature at the University of Michigan. That means promotions all along the line and an opening at the bottom, which the chief says is for me. [*As* Luigi *enters.*] And here, opportunely, is Luigi, so we'll drink to my good luck. [*He picks up the glass which* Luigi *has set before him.* Luigi *exits.*]

Georgina [*picking up her glass*]. Well, if you consider it good luck——

Clark. I do indeed, and thanks for the toast.

Georgina [*savoring the drink*]. This is quite good.

Clark. Careful! Don't commit yourself. These olives go well with it.

Georgina [*taking one*]. Thank you.

Clark. And try a little of this raw ham. [*He helps her to some.*]

Georgina. I hope it doesn't give us trichinosis.

Clark. What in hell is that?

Georgina. It's a horrible intestinal disorder you get from eating undercooked pork.

Clark. Really? Well, if we do get it, it will probably be the only thing we'll ever have in common, so let's go to it. [*He takes a large mouthful.*]

Georgina. I didn't believe that you were serious, this morning, about wanting to be a sportswriter.

Clark. If I have a fault, Georgina, it's that I incline to the serious side.

Georgina. I can't understand it. People getting all excited about which team scores the most runs or who knocks out who.

Clark. Nothing hard about that. Every time the champ comes up with a haymaker, forty thousand customers are taking a swing at the boss or the traffic cop. And when the King of Swat whams it into the bleachers, a million flat-chested runts are right in there, whizzing around the bases.

Georgina. That's nothing but escapism.

Clark. That's right. Like the girls out of college who slam the door with Nora, take a nose dive into the brook with Ophelia, or tumble into a lot of Louis Quatorze beds with Opal.

Georgina. We'll just pass over the personal implications and confine ourselves to the abstract question whether an interest in sports and an interest in literature——

Clark. There is no such thing as an abstract discussion between a man and a woman.

Georgina. Well, *that* certainly reveals a narrow and conventional mind.

Clark. Who's getting personal now? You see, every road we take leads right back to that novel of yours.

Georgina. Will you stop harping on that? What's my novel got to do——! I was certainly an idiot ever to show it to you.

Clark. But you did! And the reason you did was that

you thought you'd produced something creative and wanted to show it off.

Georgina. Nothing of the kind! I mistook you for a literary critic and I wanted——

Clark. Baloney! You were just a fond mamma, showing off her baby and blindly oblivious to the fact that it was just an old rag doll with the straw stuffing coming through. Talk about escapism! Why, there isn't a genuine moment in it—just a rehash of all the lady writers from Jane Austen to Virginia Woolf.

Georgina. All right, I've heard enough about that!

Clark. That's what you think! My God, can't a girl who's been around for twenty-three or -four years find——

Georgina. Twenty-two, if you don't mind.

Clark. I don't mind a bit. If you want to write, can't you produce something better than a lot of moony day-dreaming about an idiotic young couple who can't bear escalators and modern plumbing and who go off to the great open spaces to live in simple, unwashed happiness among the mosquitoes and shad flies? There's a tasty dish for you—*Love Among the Heifers*: a pastoral in nine cantos, with costumes by Abercrombie and Fitch.

Georgina. Anything can be made to sound silly, if you're stupid and literal about it. I happened to be writing a fantasy, about two sensitive people who find themselves hemmed in by the steel and stone of the city, and who can find freedom only in——

Clark. Skip it! Can you imagine any girl in her right mind behaving the way that heroine of yours does?

Georgina. Yes, I can. If she cared enough about the man, why wouldn't she be willing to give up a lot of meaningless things for him?

Clark. What! And go tooting off to some nebulous never-never land with that balmy Jim Lucas of a character.

Georgina. What's Jim Lucas got to do with it?

Clark. That just slipped out. But it's not so far off, at that. No wonder he thinks the story is a world-beater. Why, I'm beginning to think that maybe he sat for that portrait.

Georgina. I hope I'm not so literal-minded that I have to write about——

Clark. I know! I know! Why bother to step outside and

look at life, when it's so cozy indoors and there's always a
shelf full of books handy? For God's sake, hasn't anything
ever happened to you? Have you never been drunk? Or
socked a guy for making a pass at you? Or lost your panties
on Fifth Avenue?

Georgina. You think you're going to make me lose my
temper, don't you? Well, I'm sorry to disappoint you, but
you're not. However, I do find you even more offensive
than I had expected, so, if you'll excuse me, I think I'll just
leave you to your splendid repast, while I—— [*She starts
to rise.*]

Clark [*pushing her back into her seat*]. You'll certainly
do nothing of the kind! I told you I don't like eating alone.
And what's more, I'm going to protect these friends of
mine here. They're artists: the preparation and serving of
food is a serious business to them. [*As* LUIGI *enters.*] Here's
Luigi now, with the minestrone and a dusty bottle of
Falerno. Do you think I'm going to have his feelings lacer-
ated by having you walk out on the soup course? No! It's
time you learned some manners.

Georgina [*aghast*]. I beg your pardon! And to think that
I turned down two other invitations to——!

Clark. Well, that was your mistake. Just as it was my
mistake to pass up the Wilinski-O'Connell fight at the
Garden. But since we are here, you'll just have to see it
through. You can say or do whatever you like to me, but
I will not allow Emilio's minestrone to be slighted.

Luigi [*smiling, as he starts to serve the soup*]. Ees nice
and hot.

Georgina [*with great self-restraint*]. Very well, I shall
eat the minestrone.

Luigi. A leetle cheese, mees?

Georgina. No, thank you.

Luigi [*distressed*]. Oh, ees no good weedout cheese.

Georgina. Well, just a little then. [*As he serves her.*]
Thank you, that's very nice.

Clark. A lot for me, Luigi.

Luigi [*beaming*]. Sure ting, Meester Redfield! [*He serves*
CLARK *and goes for the wine.*]

Clark. They really do a beautiful minestrone here, don't
they? [GEORGINA *eats her soup without replying.*] You'd

think I owned the joint, wouldn't you, the way I go on? You ought to eat here three or four times a week and build yourself up. You're too damned skinny. [*She throws him a look but does not reply.*] Personally, I find the natural curves of the female body quite appealing. [*As* Luigi *approaches with the wine bottle.*] Ah, here we are! Luigi, did you know that the ancient Romans drank this wine?

Luigi. No, I didn't know. I come from Napoli. [*He fills the glasses and goes.*]

Clark [*sniffing the wine*]. I want you to taste this. But finish your soup first. I'm glad to see you concentrating on your dinner. I can't stand girls who are so busy gabbing that they just pick at their food.

GEORGINA *throws him a withering look. Apparently oblivious of it, he tears off a morsel of bread and pops it into his mouth. As they go on eating their soup the lights fade slowly on the scene. To the sound of a string quartet playing Elizabethan music, the lights come up dimly at the left on a section of a theater, consisting of eight or ten seats arranged in three rows. The seats face right and the stage of the theater is presumably off right, beyond the proscenium arch. The aisle of the theater runs right and left, downstage of the seats. All the seats are occupied, except the aisle pair in the first and third rows. After a moment an* USHER *enters at left, followed by* CLARK *and* GEORGINA. CLARK *has* GEORGINA's *script tucked under his arm.*

Usher [*stopping at the third row*]. First two on the aisle.

She hands CLARK *the stubs and programs and exits left.* GEORGINA *takes the second seat and* CLARK *the one on the aisle.*

Georgina. Well, I'm glad we're not late. I hate to come in after the curtain is up.

Clark. I knew a girl who was dropped from the Social Register for admitting that she had seen the first act of a play. She finally put an end to herself, by taking an overdose of caviar.

Georgina. Why do they come to the theater at all?

Clark. It fills that awkward gap between liqueurs and highballs.

Georgina. Please don't mention food or drink again!

Clark. Good dinner, wasn't it?

Georgina. Oh, yes, the dinner was fine.

Clark. There's some reservation there.

Georgina [*looking at her program*]. That's lovely music. I wonder what it is.

Clark. Sounds like Purcell.

Georgina [*finding it in the program*]. Why it *is* Purcell!

Clark. Sorry! I always seem to be saying the wrong thing.

Georgina. It's certainly a mystery to me—— [*She breaks off.*]

Clark. Oh, come on! Say it!

Georgina. Well, it's just that I don't understand why a person who knows as much as you do has so little knowledge of human nature.

Clark. You mean I have no knowledge of your nature?

Georgina. I mean anybody's nature! Either that or what's even worse, you take pleasure in making people feel uncomfortable.

Clark. What are you uncomfortable about?

Georgina. How would you like it if I had spent the whole evening harping on your shortcomings?

Clark. I might have found it very instructive.

Georgina. There you go again—implying that I am afraid to hear about my deficiencies. That's not what I meant at all.

Clark. Then what did you mean?

Georgina. I mean that there are ways of saying things. No sensible person objects to having things pointed out in a——

Clark. I see! We're back again on destructive versus constructive criticism.

Georgina. Yes, we are. It's one thing to be told, in a friendly spirit, how you might improve yourself in certain respects——

Clark. In other words, you like to hear about your faults in a way that highlights your virtues.

Georgina. If I listened to you, I'd soon believe that I didn't have any virtues. I don't know anything. I can't do anything. I'm just a total loss. Luckily, I don't attach any importance to your opinion of me.

Clark. Is that why you keep bringing it up?

Georgina [*indignantly*]. Well, what do you think I am, some kind of a jellyfish that's just going to sit and let you——

Clark. If you'd ever tangled with a jellyfish you'd know they're anything but submissive creatures.

She buries her nose in the program. The Usher *comes down the aisle, followed by* George Hand *and a* Young Woman *in a spectacular evening gown. The* Usher *stops beside the unoccupied row.*

Usher. These two.

Hand [*as the* Usher *exits*]. Thank you! [*Seeing* Georgina *and going up to her.*] Why, hello, Georgina! Fancy meeting you here!

Georgina. Why, hello, George! [Clark *rises.*]

Hand. This is Miss Delehanty. Tessie, Miss Allerton.

Miss Delehanty. Hi!

Georgina. How do you do? And this is Mr. Redfield. Miss Delehanty, Mr. Hand.

Miss Delehanty [*to* Clark]. Hi!

Hand [*shaking hands with* Clark]. Are you the Redfield who writes those book reviews?

Clark [*eying* Miss Delehanty]. Afraid so.

Georgina. But he doesn't read the books.

Hand [*laughing*]. Well, thank God for that! Think of what he'd say if he did read them. Well, I guess we'd better settle down, Tessie.

Miss Delehanty. Yeah! [*She and* Hand *sit in the first row.*]

Clark [*sotto voce*]. What's his name—Hand?

Georgina. George Hand. He's one of the biggest book jobbers in——

Clark. Oh, yes! I thought it rang a bell somewhere.

Georgina. Something wrong about it?

Clark. No. Not a thing. If books must be sold, there must be people to sell them. I'll bet he catches hell from Tessie, when she finds out this isn't a musical. Well, I guess that accounts for *one* of the dinner dates you turned down.

Georgina. Yes, it does. And I almost wish I hadn't.

Clark. Why did you?

Georgina. Because I already had accepted your invitation.

Clark. You could have called me off.

Georgina. Well, that is certainly a gracious remark! As a matter of fact, I would have, if I'd known where to reach you.

Clark. Always call the paper. If I'm not there, somebody's likely to know where I am.

Georgina. I'll remember that—but I doubt that I'll ever have any need for the information.

Clark. They say this Hand is quite a chaser.

Georgina. Do they? Well, I wouldn't know about that.

Clark. I thought you might.

Georgina. What made you think that?

Clark. I don't know. I get hunches like that sometimes. I have Indian blood in me.

Georgina. Well, in the future I wish you would please—— [*The music comes to an end amid scattered applause.*]

Clark [*applauding*]. Sh! Curtain going up!

The lights dim, except that GEORGINA's *and* CLARK's *faces remain brightly lighted. They look off right, where a glow is now visible as the curtain presumably rises. There is scattered applause followed by a flourish of trumpets, and then the voices of the unseen actors of* The Merchant of Venice *are heard off right.*

Antonio.   In sooth, I know not why I am so sad:
           It wearies me; you say it wearies you;
           But how I caught it, found it, or came by it,
           What stuff 'tis made of, whereof it is born,
           I am to learn;
           And such a want-wit sadness makes of me,
           That I have much ado to know myself.

Salarino. Your mind is tossing on the ocean;
           There, where your argosies with portly sail,
           Like signiors and rich burghers on the flood,
           Or, as it were, the pageants of the sea,
           Do overpeer the petty traffickers
           That curtsy to them, do them reverence,
           As they fly by them with their woven wings.

During the latter part of SALARINO's *speech, his words grow fainter, as* GEORGINA's *attention wanders from the stage.*

She sits staring into space, and only a distant murmur of voices is now heard. After a moment the theater MANAGER, *wearing a dinner jacket and looking for all the world like* MR. ALLERTON, *hurries on at the left, downstage of the seats. He makes straight for* GEORGINA *and leans across* CLARK *to speak to her.*

Manager [*tensely*]. Excuse me, are you Miss Georgina Allerton?

Georgina [*in surprise*]. Why, yes, I am.

Manager. I'm the manager of the theater. Miss Hilda Vincent, who was to play Portia tonight, has just collapsed in her dressing room and——

Georgina. Oh, how perfectly awful! Is she seriously——?

Manager. Well, I hope not. But she won't be able to go on. And we have no understudy.

Georgina. But what will you do?

Manager. That's what I've come to see you about.

Georgina. Me?

Manager. Yes, Miss Vincent is under the impression that you are familiar with the role of Portia——

Georgina. Well, I did play it once. But that was in high school, years ago.

Manager. Are you up in the part?

Georgina. Oh, I remember every word of it. But I couldn't possibly go on and——

Manager. Well, won't you please help us out and try it?

Georgina [*hesitantly*]. Well, I don't know. [*Turning to* CLARK.] Do you think I should, Clark?

Clark [*laughing*]. Are you being funny? You couldn't get up there and act that part for a first-night audience.

Georgina [*to the* MANAGER]. I guess he's right. I couldn't do it.

Manager. Please try! It's that or refunding thousands of dollars and sending away all these people disappointed. Miss Vincent told me to beg you in the name of your alma mater to——

Georgina. All right! I will! I'll try it!

Clark [*trying to detain her*]. You'll make a fool of yourself!

Georgina [*pushing past him*]. I'd rather be a fool than a coward.

Manager. That's the spirit, Miss Allerton! I know you'll come through. This way, please. [*Her head high, she follows him across the stage into the darkness at the right. The light fades out at the left, then there is scattered applause, followed by the voice of the* MANAGER, *off right.*] Ladies and gentlemen, I regret to inform you that Miss Hilda Vincent, who was to be seen as Portia tonight, will be unable to appear. [*Murmurs and exclamations from the unseen audience.*] However, there happens to be in the audience a young lady, Miss Georgina Allerton, who, though not a professional actress, is familiar with the role, and has graciously consented to replace Miss Vincent. [*Scattered applause and murmurs.*]

Clark [*loudly*]. Boo!

Manager. I am sure you will show Miss Allerton every indulgence, in view of the fact that she is going on at a moment's notice, and without even a rehearsal. I thank you.

Applause, followed by a flourish of music. Then the lights come up at right, on a small section of an elevated stage. GEORGINA, *in the dress of a* Venetian *doctor of laws, stands on the stage, facing the spectators at left, among whom only* CLARK *can be seen, as a spotlight focuses on his face.*

He grins sardonically as GEORGINA *begins to speak.*

Georgina. The quality of mercy is not strain'd;
It droppeth as the gentle rain from heaven
Upon the place beneath. It is twice blest—
It blesseth him that gives, and him that takes.
'Tis mightiest in the mightiest. It becomes
The throned monarch better than his crown.
His sceptre shows the force of temporal power,
The attribute to awe and majesty,
Wherein doth sit the dread and fear of kings;
But mercy is above this sceptred sway;
It is enthroned in the hearts of kings,
It is an attribute to God himself;
And earthly power doth then show likest God's
When mercy seasons justice. Therefore, Jew,
Though justice be thy plea, consider this—
That, in the course of justice, none of us
Should see salvation: we do pray for mercy,

And that same prayer doth teach us all to
    render
The deeds of mercy . . .

As the speech goes on, Clark's *expression begins to soften
until at the end he is moved almost to tears. When the
speech is finished there is an outburst of applause, cheers,
and cries of "Bravo!"* Clark *sniffles, then takes out a handkerchief and blows his nose.* Georgina *bows, smiles, and
blows kisses to the unseen audience. Two ushers cross
quickly from left to right, carrying huge bouquets which
they hand up to* Georgina. *Her arms filled with flowers,
she bows again. Then she disappears. There is another
upsurge of applause as the lights fade out at right. Then*
Clark *springs to his feet as he sees* Georgina *approaching
    from the right and meets her stage center.*

Clark. Georgina! You were magnificent!

Georgina [as they go toward their seats]. Don't try to
flatter me. I know you don't mean it.

Clark. But I do! I swear to you I do! You were superb:
sincere, moving, eloquent, forceful, charming.

Georgina. That's a lot, isn't it, for a girl who doesn't
know anything, a girl who can't do anything?

Clark. I take it all back, Georgina—every word of it.
I've done you an injustice, completely misunderstood
you——

Georgina. Next time, maybe you'll be a little more careful. Only I'm afraid there'll be no next time for you, as far
as I'm concerned. [*They are seated by now.*]

Clark. Georgina, you mean you want to be rid of me?

Georgina. Yes, and a good riddance too.

Portia [off right]. A gentle riddance. Draw the curtains, go.
    Let all of his complexion choose me so.

*There is applause as the unseen curtain falls. As the lights
come up again at the left* Georgina, *startled, begins to
applaud. The Elizabethan music is resumed and continues
    throughout.*

Clark [to Georgina*].* Well, I'm glad you're back with us.
[*The other spectators begin to rise and file out.*]

Georgina. It's good, isn't it?

Clark. Why, I don't believe you heard a word of it.

Georgina [*indignantly*]. Why, I heard every syllable. What do you mean——?

Clark. Go on! You were off in some Cloud-Cuckoo-Land.

Georgina. I was nothing of the kind!

Clark [*looking toward* HAND *and* MISS DELEHANTY]. Sh! We mustn't give them the impression that we're not en rapport. Besides, I'm dying to know how Tessie interprets the casket plot.

Hand [*as he and* MISS DELEHANTY *join* CLARK *and* GEORGINA]. Say, that Vincent girl is a good Portia, isn't she? Why, to meet her at a cocktail party, you'd never think she had it in her.

Clark. The world is full of girls like that. You have to live with them to know them. Miss Delehanty, how about a cigarette?

Miss Delehanty. Yeah, why not?

Clark [*as they go left*]. Well, there might be a number of reasons. Let's look at it, first, from the purely esthetic angle—— [*He and* MISS DELEHANTY *exit.*]

Hand. So you turned me down for a book reviewer!

Georgina. I had already said yes to him when you——

Hand. Never mind, I can take it. But remember, we're playing a return engagement tomorrow at the Canard Rouge. I've dug up a lot more dope about Mexico. It seems that——

Georgina. Save it until tomorrow. We really should join the others.

Hand [*as they go left*]. Yes, I guess so. Kind of brash, this Redfield, isn't he?

Georgina. Oh, yes—very!

As they exit the lights fade on the scene and the music changes to a jazz rhythm. The lights come up, center, on a table in a night club. A HEADWAITER *appears, at.left, followed by* GEORGINA *and* CLARK, *who still carries the script.*

Headwaiter. How about this?

Clark. Yes, this'll do. [*He and* GEORGINA *seat themselves at the table.*]

Headwaiter. Can I take your order?

Georgina. Nothing for me. I've only got about a half-hour——

Clark. That's time enough for a drink. Scotch and soda?

Georgina. Now, don't spoil things by beginning to ask me what I want.

Clark [*to the* HEADWAITER]. Two Scotches and soda. And two smoked whitefish sandwiches on rye toast.

Georgina. Do you really think you can eat two sandwiches?

Clark [*to the* HEADWAITER]. Well, just bring one to start with.

Headwaiter. Yes, sir. [*He exits. The band selection comes to an end.*]

Clark. Now we can really relax and talk things over.

Georgina. I couldn't relax even if we had anything to talk over. I don't know why I let you drag me here, when I have to——

Clark. I know! I've got my eye glued on the time. Where is it that you have to be at midnight, Cinderella?

Georgina. My, but you ask a lot of questions, don't you?

Clark. Newspaperman. Get the story or get another job.

Georgina. Well, if you must know, I'm going to the airport to see somebody off.

Clark. Good! I'll go with you!

Georgina. You'll do nothing of the sort.

Clark. Well, that's settled! [*He suddenly laughs aloud.*]

Georgina [*vexed*]. Am I missing something again?

Clark. I'm thinking of George Hand.

Georgina. What's so funny about that?

Clark. On the way out of the theater, he asked me where we were bound for, and I said we were going to the Blue Grotto and why didn't he join us there. I can just see him turning that gloomy joint upside down in search of us, while Miss Delehanty sits wrapped in her thoughts—the naked creature!

Georgina. Well, of all the adolescent——! [*She laughs in spite of herself.*] I'm only laughing at the picture of Miss Delehanty——

Clark. It's all right. Don't apologize. Is this George Hand trying to seduce you?

Georgina. Heavens, who's talking book language now?

Clark. Well, I've learned that I mustn't always use the

first word that springs to my lips. Of course, if you'd rather
I asked you if he's trying to——

Georgina [*hastily*]. No, I wouldn't! He's asked me to go
to Mexico with him. You can put your own interpretation
on that.

Clark. I have. It doesn't worry me.

Georgina. Why should it worry *you?*

Clark. I've just told you it doesn't. I mean it's not what's
worrying you either.

Georgina. Who said anything was worrying me?

Clark [*preoccupied*]. Nobody. Tell me something, Georgina. Are you a virgin?

Georgina. Didn't you say that the Newspaper Guild
limits your working hours?

Clark [*thoughtfully*]. It really doesn't matter much.
Well, I'm glad we went to that play. Because suddenly
everything clicked. Do you remember my telling you that
you were off in a trance?

Georgina. I was off in some Cloud-Cuckoo-Land, you
said.

Clark. Yes. I happened to look at you and I saw that you
were no longer Georgina Allerton, that college grad who
plays at running a bookshop. You were suddenly being
somebody up there on the stage, who was pretending to be
Portia of Belmont who was pretending to be a doctor of
laws in an imaginary Venetian court of justice.

Georgina. Well, that's what art is supposed to do for us,
isn't it? Make us identify ourselves with——

Clark. No! Art should reveal reality to us. It shouldn't
be something that we use to screen ourselves from reality.

Georgina. Is that what you're trying to tell me—that I
hide from reality?

Clark. Yes. Sitting there beside you in the theater and
looking at you——

Georgina. Weren't you interested in the play?

Clark. What's that got to do with it?

Georgina. I was wondering what made you look at *me.*

Clark. Let's stick to the point, please.

Georgina. I'm sorry!

Clark. The point is that you're a daydreamer. You live
in a world of fantasy instead of the world of reality.

Georgina. What is this reality you keep talking about?

Clark. I was hoping you wouldn't ask me that because I'm not sure that I know the answer. But I'm pretty sure it means living your life out and not dreaming it away.

Georgina. If a dream is real to you, why isn't it as real as something you do?

Clark. Because dreaming is easy and life is hard. Because when you dream you make your own rules, but when you try to *do* something, the rules are made for you by the limitations of your own nature and the shape of the world you live in. Because no matter how much you win in your dreams, your gains are illusory, and you always come away empty-handed. But in life, whether you win or lose, you've always got something to show for it—even if it's only a scar or a painful memory.

Georgina. Scars are ugly and pain hurts.

Clark. Without ugliness, there would be no beauty. And if you're afraid to know pain, you'll never know the value of pleasure.

Georgina. You're a tough guy, aren't you?

Clark. Well, I've had to fight my own way through life, ever since I can remember. You either get tough, or else you go under.

Georgina. It's not the way I was brought up. I always had people to protect me.

Clark. If you bandage a muscle long enough, it withers. And that goes for your emotions too. If you keep smothering them with dreams, they'll die after a while.

Georgina. Don't say it. It's what I'm afraid of.

Clark. Then it's time somebody said it.

Georgina. I know. Push her off the dock and she'll learn to swim. But suppose I'm not the one that gets tough. Suppose I'm that one that goes under.

Clark. All right then. If that's the way you feel about it, go on sitting on the end of the dock for the rest of your life and let the moonbeams turn your blood to water.

Georgina. No, I mustn't do that, must I? Keep on telling me. I mustn't do that. Only what do you do, if the thing you always dreamed suddenly faces you? Suppose— well, suppose you cared very much for someone. Couldn't get him out of your thoughts, day or night. And all the while you knew it was hopeless, knew you could never have him. But still you went on, weeping and longing and dreaming. And then, just like that, what you thought could never be suddenly became possible. What you had prayed for was yours for the asking. Only it was all different— not a bit the way you dreamed it. And he was different too. But it was reality; it was no longer a dream. And that's your recipe—reality. So that's what I go for, according to you.

Clark. Not according to me at all.

Georgina. But you said——

Clark. I said live your life. Lots of people have a beautiful time, yearning unhappily for the pot of gold at the end of the rainbow. But when the rainbow fades, and the pot turns out to be full of ashes, they don't have to hug it to their bosoms. They can leave it be and say, "Well, looks like I staked out the wrong claim." That is, if they have any guts and any sense of humor they can. If you can make a dream come to life, grab hold of it. But if it dies on you, roll up your sleeves and give it a decent burial, instead of trying to haul the corpse around with you.

The band begins to play another dance tune.

Georgina [*rising*]. Thank you, teacher.

Clark [*also rising*]. Do you have to go already?

Georgina. Well, the bus to the airport won't wait.

Clark. Why is it so important that you go?

Georgina. I told you I'd promised somebody I'd see them off.

Clark. What would happen if you didn't?

Georgina. Nothing would happen, I guess. Except that they might be disappointed.

Clark [*as the waiter appears with the drinks and sandwich*]. Well, if you do go, I'll have to eat and drink alone, and I've told you I don't like that.

Georgina [*hesitantly*]. Well, if I don't go, I should at least phone the air terminal and say I'm not coming.

[*The waiter exits.*

Clark. Why? If you don't show up, they'll figure out that you're not there.

Georgina. Yes, I suppose that's true.

Clark. Of course, if you enjoy unnecessary telephone conversations——

Georgina. No, I really don't.

Clark [*resuming his seat*]. Then let's sit down.

Georgina [*complying*]. I wonder why I listen to you.

Clark. I have a magnetic personality. [*Raising his glass.*] God, I've talked my throat dry. Here's to you.

Georgina [*raising her glass*]. And here's to you. I'm sorry your throat is dry, but I'm glad you talked to me. Do you mind telling me why?

Clark [*with a shrug*]. I don't know. I guess I hate to see anybody with such pretty legs walking around in a trance. [*Taking a bite of the sandwich.*] Say, this is damned good!

Georgina. Could I have a bite?

Clark [*pushing the plate over*]. Why, sure! Maybe I'd better order another one.

Georgina. No, let's finish this one first. [*Taking a bite.*] It *is* good. You're always right, aren't you?

Clark. About ninety per cent of the time. Well—say, ninety-five. I hope I'm right about that Wilinski-O'Connell fight. I'm backing Wilinski on the short end of a two-to-one bet.

Georgina [*her mouth full*]. It's too bad you didn't go.

Clark. Oh, that's all right. This is fun, for a change.

Georgina. Gee, thanks.

Clark. You should eat more. You're too skinny.

Georgina. You told me that before.

Clark [*looking at her*]. Jim Lucas?

Georgina [*startled*]. What?

Clark. You heard me. I said Jim Lucas.

Georgina. How did you guess?

Clark. I have a knack for putting one and one together.

Georgina. He's going to Reno to get a divorce.

Clark. Well, what the hell else would anybody go to Reno for?

Georgina. He wants me to join him there.

Clark. And are you going to?

Georgina. Maybe.

Clark. Say, I'd like to have a piece of the agency that handles your travel arrangements. And if you do get there, what then?

Georgina. We'd get married and get ourselves a ranch.

Clark. A ranch. [*Suddenly.*] My God, it's right straight out of that novel of yours.

Georgina. Just pushing the girl off the dock isn't enough for you. You have to kick her off. [*Rising.*] Get up!

Clark. Why?

Georgina. I feel like dancing.

Clark. With me?

Georgina. Well, I'm a shy girl. I'd feel funny about accosting some stranger. Don't you like to dance?

Clark [*rising*]. It depends upon with whom.

Georgina. You have a charming way of saying things. Years of experience, I suppose.

They dance back and forth across the stage, a spotlight following them.

Clark. Well, working on a newspaper, you get around.

Georgina. That's what I mean.

Clark. Your eyes aren't too bad either.

Georgina. Now don't feel that you have to overdo it.

Clark. That's a sound criticism. Overstatement is one of my worst faults.

Georgina. I'm sure you have plenty of bad ones.

Clark. Well—enough.

Georgina. Is that why no girl has ever married you?

Clark. I've never asked one to.

Georgina. Never met anyone worthy, I suppose.

Clark. That's partly it. But it's also because I think I'd make a lousy husband.

Georgina. Would you? Why?

Clark. Well, in the first place—— [*Breaking off.*] Do you really want to know?

Georgina. Well, it gives us something to talk about.

Clark. We wouldn't have to talk.

Georgina. That's true. Only you don't seem very happy when you're not talking.

Clark. Well, that's the first thing. I'm gabby.

Georgina. Maybe that's because you really have a lot of things to say.

Clark. That doesn't follow. The world is full of windbags. Then again, I'm blunt and caustic. I come right out with things.

Georgina. That might be honesty.

Clark. As for egotism—that's my middle name.

Georgina. It's a quality that a lot of creative people seem to have.

Clark. I'm a hard guy to know.

Georgina. Complex people usually are.

Clark. I'm lacking in reverence.

Georgina. It could be that you're too penetrating to be taken in by sham.

Clark. It bores me to listen to other people's troubles.

Georgina. Perhaps you think they should stand on their own feet and solve their own problems.

Clark. The idea of supporting a wife irks me.

Georgina. A man who is independent himself might not respect an able-bodied woman who was willing to be a dependent.

Clark. I'm an unpredictable bastard. If I have a strong impulse, I'm as likely as not to follow it.

Georgina. That could denote imagination and courage.

The music comes to an end. They stop dancing and applaud mechanically, both transfused with new-found emotion.

Clark. You dance all right.

Georgina. Thank you. So do you.

Clark [*as they go back to the table*]. Why don't we order another drink?

Georgina [*seating herself*]. That's a wonderful idea.

Clark. You order it. I want to make some phone calls. [*Fishing in his pockets.*] Have you got any nickels? You know how I always get stuck in phone booths without nickels.

Georgina [*opening her handbag*]. I think I have. How many do you want?

Clark. Oh, three or four. [*She hands him some nickels.*] Thanks. And don't forget to order the drinks.

Georgina. I won't.

Clark. Oh, better order another sandwich too.

Georgina. All right, I will.

Clark [*picking up the remains of his sandwich*]. I may as well finish this, while I'm phoning.

He takes a bite as he exits. As GEORGINA *sits gazing after him the lights fade out on the scene. A persistent knocking is heard offstage right. The lights come up center on the empty stage. A* MAN *in slippers and an old-fashioned nightshirt comes on at left, carrying a lighted kerosene lamp.*
He looks like MR. ALLERTON.

Man [*peering off right as the knocking continues*]. Consarn it all, who's there?

Clark [*off*]. Is Justice of the Peace Billings in?

Billings. Where in tarnation do you think I'd be this time of night?

Clark [*off*]. Well, open up and let us in.

Billings. What in thunder for?

Clark [*off*]. We want to get married.

Billings. Well, jiminy crickets, can't you wait till mornin'?

Clark [*off*]. No, we can't. It's an emergency.

Billings [*as he goes off right*]. Some folks ain't got the sense they was born with.

A sound of bolts opening and a door creaking. Then BIL-
LINGS *reappears, followed by* CLARK *and* GEORGINA.

Clark [*producing a paper*]. Here's the license, Judge. Now give us the works.

Billings [*peering at the license as a cuckoo clock sounds two*]. Well, I'll be danged! Two o'clock. Time you young folks was in bed, 'stead of gallivantin' around.

Clark. We know it. But we thought we ought to get married first.

Billings [*reading the license*]. Do you, Georgina Allerton, aim to take this bachelor, Clark Redfield, to be your lawful wedded husband?

Georgina. I do.

Billings. And do you, Clark Redfield, hanker to take this spinster, Georgina Allerton, to be your lawful wedded wife?

Clark. That's what I'm here for.

Billings. To love and to cherish. To honor and to obey.

Clark. No!

Georgina [*simultaneously*]. No!

Billings. What's that?

Clark. Cut out that "obey."

Billings [*grumpily*]. It's part o' the ceremony. Folks ain't expected to take it serious.

Georgina. We're very serious people—very serious and very honest.

Billings. When I do the marryin', I don't want no back talk. In sickness and in health. In joy and in sorrow. Until death do you part.

Clark. I do.

Georgina. I—— [*She stops as a clatter of horse's hoofs is heard off left.*]

Jim [*off*]. Whoa! [*The hoofbeats stop and* JIM *rushes on, dressed as a cowboy.*] No! No! Stop!

Georgina. Jim!

Clark. Oh, so you're here, are you?

Jim. Yes, I am! And just in the nick of time, it seems.

Clark. What do you want?

Jim [*ignoring him*]. Georgina, do you realize what you're doing?

Georgina. Well, not altogether, Jim. But it gives me such a wonderful feeling, as though I were really alive for the first time.

Jim. You're just yielding to a romantic impulse, just throwing yourself away.

Clark [*to* JIM]. You keep out of this, Lucas. You're all washed up, as far as this girl is concerned; and I'm taking over now.

Jim. Answer him, Georgina!

Georgina. I don't know what to say. I never met anyone like him before. He's a tough guy—he really is. He scares the daylights out of me.

Jim. All right. I'll answer him then. [*To* CLARK.] She's mine—mine! Do you understand?

Clark. How do you figure that?

Jim. Because she loves me—she's always loved me. For years she's built her whole secret life around me—yearning, dreaming, hoping against hope. And now I'm free and I want her, and I'm going to make her mine.

Georgina [*to* CLARK]. It's true what he's saying. He wants me, and I've always loved him and——

Clark. Scuttlebutt! He doesn't know what he wants and never will. And you don't love him and never did. You've just been in love with some Romeo of your imagination, that never was on land or sea.

Georgina. Do you think so? Do you think that's the way it is?

Jim. Don't listen to him, Georgina.

Georgina. I have to listen to him, Jim. He may be right. He is—ninety-five per cent of the time.

Billings [*impatiently*]. Well, young lady, I'm goin' back to bed. The law don't require me to stay up all night, waitin' for folks to make up their minds.

Georgina. No, wait! It's true. I've got to make up my mind. If I don't now, I never will. All right, Judge, proceed with the ceremony.

Billings. Well, that's better. Do you, Georgina Allerton——

Jim. No, Georgina. You mustn't do this.

Billings. You keep out of this, young feller, unless you want to spend the night in the lockup.

Clark. Go on, cowboy. Beat it.

JIM *looks appealingly at* GEORGINA, *but she averts her head, and he exits dolefully.*

Georgina. All right. I'm ready. In sickness and in health. In joy and in sorrow. Until death—— [*She breaks off as the jazz music from the night club blares forth.*] No, no! Stop it, Georgina! You mustn't go on like this! You mustn't! [CLARK *and* BILLINGS *have gone, and as the night-club scene appears again she goes back to her place at the table.*] I'm at it again—drugging myself with dreams. And when I come to, all I'll get from him is a slap in the face. He doesn't care a damn for me. He's just having fun with me—just giving me the run-around, that's all. He's calling up to find out if he won his bet on Wilinski—that means more to him than I do. [*Springing to her feet.*] No, I can't take it! I'll never see him again. I'll go before he gets back. I'll—I'll—oh, I don't know. Anything—anything not to hear the bitter truth from him. [*She starts to exit.*]

Clark [*entering*]. I won! Wilinski knocked him out in the—— [*Looking at her.*] You look as though you think you're going somewhere.

Georgina. Yes, I am. Good-by, and congratulate Wilinski for me.

Clark. We'll send him a joint wire. Where are you going?

Georgina. I'm going to take a taxi to the airport and get on that plane with Jim.

Clark. Why?

Georgina. Because you've convinced me that doing something is better than doing nothing. And if I don't go away with Jim, I haven't anything.

Clark. Well, of course, if that's what you want to do! Only I wish you'd told me just a few minutes sooner.

Georgina. What do you mean by that?

Clark. Well, you know those impulses I get. I suddenly decided to round off the evening by blowing in that dough I won on Wilinski. So I ordered one of those rented limousines to come around and pick us up. The guy wears a peaked cap and gauntlets. It's pretty damned impressive.

Georgina. Where were you planning to go?

Clark. Oh, I thought we could decide that as we went along. We could whirl around Central Park a couple of times, and then maybe work our way up to Bronx Park—or even beyond. It's a nice night for a ride, and, sitting back in a car, you get a chance to talk. I haven't been able to get in a word edgewise all evening. [*He pays the check.*] Oh, didn't you order that sandwich?

Georgina. Oh, I'm sorry! I forgot all about it.

Clark. Daydreaming again?

Georgina. Afraid so. About you and me.

Clark. Why, you're improving. I think this one may really pay off.

A liveried CHAUFFEUR *enters.*

Chauffeur. Excuse me, are you Mr. Redfield?

Clark. Yes. Keep your motor racing. We'll be right with you.

Chauffeur. Yes, sir. [*He exits.*

Clark [*looking after him*]. What did I tell you? Well, are you ready?

Georgina. Clark—Clark, I'm a serious girl. I wouldn't know how to take any more jokes.

Clark. Well, I have my serious moments too. Look, if you don't want to ride around with me, I'll drop you at the airport and take a spin by myself. Only let's get going. You have to pay these birds whether they're moving or standing still.

He takes her arm, and, as they exit at the right, the lights fade quickly on the scene. A telephone rings at the left and the lights come up, revealing MRS. ALLERTON *in bed as she turns on the lamp on the night table beside her. In a twin bed, on the other side of the night table,* ALLERTON *groans and turns over.*

Mrs. Allerton [*picking up the telephone, sleepily*]. Hello!

She sneezes and gropes under her pillow for a cleansing tissue as the lights come up quickly at the right on a double bed. GEORGINA, *telephone in hand, is seated on the bed with* CLARK *close beside her.*

Georgina. Hello, Mother! Goodness, you sound worse.

Mrs. Allerton [*irritably*]. What's that? What number are you calling? [ALLERTON *groans again.*]

Georgina. It's Georgina, Mother.

Mrs. Allerton. Well, for goodness' sakes! What time is it?

Georgina. About three-thirty, I guess. Listen, Mother, I'm——

Mrs. Allerton. What are you calling up at this hour for? Are you in jail?

Georgina. No, I'm in Greenwich.

Mrs. Allerton. What are you doing there?

Georgina. I just got married.

Mrs. Allerton [*sneezing*]. You just got what? Talk a little louder. This damned cold seems to have gone to my ears.

Georgina. I said I just got married.

Mrs. Allerton. Well, for God's sake! George, did you hear that? She's married. [ALLERTON *mumbles unintelligibly.*]

Georgina. I thought you'd——

Mrs. Allerton [*angrily*]. Wait a minute, will you? I can't talk to two people at once. [*Poking* ALLERTON.] George, will you please wake up? She's married.

Georgina [*to* CLARK]. She's furious at me for waking her up.

Clark. I don't blame her.

Allerton [*raising himself to a sitting position*]. Who's married?

Mrs. Allerton. Georgina, of course! Who do you suppose?

Allerton. To whom is she married?

Mrs. Allerton. How the devil should I know?

Allerton. Well, ask her.

Mrs. Allerton [*at the telephone*]. Georgina, your father wants to know to whom you're married.

Georgina. Oh, to a man I know.

Mrs. Allerton. Well, I should hope so. [*To* ALLERTON.] I can't get a thing out of her.

Allerton. Let me talk to her. [*Taking the telephone.*] Hello, Georgie.

Georgina. Hello, Dad! I'm married!

Allerton. Can you tell us who your husband is?

Georgina. His name is Clark Redfield. He took me to dinner and the theater and then——

Mrs. Allerton [*to* ALLERTON]. Well, who is it?

Allerton [*to* MRS. ALLERTON]. I didn't get the name. Someone who took her to dinner and the theater and——

Mrs. Allerton. Good grief! [*Snatching the telephone.*] Don't tell me it's that boorish, conceited newspaperman!

Georgina [*happily*]. Yes, that's the one. Wait, I'll let you talk to him. [*She hands* CLARK *the telephone.*]

Clark. Hello, Mrs. Allerton. This is your new son-in-law, Clark Redfield.

Mrs. Allerton. Clark who? Talk a little louder, can't you? [*She sneezes.*]

Clark. Redfield. Red as in Russia, field as in football. Have you got a cold?

Mrs. Allerton. Only a newpaperman could ask such a foolish question. [*She sneezes.*]

Clark. Have you ever tried a little——

Mrs. Allerton. Look, young man, don't give me any of your advice. You're going to need all you've got for that girl you've married. [*To* ALLERTON.] I think she's going to have her hands full with him.

Clark. What's that?

Allerton. Let me talk to him. [*Taking the telephone.*] Hello. This is Georgina's father.

Clark. Oh, yes. This is her husband.

Allerton. Yes, so I understand. I just wondered whether you have any plans.

Clark. Do you mean future plans or immediate plans?

Georgina. Let me talk to him. [*Taking the telephone.*] Good night, Dad. Tell Mother——

Allerton. You'd better tell her. [*He hands the telephone to* MRS. ALLERTON.]

Georgina. I just wanted to say good night, Mother.

Mrs. Allerton. Have you got everything you need?

Georgina. Yes, we bought toothbrushes and popcorn in Mamaroneck.

Mrs. Allerton. Well, if it's chilly up there, don't let him talk you into leaving the window open. [*She sneezes.*]

Georgina. I won't. Good night. [*She hangs up.*]

Mrs. Allerton [*hanging up*]. I hope I didn't sound too damned mushy. [ALLERTON *sneezes loudly as the lights fade quickly.*]

Clark [*looking at his watch*]. It's three-thirty. I'm not used to being up so late. [*He puts out the lamp beside the bed, leaving the scene in semidarkness.*]

Georgina. Wait! There's just one thing I'd like to know. Do I have to give up dreaming altogether? Couldn't I just sort of taper off?

Clark. Well, I'll be reasonable about it, as long as you run your dreams instead of letting them run you.

Georgina. I know! If you can dream and not make dreams your master! Do you think Kipling will live?

Clark [*as he pulls down an imaginary shade*]. Look, I didn't come all the way up here to discuss literature!

The stage is plunged into darkness. The curtain falls.

Curtain.

DRAMABOOKS
(Plays)

WHEN ORDERING, please use the Standard Book Number consisting of the publisher's prefix, 8090-, plus the five digits following each title. (Note that the numbers given in this list are for paperback editions only. Many of the books are also available in cloth.)

Elmer Rice: Three Plays (Adding Machine, Street Scene, Dream Girl) (0735-5)
The Day the Whores Came Out to Play Tennis . . . by Arthur Kopit (0736-3)
Platonov by Anton Chekhov (0737-1)
Ugo Betti: Three Plays (The Inquiry, Goat Island, The Gambler) (0738-X)
Jean Anouilh Vol. 3 (Thieves' Carnival, Medea, Cécile, Traveler Without Luggage, Orchestra, Episode in the Life of an Author, Catch As Catch Can) (0739-8)
Max Frisch: Three Plays (Don Juan, The Great Rage of Philip Hotz, When the War Was Over) (0740-1)
New American Plays Vol. 2 ed. by William M. Hoffman (0741-X)
Plays from Black Africa ed. by Fredric M. Litto (0742-8)
Anton Chekhov: Four Plays (The Seagull, Uncle Vanya, The Cherry Orchard, The Three Sisters) (0743-6)
The Silver Foxes Are Dead and Other Plays by Jakov Lind (The Silver Foxes Are Dead, Anna Laub, Hunger, Fear) (0744-4)
New American Plays Vol. 3 ed. by William M. Hoffman (0745-2)
The Modern Spanish Stage: Four Plays, ed. by Marion Holt (The Concert at Saint Ovide, Condemned Squad, The Blindfold, The Boat Without a Fisherman) (0746-0)
Life Is a Dream by Calderón (0747-9)
New American Plays Vol. 4 ed. by William M. Hoffman (0748-7)

THE NEW MERMAIDS
Bussy D'Ambois by George Chapman (1101-8)
The Broken Heart by John Ford (1102-6)
The Duchess of Malfi by John Webster (1103-4)
Doctor Faustus by Christopher Marlowe (1104-2)
The Alchemist by Ben Jonson (1105-0)
The Jew of Malta by Christopher Marlowe (1106-9)
The Revenger's Tragedy by Cyril Tourneur (1107-7)
A Game at Chess by Thomas Middleton (1108-5)
Every Man in His Humour by Ben Jonson (1109-3)
The White Devil by John Webster (1110-7)
Edward the Second by Christopher Marlowe (1111-5)
The Malcontent by John Marston (1112-3)
'Tis Pity She's a Whore by John Ford (1113-1)
Sejanus His Fall by Ben Jonson (1114-X)
Volpone by Ben Jonson (1115-8)
Women Beware Women by Thomas Middleton (1116-6)
Love for Love by William Congreve (1117-4)
The Spanish Tragedy by Thomas Kyd (1118-2)

SPOTLIGHT DRAMABOOKS
The Last Days of Lincoln by Mark Van Doren (1201-4)
Oh Dad, Poor Dad . . . by Arthur Kopit (1202-2)
The Chinese Wall by Max Frisch (1203-0)
Billy Budd by Louis O. Coxe and Robert Chapman (1204-9)
The Firebugs by Max Frisch (1206-5)
Andorra by Max Frisch (1207-3)
Balm in Gilead and Other Plays by Lanford Wilson (1208-1)
Matty and the Moron and Madonna by Herbert Lieberman (1209-X)
The Brig by Kenneth H. Brown (1210-3)
The Cavern by Jean Anouilh (1211-1)
Saved by Edward Bond (1212-X)
Eh? by Henry Livings (1213-8)
The Rimers of Eldritch and Other Plays by Lanford Wilson (1214-6)
In the Matter of J. Robert Oppenheimer by Heinar Kipphardt (1215-4)
Ergo by Jakov Lind (1216-2)
Biography: A Game by Max Frisch (1217-0)
Indians by Arthur Kopit (1218-9)
Narrow Road to the Deep North by Edward Bond (1219-7)
Ornifle by Jean Anouilh (1220-0)
Inquest by Donald Freed (1221-9)
Lemon Sky by Lanford Wilson (1222-7)
The Night Thoreau Spent in Jail by Jerome Laurence and Robert E. Lee (1223-5)

For a complete list of books of criticism and history of the drama, please write to Hill and Wang, 72 Fifth Avenue, New York, New York 10011.